THE
IRON
CURTAIN

THE IRON CURTAIN

MY RUGBY JOURNEY FROM LEAGUE TO UNION

**PHIL LARDER
AND NICK BISHOP**

First published by Pitch Publishing, 2015

Pitch Publishing
A2 Yeoman Gate
Yeoman Way
Durrington
BN13 3QZ
www.pitchpublishing.co.uk

A CIP catalogue record is available for this book
from the British Library.

ISBN 978 178531-039-3

Typesetting and origination by Pitch Publishing
Printed and bound in Great Britain by TJ International

Contents

Acknowledgements

THIS book is dedicated to my dear mum and dad, Maurice and Edith, who introduced me to the great game of rugby league, to Alan Davies who inspired me whilst playing for Oldham and Great Britain, to Ione Gibbons who directed me to the advert for RL's first director of coaching where my voyage began, to Jonathan Davies and Richie Eyres who opened the way into my first coaching role at Widnes RL, to Great Britain coach Maurice Bamford who appointed me as his assistant, and to his successor Malcolm Reilly who was at the helm when we finally beat Australia.

To Fran Cotton who had the vision to appoint a rugby league coach to improve England's defence, to David Shaw who smoothed the way into the 'other code', to Dean Richards and the Leicester Tigers who did so much to help me learn the new game, to Clive Woodward who took me on an incredible journey and to Andy Robinson, Dave Reddin, Phil Keith-Roach, Dave Alred and Simon Hardy who helped England to be number one in the world. To the great players, in both codes of rugby, at both club and country, who gave so much in the arena and were a joy to be with during every working day.

Above all to my wife Anne who has always been my strength and greatest supporter, to Matt, Dids and Anna who have always made us so proud and are our best pals.

Finally to my young grandson Freddie, and all the youngsters like him, who are taking their first tentative steps in sport, and to all the coaches who are guiding them along the way. Enjoy. I hope you have as much fun as I have had.

I would like to thank Alun Carter who first persuaded me to replace a rugby ball with a pen, and then quickly introduced me to Nick Bishop. Nick has been an inspiration as my co-author, has completed copious research and opened my eyes to many events that had happened behind the scenes.

Both the authors would like to thank all those who contributed so generously to the book, including Martin Johnson, Neil Back, Mike Ford, Andy Robinson, Stuart Lancaster, Will Greenwood, Dave Reddin, Dave Alred, Simon Hardy, Phil Keith-Roach, John Huxley and Roger Halstead; to all at Pitch Publishing, especially Paul and Jane Camillin for their help in the production of this work.

Prologue

I AM sitting on the grass as dusk begins to fall, with my back leaning against one of the goalposts at Stadium Australia. I do not know what the time is and cannot even remember the date. I'm exhausted, battered and bruised from a game I haven't even played. The anxiety and tension of the last two and a half hours has been almost too much to bear. After all the turmoil of the game, I need to look down at the medal on my chest and check that it is still gold.

My thoughts drift back to the final of the 1995 Rugby League World Cup against my old nemesis Australia. For years afterwards, the bitter memory of that loss followed me across my career and the pain did not diminish with time. I blamed myself and it tormented me. I thought it was the biggest game I would ever be involved in and I would be going to my grave knowing that I had blown it.

This evening I have finally caught up with my own personal white whale, in a World Cup Final against Australia in Sydney. The feeling of humility, the sheer good fortune of having been given a second chance is overwhelming. On the other side of the globe, the curse has finally been lifted, and I feel nothing but relief and exhaustion.

My phone rings and it is Jack Gibson, the master-coach himself. Jack does nothing to dispel the feeling that the past might yet be up for revision:

'Well done Phil,' he growls, and there is a pause before he adds threateningly '...but we almost did ya! Not bad for a game of union. You've done a top job. That England defence... well, Mass [Jack's coaching partner Ron Massey] and I are proud of you. If you are staying on next week, come and have a look at us. Be great to see ya.'

That's Gibbo, hard to impress and brusque to the point of rudeness. No-one's opinion on rugby matters more to me.

I remember all those other Aussies who have [ironically] shaped the development of my rugby career by so generously 'showing me the lot'. Gibbo, Mass, Frank Stanton, Peter Corcoran and Frank Johnson, who passed away ten years ago – God rest his soul. Nothing was too much for them. They had patiently guided me through a rugby universe that was so much more advanced than anything I could have possibly imagined.

My thoughts wash towards my first encounter with Clive Woodward at Shelley, the meeting which triggered my move across the 'iron curtain' from rugby league to rugby union.

'Phil, I'm not too concerned about the Five Nations,' Clive had said.

'I want us to take on the giants from the southern hemisphere. They are the teams we must measure ourselves against. Beating the likes of Australia, South Africa and New Zealand, *that* must be our aim.'

Clive didn't know it at the time, but he had me at *Australia*. Everything else faded out into the white noise of irrelevance after that. Immediately I was hooked. Mentally, I had always listed reasons by the dozen why we would never be able to overtake the Kangaroos in rugby league and argued myself into a state of complete submission, but in union Clive was now telling me that it was possible.

Clive had played at Manly, the suburb of Sydney where I first met with Frank Stanton [then coach of the Kangaroos] and Frank Johnson to discuss the future of British rugby league. We shared the Australian connection and now we'd achieved the unthinkable, beating them on their home patch and in front of their own people to lift the biggest trophy in our sport... How many England coaches have tried to do that and failed?

My reverie is interrupted by a scream in my ear and a microphone jammed into my face:

'Phil, can I have an interview? It's going live to the UK with Radio 5 Live.'

'Sure,' I blurt out automatically.

For the life of me, I cannot remember a word I say, and the whole interview passes in a dream-like blur, a vague token of the reality to which I know I will soon have to return. Later I will recall talking about the support we'd received, and that at least does have some real truth behind it.

Up in the stands, there is a familiar sight that offers some comfort. The English spectators who invaded Sydney on the week of the final brought with them some of the biggest red and white flags I have ever seen. I saw one being carried head high down on the beach at Surfers

Paradise. At least 50 people were needed to hold it aloft. That same flag had been hoisted over heads before kick-off, now it has reappeared again after the game.

The spectators have been phenomenal, especially on the Gold Coast and here in Sydney. Little red and white flags fluttering vigorously wherever we go, slaps on the back and the inevitable photos to prove that 'I was there'; it must have cost them the earth, and I hope our win has made it worth their while. They do not realise how important they are, because whatever we achieve ultimately belongs to them. We are all England.

I join the boys walking round the pitch and we are waving at everyone. Even the Aussies smile back and applaud us. Finally I see my wife Anne, my sons Matt, David and his girlfriend Jamie in the crowd and my eyes begin to fill up. I hope that I have made them proud – and Anna and mum back home, and my dad looking down from the skies beyond all of us.

I remember my dad talking to me when I was still a teenager, worrying about what I would do when I left school, as my life opened up before me:

'Phil,' he said, 'don't make it too difficult for yourself, have patience and it will simply drop into place.

'Take the time to find out what you are good at and what you enjoy doing… follow your passion in life. When you know, grasp the nettle, forget everything else and give it your all.'

Remembering those words and looking around at all the other England coaches and players who have done exactly the same, now passing the William Webb Ellis trophy overhead from one eager set of hands to the next, I begin to understand what a 'lap of honour' really means. The honour is not in the personal nature of the triumph, no matter how many demons you have to exorcise in the course of your personal life. It is in the passing of the cup, the sharing of the experience with the people you have learned to love as members of your real, extended family. That is what 'winning' really means.

Chapter one

Watershed moments

THERE is no place like the true home of Oldham RLFC, the Watersheddings. Of the Sheddings, the great Yorkshire fast bowler Fred Trueman is reputed to have said: 'Rugby league without the Watersheddings would be like a horror film without Boris Karloff.' No-one knows if Fred really made such a statement, but he wasn't far off the truth if he did. With the Sheddings, you got exactly what you paid for – a hard game of rugby league in the raw, unvarnished. There was never any effort made to tease the spectators into a heightened state of anticipation, no pre-match entertainment, no dancing girls. Even when the club adopted a mascot in the mid-90s he promptly drove an opposing fan who had invaded the pitch into the mud near touch with a great low chop tackle – and 'Braddy' meant it too! There were no frills, no corporate boxes or hospitality packages or picnics in the car park, and there was absolutely nowhere to hide from the biting cold that started with your hands and feet and seemed to work its way inevitably into your very core. There was none of the nonsense you get nowadays.

It was all about the match and everything was pared back down to the bone. It was a test of survival as much as enjoyment, and much depended on your ability to endure the unique climate of the Sheddings. It was always cold, bitterly cold when Phil Larder went to watch as a boy, then later to play there as a man – so cold even a referee [Robin Whitfield] wore a thick woolly scarf for an entire game back in the 90s. It was only when Phil went to his mum and dad's house from Huddersfield that he realised how cold it was in Oldham! More often than not the proceedings would be covered by a blanket of fog descending like some kind of divine punishment from the western escarpment of the Pennines – especially when the club were threatening to reach a Challenge Cup Final, God forbid. As the rugby league press officer John Huxley recalls, 'The Sheddings was the only ground, along with Thrum Hall in Halifax, which was "at altitude". It tended to experience some sudden and extreme shifts of climate as a result. I can remember matches which started in brilliant sunshine and finished in sleet or snow on the same afternoon. The cold would come down very quickly on to the Sheddings' little knoll, like a vengeful fury.'

It was the only ground where you could get saturated without it ever raining. As the rugby league journalist Dave Hadfield put it in his tour of league country,

> 'Watersheddings… had a grimness of aspect and an absence of creature comforts which made Thrum Hall seem like watching a match from a tart's boudoir by comparison. Never has a ground been more aptly named, because I can never remember a dry day at Watersheddings. Its altitude could also have another effect on occasion. I remember going to watch a New Zealand tour game on a day when it was cracking the flags in Bolton, people were sunbathing in Bury and still in their shirtsleeves in Rochdale, but Watersheddings was frozen solid.' *[Up and over: a trek through rugby league land]*.

Upwards of 20,000 people would huddle together on the terraces in the wooden stands for the really big games – reputedly nearly 30,000 crammed into the ground for one cup-tie in the 50s against Huddersfield – squeezed in so tight nobody could so much as turn their head to look over a shoulder. This was only the beginning of the gladiatorial ritual. As Mike Ford [an Oldham and Great Britain rugby league scrum-half in his playing days and an international union coach for Ireland and England thereafter] recalls,

> As a player, after you'd changed into your red-and-white hoops in the cricket pavilion, you'd have to walk a good hundred yards or so to get to a small holding room or cellar underneath the main stand. That cellar was Alex Givvons' underground kingdom – and believe me, you didn't want to cross Alex, or forget to give

him a pack of cigars as the fee for passing through his territory. You'd end up going on the field in any old odds and sods of kit, your socks wouldn't match or your shorts would be big enough to fit Jim Mills... But it was a test just to get as far as Alex.

You had to push through the spectators, who were already shoulder-to-shoulder, to get to the cellar. It became a very intimate experience because you were face-to-face with the people you represented and who were there to support you... You could see the looks on their faces and they'd make little comments to you both before and after the game. If we won well, it was great to see all the flushed faces and feel all the back-slaps and hair-ruffles as we passed through – but woe betide us if we lost badly! We'd get it both barrels as we struggled to find a seam in the crowd to get back from the tunnel back to the pavilion, and sometimes players were held to account physically by the supporters... so it was by turns warm or punishing, but always a very personal experience. Sheddings was unique, a complete one-off in this respect.

Whether they'd been squeezed together more for warmth or local expectation, that crowd would move in ripples like a muscle flexing and the stands would creak and resound with the pounding of a thousand hobnail boots. They would lurch forward as one to curse the referee when he penalised Oldham unjustly, or freeze like statues when the opposition scored. The pressure would only ease at half-time, when you were carried away from the stands involuntarily to queue for the delicious hot oxtail soup they served from the corrugated shack in the corner of the ground. Then the human caterpillar would bear you back to your spot on the terraces for the second half.

On occasion, the monster would show mercy. Phil Larder recalls one championship decider between ourselves and Hull FC. There was a bit of commotion and a few voices were raised before the game:

'There's young lads tha' can't see!' Suddenly I felt myself being hoisted into the air until I was flat on my back. I could just turn my head enough to look across the sea of caps, enough to see other small boys just like myself, being passed down overhead from the back of the stand to the front of the terracing. What an amazing feeling! Looking back on it now, it represents to me the sense of togetherness that gave the Sheddings its character,

however cold it got. The kids watched that game in a privileged position, sat on the side of the pitch next to the wall because the ground was full to overflowing, watching tackled players whizz past into touch or cutting a trench through the mud towards us. The smell of liniment was only inches away.

The monster had a conscience after all. As time wore on, bits lost or torn off the stands were neglected, or replaced by odd ill-matching materials so that the Sheddings did indeed start to resemble Frankenstein's patchwork creation. Legend has it that one Oldham supporter was thrown off the top deck of a stand by a Warrington man, who then chucked his crutches after him apologetically.

The ground was like a living curse, and the curse was nowhere more active than in the Challenge Cup. Even when Oldham were at their peak in the 1950s and 60s, with many a Great Britain international in their ranks, Wembley remained the great taboo. In one semi-final against Swinton, they were ahead and the referee had his whistle in his mouth when the curse struck. A Pennine fog came down swiftly like the hand of God and the game had to be abandoned. Oldham lost the replay. In another semi against Warrington in 1990 they scored a try to draw level and had a kick to win it at the death. The ref disallowed the try for a mysterious offside and ORLFC lost 10-6. A win would have taken them to Wembley the day before Latics played in the FA Cup Final. As he walked off to a barrage of abuse the ref said calmly: 'You've already got one team at Wembley haven't you?' That man was the scarf-wearer back in the day, Robin Whitfield. After that, the Oldham fans resigned themselves to the inevitable in song,

'Wemb--ley, Wemb--ley,
Most famous place in London
That we have never been.'

Curse or no curse, Watersheddings had a meaningful place in the local community. For more than 40 years it was also the home of the local cricket club and other legendary rugby league figures like Don Vines and Jim Sullivan moved on to success in sports other than rugby there. 'Buller' played baseball after an illustrious career as probably one of the greatest full-backs to play rugby in either code. He played for Great Britain before his 18th birthday, while Vines [an Oldham Rugby League man] became a 'heel' or villain in professional wrestling, fighting 'the Outlaw' at the Sheddings in a grudge match after playing prop for Wakefield and Great Britain in the late 50s and early 60s.

The ground was a civic institution and a centre of sporting activity in the area, and the success of the rugby team had a positive spill-over effect on the other sports based at the ground. As *The Athletic News* noted as far back as 1887, 'In 99 cases out of every 100… football helps cricket over the stile of financial embarrassment.' When the Sheddings quite literally began to fall to pieces, and Oldham RLFC were forced to sell it to pay off the club's debts in June 1994, it was a dark day for not only local rugby supporters but the community as a whole. John Huxley recalls that, 'The Greyhound stadium was adjacent to the rugby ground, and cricket and baseball were played at the ground itself in the spring and summer. The lounge bar at the club was where all the good and great of Oldham used to come and commune – men like "Rocky" Farnsworth and Frank Disken "the Maharishi of rugby league", who famously once brought two southern union men [Rosslyn Park's Bob Mordell and Adrian Alexander from Harlequins] to the club in the early eighties and who first introduced Phil to Dave Alred, a future coaching colleague in union, in 1984. Socially, Watersheddings was a hub for the local community and one that was never satisfactorily replaced when Oldham RLFC had to move across town to Boundary Park.'

Not that you'd guess it now, now that the whole place has been re-developed as a new-build housing estate, all neat lawns and detached living. They've left the old wooden entrance gates there as part of the perimeter fence but they stick out like a sore thumb – beyond the sense of sheer oddity they only give up their secret to the genuine Oldham supporter, one who has known the history of sport in the area for 20 years or more.

The one solid reminder that this is in fact a burial ground full of rugby memories, and particularly of the many crushed Oldham dreams that lie just beneath the surface of the tarmac, is a small blue plaque that commemorates its significance to the community. It is one of many in the borough which remember events and people as diverse as the Peterloo massacre of 1819, Bradbury sewing machines and Joseph Lees, the originator of the fish 'n chip dinner in Market Hall, Albion Street. The plaque reads modestly,

> 'On the site of the housing development to the east of this park
> was the famous Watersheddings rugby ground, which served the
> Oldham club from its opening on 28 September 1889, until the
> last first team match on 19 January 1997.'

For Phil Larder, the name 'Watersheddings' evokes a string of memories that he can count like rosary beads. Most of the touchstones of his rugby life happened there, whether it was as either a spectator, or later as a player for Oldham.

> I often revisit them in my mind and they have not lost their significance over time. I grew up in an era when rugby league was thriving and was the number one winter sport in the north of England. Soccer's Oldham Athletic played at Boundary Park but could not compete with the passion generated by league or the numbers of spectators the Sheddings attracted. Oldham was very much a rugby town. All my pals played sport at every opportunity whether on the old disused bowling green in the centre of Moorside or in the school playground, but although we enjoyed playing both soccer and cricket, it was rugby league that we lived for.

It's different now. Oldham finally left the Watersheddings in 1997, only five years after the Latics secured promotion to soccer's Premier League. They bounced around in exile for the next dozen years, playing home matches outside the borough and even suffering the ignominy of being kicked off Boundary Park, a home they shared with the Latics for a while, in 2009. Now they play in the third tier of the rugby league on an old disused piece of ground in Limeside with a stand made out of old spars from Wembley stadium and old seats from Wilderspool.

> What a way to go out! I'm very thankful I played in an era before league in the area was on its uppers, and when rugby was still the lifeblood of the town; before sporting interest rolled comfortably downhill into Boundary Park, and the easy sunshine of soccer replaced the Pennine growl of the Watersheddings, with Alan Davies emerging suddenly from the endless fog to deliver another brilliant try-scoring pass to his wing. Give me that, any day of the week.
>
> Back in the late 50s and early 60s, more than half of the Oldham team were Great Britain internationals, and Great Britain were at the top of the pile then, the best team in the world. We could beat Australia, and we could do it regularly. I was at Moorside junior school and I would walk from my house with my school mates to the ground, which was only half a mile or so

away. I'd be wearing my worn Oldham jersey, all the others would be in their soccer shirts. Eight or nine of us would plant ourselves on a set of steps at the back of the double-tiered stand near the Pavilion end of the ground. We'd beat our shoulders and rub our hands at the thought of the treat in store, and at just the right moment we'd open the shutters at the back of the stand and look out on the players as they walked down to the stadium from the Pavilion. We'd catch a glimpse of our favourites waiting to come out from below the stands. 'There's "Rocky" Turner!' one would say; or I'd shriek, 'Alan Davies just winked at me!' and those moments were treasured in the memory, better than autographs and more warming than Bovril... The games themselves were often thrilling, because Oldham played a brand of open rugby that was exciting to watch, and they had won every competition in England bar the Challenge Cup. That kept us warm on even the coldest of winter afternoons, too.

Phil's mum and dad were also avid Oldham fans, which meant that he went to see as many away games as he did home. When Griff Jenkins took over the coaching, he moved the training to Counthill school. Counthill was a short gallop across the fields for Phil, so he ended up watching every game that Oldham played, home and away, and every training session too. Phil Larder was in rugby league heaven as a schoolboy, and his main memories are of those eager fog-bound journeys to and from a session or a match.

Although there were many great players in the Oldham team – Derek Turner, Bernard Ganley, Syd Little and Frank Pitchford just to name a few – my idol was a man who played right centre for both the club and Great Britain, Alan Davies. I watched every move that he made, or thought I did, whether he was playing for Great Britain in partnership with Wigan's captain Eric Ashton, or for Oldham making strong powerful bursts, drawing his man and cleverly creating scoring opportunities for his winger John Etty.

Alan, the son of a miner, was born in Leigh on the outskirts of Wigan. He was a hard running centre with a great eye for a gap, but what thrilled me above all else was his ability to run on that outside arc, pull both the opposing centre and wing into him before making a perfectly timed and weighted pass to put his winger away down the touchline. John Etty regularly topped the try-scoring charts of the day, but it was mostly because of Alan Davies' skills.

I wanted to be just like him. A couple of years into my career with Oldham, I remember stopping off at my parents' house on the way to play in the Lancashire Cup Final against St Helens at Wigan's Central Park. There in the living room, was a framed photograph of Alan Davies in his pomp, with a well-wishing underneath it… It hadn't been there before and it took me by surprise. It was only at that moment that it dawned on me that I might be worthy successor to the number 3 jersey that Alan had worn with such distinction, and that I was now becoming a part of the living fabric of Oldham Rugby League history, just like him. It was quite a humbling moment.

League has always historically been more focused on providing a good attacking, try-scoring spectacle than its cousin union. It does not allow either set-pieces [like lineout or scrum] or a contest at the tackle to interfere with this aim. Even back in 1888 it was noted that: 'The acme of good play is when a skilful three-quarter finishes up a dashing run by dodging a full-back and planting the ball over the line. In the North, no other part of the game is applauded more than this…'

Phil did not realise it at the time, but Alan Davies – and the way he was watching Alan Davies – was to have an important impact on his subsequent career in rugby, and in both codes. John Huxley says that:

> In the late 60s and early 70s, Phil Larder took over the role played by Alan Davies in the previous generation of Oldham players. In Oldham's renowned open, handling style of game, Phil was the elegant passer and very clever 'sniffer' of opportunities for the wing outside him, a Welshman by the name of Mike Elliott. They were a great combination both on and off the field, and with Phil's endless midfield coaxings, Elliott became the top try-scorer in club history with 153 tries. Phil wasn't in Alan Davies' class as a player mind you, but he helped carry the torch on for the kind of football the Oldham supporters loved and respected.

Mike Ford recalls watching Phil Larder playing for Oldham as a boy:

> Phil was exactly like Alan Davies when he had the ball in hand. He was one of the best in the league at setting up the winger

outside him. He was quick, very quick, and he could also step his opponent when he moved out on to the winger. Unfortunately, as a defender Phil wasn't the best and we were looking through the cracks in our fingers when attacks went to his side of the field… so it became a case, for us Oldham supporters, of hoping that Phil's creative contributions would outweigh his defensive lapses!

Like most spectators, Phil's eye as a spectator had followed the team in possession, so when Oldham played Wigan and Oldham had the ball he would watch Alan Davies; but when Wigan were in possession, instead of watching Alan Davies defend [and Davies was a great defender] Phil found himself drawn to what Eric Ashton was doing with the ball.

Defence was an afterthought. My problem was that I had never received any rugby coaching. I went to a soccer-playing school and only played a couple of games of rugby as a kid for Werneth, a team built by rugby league historian Tom Webb. Everything I did, I had learned from being a spectator watching Oldham RL.

A rugby ball has a hypnotic effect on the spectator, so that he or she will tend during a game to follow the team in possession. It is entirely natural and pervasive even in the present day [with its saturation TV coverage], that live spectators, armchair critics and media commentators tend to follow the man who is doing something with the ball, rather than the man who is trying to stop him. Because of the nature of narrow angle TV coverage, the ball is everything. The 'unseen work', what people are doing away from the ball and out of shot [which is just as important, if not more so from a coaching point of view] tends to be neglected. A long way into his rugby future as a coach, Phil would always ask his analysts for film footage from behind the posts, as well as looking in from the sideline, so that he could assess the contribution of players away from the ball. One of the stiffest challenges he would face when he switched codes was to persuade the management, coaching staff, players and spectators of the essential contribution that a well-organised defence – the contribution of the people 'out of shot' – can make to the ultimate success of the team.

Phil's dad saw his son's future in union rather than league. Phil started playing first-class rugby union at Broughton Park and was a regular first team player by the time he was 16, running out on to the field alongside established internationals like Barry Jackson and Barry

O'Driscoll. By the time he graduated from Loughborough University in 1965 [aged 20], he was approaching veteran status, having played for both Manchester and Sale and becoming a regular on the vibrant northern sevens circuit.

On the professional front, Phil had decided on a career in teaching. An opportunity opened up in Saddleworth comprehensive school in the year after Phil finished at Loughborough. Saddleworth is often known laughingly as 'the best part of Yorkshire' by Lancashire folk because it has a Lancashire postcode and was integrated into a new local authority in 1974 – despite being historically a part of the West Riding of Yorkshire! In fact the white rose and the red have argued over Saddleworth's soul ever since the Middle Ages. There are now two signs, less than 50 yards apart, one facing west to Yorkshire and the other east towards Lancashire. As one poor fellow put it, 'I live in a house between the two signs, so where does that leave me? In no man's land?...' The idyllic network of small villages with names like Dobcross, Diggle and Delph are still overshadowed by others of more ancient, even biblical menace further up the Pennines – Jericho, Shiloh and Blunder Ho. So the young Phil Larder found himself on the outskirts of Oldham, living and working on the border between two age-old antagonists. It was quite symbolic, because the tug of war he was experiencing between the two rival rugby codes at the time reflected that geographical divide.

I had been offered a post as the head of PE, and I took it without hesitation. I went on to work at Saddleworth for 16 mostly happy years, and one of my pupils in the 70s was Mike Ford, whose rugby career – playing for Oldham Rugby League and going on to be the England rugby union defence coach – was to bear a strong resemblance to my own. Mike was probably the best rugby player that Saddleworth produced during my time there. I will always remember one cup final when as a young fourth year student I promoted him to the senior team for the final of the Oldham Schools Cup. The winners would represent Oldham in a national competition. Our opponents and closest rivals Fitton Hill were unbeaten, but I remember Mike completely controlling the match with his kicking game and walking away with the man of the match award. Mike was like a master puppeteer even at that young age, pulling the strings to which all the players danced that day.

After an illustrious professional playing career in league he followed my example and switched codes to become a defence coach first with Ireland and later on with England. I've always felt there was a strong link there and I recommended Mike for the defensive role with Ireland when all the home unions 'went shopping' for an ex-RL defensive coach after the 2001 British & Irish Lions tour ended. Like me, Mike was a great attacker although his defensive qualities were better than mine. It was a case for both of us of crossing the great divide between codes: we both finished our playing days in league and then spent the most significant part of our coaching careers in union. It must be something in the water at Saddleworth…

Mike Ford himself has some vivid memories of Phil Larder the PE teacher:

> Phil was incredibly competitive and intense, and even though we were just a bunch of teenagers I think he tended to view us and treat us as semi-professional athletes! There was the same level of support but also the same sense of expectation. When he took over the PE department at Saddleworth that intensity improved all aspects of all the sports in which the school engaged. Everyone could feel it. Sport suddenly became important, maybe even on occasion more important than your work in the classroom, and it became a form of expression for Saddleworth as a school. I think it was a unique situation within the schools in our area. Phil treated the boys as adult athletes. It was as if a professional coach had been injected into a school [non-professional] setting.
>
> It didn't matter what sport Phil was teaching – and he taught soccer, cricket, cross-country and basketball as well as rugby in my time at the school – the intensity would always be there. When he umpired our cricket matches, he'd be as much on-field coach to the Saddleworth boys as arbiter, offering little snippets of advice… He'd say, 'Come on Fordy, he's moving too far across his stumps…' I'd adjust my line a little, clip leg stump or the batsman would get a tickle down the leg-side to the keeper, and the finger would go up. Phil would say out of the corner of his mouth, 'I told you they couldn't handle the ball coming back into them!' We'd feel under pressure and that there was nowhere to hide, but that brought the best out of us because we were always given every possible aid to success. I guess you'd call it a 'no excuse' culture nowadays.

I can remember a big cross-country race, all the Oldham schools were involved, and there were teams of eight or nine athletes representing each school. There must have been well over 100 athletes competing in all, but the problem was that the race started in a very narrow lane in which only a few runners could line up abreast of each other. This meant that some of the boys would inevitably be starting well behind the line. All the other schools were out limbering up at least 30 minutes before the race got underway, but Phil had the Saddleworth team warming up in the nearby sports hall. He told us to wear our watches and make sure that we were near the start-line by 1.55pm for the beginning of the race. At the last possible moment, he called us out of the hall. We came trotting out resplendent in our green-and-yellow running kit and looking and feeling very much like the 'A' team, and took up position. The whistle was blown… I swear we must have had a 70 yard start on some of the kids at the rear!

But that was Phil, he wouldn't cheat or countenance cheating from anyone else in one of his teams, but he would maximise every little advantage going because he absolutely hated losing. At rugby our perennial rivals were Fitton Hill, and they had been generally the best schools side in the district. That all changed when Phil joined as PE head. In his first year we lost 9-12 and Eddie Barton was in charge of the Saddleworth team. Even though they were good mates, Phil took it to heart and made sure we didn't lose to Fitton Hill again in my time there… Once Phil saw a priority and his focus settled on a particular aim, nothing would stop him until he had achieved it.

I guess it was a sign of the link between us that Phil finished teaching at the school on the same day that I left it as a pupil. Before leaving I hadn't been able to decide whether I wanted to pursue a career in soccer or rugby league. Eventually I chose soccer, and found that Phil had already devised a programme for me to maximise my conditioning – a programme individually-tailored to my needs, with an athletics trainer, spikes, a nutrition course… – everything had been thought of and thought through in meticulous detail. Even then he would be fretting that the course wasn't sufficiently soccer-specific, or didn't contain enough sprint training… But that was Phil to a 'T' – intensely loyal to those in whom he saw potential, and who were prepared to work to make it happen, and professionally attentive to detail, even in a school setting. It was some education for a teenager like myself, and moreover it continued even when I was looking for work much higher up the professional scale as a coach in union. I always knew Phil's helping hand would be there whenever I needed it.

It was becoming hard for Phil to reconcile the demands of a new full-time job looking after a department at school, with playing rugby union in his spare time. Although he enjoyed playing the game, equally he couldn't afford the time away from work, and the long journeys down to places like Bath and Rosslyn Park were becoming a chore. They interfered with his school duties, particularly the management, refereeing and preparation of the many representative teams which are at the core of a PE teacher's role. In the winter, Saddleworth supported six soccer teams, three rugby league sides and four basketball teams, in addition to its numerous cross-country and badminton fixtures. Missing Saturday morning games because he was playing rugby in the Midlands or the south of England set a poor example to his young charges at school.

Although he did not always care to admit it to himself, Phil had never felt instinctively comfortable in the union code:

> I felt that I was playing union like a league player and that I'd never really understood the game, even when I was enjoying it! In league I knew just what to expect, so I was back in my comfort zone…

It was therefore with a sense of relief that Phil received an offer to turn professional as a rugby league player for Leigh RLFC. Their coach, the former Great Britain captain Alan Prescott was very persuasive, but when Oldham threw their hat into the ring his mind was made up. The club scout Derek Foy had spotted Phil's potential at the Manchester sevens tournament but negotiations were protracted, with no less than four meetings with the committee.

> On the first occasion I'd just grabbed some lunch from the school canteen before hurrying off to meet with the Oldham RLFC committee representatives in a local pub. They said that I could have anything I wanted to eat, but I was too bloated to accept! I knew better after that, and came 'empty' the next time.

Although league didn't become a full-time professional sport until the advent of Rupert Murdoch's Sky-sponsored Super League in 1996, it had always been semi-professional. At Oldham training was two evenings per week, the same as Phil had been used to in rugby union, and apart from the Cumbrian clubs [Workington, Whitehaven and Barrow] all the other clubs were no more than a stone's throw away. The extra money Phil was paid by Oldham allowed him to invest in a new house with his partner [and wife-to-be] Anne and to buy a new car. Furthermore he was able to save all his matchday fees and live off his wages as a teacher.

Some of the stars of the era earned a lot more than the average, as I soon found out. While I was signing for Oldham in the away dressing room of Cheshire club Davenport after losing in the final of their charity Sevens to Newport, in the changing room opposite, just a few feet away from me was David Watkins, the Welsh rugby union international and captain of the British Lions in Australia one year previously. He had captained Newport that day and was signing on the dotted line for Salford RLFC. Afterwards I had a pint with David and was well pleased to learn that I had commanded the same signing-on fee as him – at least until I counted the noughts on his cheque!

David Watkins was to prove my nemesis. After the first three games of the new season Oldham were undefeated and I had won two 'man of the match' awards playing in the centre. I was at the top of my game and I was feeling supremely confident I could handle the young Welshman, having already played against him in the final of the Davenport Sevens in the other code. After my start in professional rugby I was beginning to wonder whether I should have been the one with the extra nought on my paycheque.

In the event, Dai Watkins taught me the hardest of lessons, one that I would never forget – even though I probably ended up overusing it as an example in my frequent seminars on defence at the RFU! That Oldham-Salford match would shape my thinking about rugby and send out consistently powerful ripples throughout my later career as a coach. I had assumed that David would be playing at stand-off, but Salford decided instead to blood him in the centre, with their experienced league international Ken Gill filling in at number 6. So after the first few play-the-balls at the Willows we found ourselves looking across

26

at each other and it was obvious we would be in direct opposition for the rest of the game.

The first time he had the ball on my side of the pitch he ran directly at me, veering away on an outside swerve at the last moment. I was pretty quick back then and accelerated to keep pace but he almost got around me. As a result I was only able to make a weak tackle several yards downfield. As we both struggled to our feet our eyes met and there was a faint grin on his face – as if to say, 'I've got your number now!'

On the second occasion Dai received the ball, I said to myself 'I'll stand a bit wider this time, to stop that outside break.' He came towards me, I leaned in and suddenly he was gone – I'd been left flat-footed and he'd stepped me on the inside, rounded our full-back Martin Murphy – who was an outstanding tackler – and scored under the posts. It was like that for the rest of the game – if I positioned myself as I habitually did, on the inside half of his body, he could take me on the outside shoulder with his acceleration and swerve; when I adjusted and stood wider I could not handle his side-step. The ground was heavy but it was as if David skipped along the top of the surface while I was stuck in the mud.

He was at another level – sheer lightning... It got to the point where I wanted the ground to open and swallow me up. I felt that everyone in the crowd could see my own defensive frailties as clear as daylight, and that it was a personal humiliation. Moreover, I felt it was my individual inability to mark Watkins that had cost my team the game.

Salford hammered Oldham and Phil reluctantly had to admit that Watkins fully deserved that extra nought on his cheque. David Watkins of course went on to become an all-time great as captain and coach of Great Britain, which was a massive accolade for any player, but particularly one whose early background lay in rugby union. Moreover, Oldham has in the current era become virtually a feeder club to the Salford Red Devils in Super League with a number of its players dual-registered. With the ambitions of Dr Marwan Koukash as a sporting benefactor in the region, it may not be too long before both clubs exist under the umbrella of single ownership. As it turned out, Phil's own difficulties with Dai Watkins, and the overall result of the 1967 match were both quite prophetic in relation to the very different futures of two great RL clubs 35 years later.

The match helped change Phil's thinking about the game in both codes for good, even if he wasn't fully aware of it at the time. It wasn't until he visited Jack Gibson in Australia in the 1980s that this thinking began to gestate and take a solid form. But Phil did find himself looking at on-field issues more from a defensive point of view, and the experience with Watkins was far more informative than any defensive 'training' Phil had received previously:

> I was aware that I was not a good defender, so I approached one of our coaches Alex Givvons, and asked if he could give me some defensive pointers or training. Alex looked back at me puzzled, then said 'Righty-o then' and took me out on to the pitch with our big second row, Bobby Irving. Then he just lined up Bobby ten yards away from me and had him slam into me at top pace! This wasn't what I had in mind. Because anyone can tackle a bloke running straight for you, it's just a matter of bottle. With England RU, we used to call 'coconut' when this happened because it was just like a coconut shy. You just had to knock the bloke off. But I wanted to know how to defend, not just how to tackle, and that was a team event.

The Watkins experience pushed Phil to see the shape of a bigger coaching picture. He was no longer observing just the great Alan Davies draw and pass, so in a sense he was moving beyond the experiences of his rugby 'nursery'.

> When you have undergone a traumatic experience like I did against Dai Watkins, a certain cast of mind [like mine] begins to worry itself into the ground, working overtime to find a solution. For example, I was convinced it would have been very difficult for any defender to have handled Watkins man-on-man consistently, so when I began coaching I started looking for organisational solutions with defenders working in threes – with the middle man playing slightly inside the attacker but protected against both David Watkins' outside break and his side-step by other defenders on either side of him.
>
> Was my humiliation against David Watkins the grit around which the 'pearl' formed?... the pearl of the defensive system I evolved with the England rugby union team in a new millennium? It's hard to say because there were many other factors involved,

and I possibly over-dramatised the episode when using it as a teaching tool in my rugby union seminars subsequently.

But it was definitely a formative experience, coming so early in my league playing career. At some level, I realised that one man is not enough to stop a really talented attacker on his own. He has to have the support on his inside and on his outside, he has to have team-mates who will help him out. I began to distrust man-on-man defence and moved towards zonal thinking, and with England we always understood that the most important defender was the one protecting the inside shoulder of the player directly under attack. It was the responsibility of that inside defender to control the spacing and talk the man outside him through an attacking play.

I may not have stopped David Watkins that day at the Willows as a player, but I dedicated the rest of my rugby lifetime to stopping him as a coach. I played for 20 years in first class rugby union and rugby league. I trained regularly and I was never dropped from the first team. In all I must have taken part in well over 700 training sessions under the direction of a multitude of coaches – some good, some bad, but all of them passionate, enthusiastic and ambitious. Never once during that time was I, or the team of which I was part, subjected to a rigorous and coherent session on defence. That was the size of the task I was to undertake, unknowingly, when I first made the move into coaching.

Chapter two

Show him the lot – the 1982 Invincibles

IT was a time of rapid expansion. When Phil started teaching at Saddleworth in 1966, it was a small secondary school with at most 500 students; within five years that number had risen to 1,500 and the school was then a comprehensive. At the same time, the number of sporting teams representing the school had grown from a mere three to a massive 25, and his responsibility as head of physical education had grown with it. Sport at the school was thriving, and the leading lights of the PE department – Eddie Barton, Mark McLoughlin, Sue Preston and Julia Ruddy – needed all the help they could get. The soccer and cricket fixtures were expanded into every age group. Cross-country, athletics, swimming, basketball, badminton and rugby league were included in the after-school curriculum and Saddleworth began to compete vigorously in the Oldham schools leagues.

Although I enjoyed every aspect of teaching PE, it was the work I did with the more talented pupils in the lunch hour, after school when the afternoon lessons had finished and on Saturday morning that really got me going. I soon realised that I had the ability to improve individual performance and inspire greater effort from my students, traits which were to serve me so well when I moved into professional coaching a few years later. Eddie

Barton, who also played professional rugby league for Oldham and later Barrow, introduced a club for pupils with learning difficulties. When I left the school, it was he who drove rugby excellence at Saddleworth forward. Eddie was able to guide a young Kevin Sinfield through his formative years so well that he was to become the captain of the hugely successful Leeds Rhinos and Great Britain sides. I know Kevin has never forgotten him: 'Eddie Barton, or "Sir" as we knew him, is a fantastic man, who gave up his time selflessly to help anyone who needed it. He was a lone soldier in creating the opportunity for myself and others to play rugby league at school, and he did it in a way that kept the fun factor very much alive. His values were exemplary and he was an absolute gentleman. On behalf of all rugby players at the school who played for Eddie I would like to say thank you.' [Kevin Sinfield]

With my own playing career coming to an end, I began to suspect that classroom-based teaching would no longer provide the job satisfaction I was looking for. I had thought about retiring in 1980 having played 350 games for my hometown team Oldham, only to change my mind and join Whitehaven's push for promotion from the second division instead. Whitehaven were losing their final game against Doncaster with only seconds remaining when I managed to crash over in the corner and then convert the try from the touchline to win the match and secure promotion. I should have been satisfied with that fairy-tale ending at 36 years of age and taken my final bow! But I didn't take the hint, signed on for another year and Whitehaven were promptly relegated back down to Division 2 the year after they'd gained promotion. That was the cue for me to finally call time on my playing career, but I couldn't cure my obsession with rugby so my only 'fix' was coaching…

At first it was the burgeoning talent and competitiveness of the Oldham schools that drew Phil towards coaching. Traditional powers such as the two Catholic schools of St Anselm's and St Albans were now joined by others like Fitton Hill, coached by Iain 'Corky' MacCorquodale [who went on to become a goal-kicker of legendary status with Workington Town], Breezehill overseen by Eric Fitzsimmons [a notorious 'double agent' who played professionally for both of Oldham's football teams in league and soccer, and who was to become one of the coaches on the National Coaching Scheme years later], and Counthill under the auspices of Bill Hainsworth – particularly in the years when the Sculthorpe brothers were pupils at the school. It was the beginning of a powerful family alignment between the Larders and the Sculthorpes. As the Great Britain coach, Phil was to hand Paul his international debut in 1996 at the tender age of 19 years old, while his youngest son David went on to play alongside Danny Sculthorpe at Rochdale Hornets.

As a result the Oldham schools representative teams became highly competitive, rivalling Wigan, Hull and St Helens for trophies and having its players selected for the English schools team which played an annual fixture against France.

Although rugby league dominated in the schools, there was a friendly relationship between the rival codes in the town and Oldham Rugby Union Club always made their ground readily available for the end of season cup finals. In 1981, after Saddleworth had defeated Fitton Hill in the under 13s final, the club chairman Terry Hirst [whose son Graham had captained Saddleworth] suggested that I should go one step further and enter the Saddleworth School RL team in the Lancashire Schools rugby union knockout competition the following year.

My first stab at coaching a side playing union was highly instructive for all concerned. The boys had their eyes opened on their visits to some of the large grammar schools with their superb facilities and grounds… 'Oohs' and 'Aahs' were in plentiful supply! However we managed to do some eye-opening of our own with the ambition and accuracy of our handling game in the matches themselves. We not only won the under 13s cup, but also the two teams I entered in the sevens competition sailed through the knockout stages to face one another in the final!

The boys would come up to me and say,

'Why do they keep kicking the ball back to us all the time, Mr Larder?'

'Beats me…!' I'd reply with a shrug of the shoulders. I probably still don't know the answer to that one to the present day…

After the exploits of Phil's league boys in the under-13s cup in their first season, the road was not so smooth for Saddleworth when they entered a team in the union competition thereafter. Mike Ford remembers that,

We loved to bring our handling and passing skills to the party, but we didn't have much of a clue about the rules of union, which to be fair are pretty complex in any case. The worst scenario for us was a bleak wet and windy afternoon, when the aspects of union we were least familiar with – like the scrum and the maul – became more important.

But I don't think the other proper union-playing schools wanted to be beaten by a bunch of leaguers again anyhow. There was one occasion – on just such a wet-and-windy day – when our boys trotted off the field at half-time for a nice warming cup of tea in the changing sheds. We'd forgotten that most of the teams we played tended to stay on the pitch and suck oranges at the break. So when we came out refreshed for the second half, we found that the ref had already blown the whistle and the game was already underway without us!

Phil had also been coaching the Oldham under-16 [league] town team which won promotion to the first division in his first year in charge, following it up with victory in the English Schools Knockout Cup Final against an outstanding Hull side – Lee Crooks, Andy Dannatt and all – at the Sheddings in front of 2,000 roaring, stamping spectators. It was a sharp reminder of the good old days, and it encouraged his home-town club, who had been based at the Sheddings for so long, to invest in a new youth team. They succeeded in signing up several age-group internationals and when they offered Phil the opportunity to become coach, he was sorely tempted to take them up on it.

Although at the time of the offer Phil had to decline – the school colts also played on Saturdays so there was an obvious conflict of interests – the die was already cast. The great mystery of Saddleworth, of a world with a foot in both camps, had already invested Phillip Larder – and sooner than he ever thought possible, a choice would have to be made. One evening in the summer of 1982, as Phil sat discussing the future with his wife Anne, the phone rang twice. It was Ione, one of Anne's closest friends, with the timely information that there was a job advertised in *The Manchester Evening News*. 'Director of Coaching, Rugby Football League, full-time, applications invited.'

I applied without hesitation, but after the initial acknowledgement I began to fear the worst. The wires went quiet for at least two months, and in the media the popular front-runner for the post was John Mantle, two years ahead of me at Loughborough and an ex-Wales RU international. I knew John well and I began to write off my chances – just before a letter dropped on to my doormat, inviting me to an interview at the George hotel in Huddersfield.

Everyone who loves rugby league knows that the George was the landmark venue where the division of rugby's soul first took place. Twenty-one clubs from Lancashire and Yorkshire seceded from the union on 29 August 1895 over 'broken-time payments' and formed the Northern union, which over time became the Rugby Football League. It even housed the Rugby League Heritage Collection in its basement before the hotel doors closed, apparently for the last time, early in 2013. It has since been brought back from the brink and revived by a local businessman.

At the time, I didn't feel that my interview had gone well. I was nervous and I felt that lack of confidence had communicated itself to the interviewing panel… So it came as a great surprise when Maurice Oldroyd [the chief executive of BARLA], rang me to say that the job was mine. Apparently the interview panel had been impressed with the way that I had developed rugby league at Saddleworth School and by my coaching of the Oldham schools town team.

I was completely lost in those first few weeks as I struggled to come to grips with the sheer range of my responsibilities and the sensitive political background to the job. I had no idea of the impact of having two separate governing bodies in the sport until I experienced it first-hand and it was at the root of many of the problems in the sport in the UK. The Rugby Football League controlled the professional arm while BARLA [the British Amateur Rugby League Association] managed the rapidly-expanding amateur section. The officials from both were at odds with each other most of the time and it got so bad that Maurice Oldroyd was not even invited by the RFL to its Wembley showpiece, the Rugby League Challenge Cup Final.

I also hadn't fully understood the scope of my role, which carried a far wider remit than progressing coach education and qualification in the sport. I was to be responsible for the overall development of playing and coaching standards at every level from junior rugby to professional rugby league and there was no doubt I felt tremendously stimulated by the challenge! But three days before I turned up for my first day of work, I'd injured my leg in training for my very last game of rugby league. I missed the match and limped into the BARLA headquarters in Huddersfield feeling underpowered both mentally and physically.

It was a sign of the times. 'Limping along' was the state of rugby league in the UK at that time. Although benevolent influences like David Oxley and Maurice Oldroyd [the heads of the respective governing bodies] did their best to protect Phil from the political background and hack out an administrative pathway that enabled positive decisions to be made for the future of the sport, they could not protect him from the traumatic evidence of the 1982 tour by Australia. The game in England was the sick man of rugby league, and that tour and those Kangaroos were the harsh medicine of change.

I began by attending all the rugby league coaching courses that took place that summer, observing both national and regional coaches at work and developing a feeling for what the student coaches expected to gain from the course. I also attended other sports courses to provide a point of comparison, and with the help of sensible folk like Sue Campbell [who headed up the National Coaching Foundation], I slowly started to cut a pathway through all the bulls**t – and believe me, theoretical dogma was plentiful in sports administration in England at that time.

Although Laurie Gant and Albert Fearnley [the two national coaches who ran the course] were well liked and respected, the content of their course did not go far enough. The introductory course, quite rightly, concentrated on developing the basics skills of rugby league, but a student who wanted to earn the highest coaching badge had to do nothing more than attend the same course all over again. There was no sense of progression, or of a clear vision behind the scheme. I had initially hoped to get Albert and Laurie on board, but when they made it clear they had no intention of developing the courses further, and expected me to be no more than an administrator, I could see that our views were terminally at odds. If I had not fired them, the coaching scheme would never have developed. All the regional coaches apart from Maurice Bamford and Australian Garth Budge followed suit and resigned, and Maurice and Garth were the only two I wanted to keep! This was good news because it allowed me to start with a clean slate and appoint my own staff.

The process of getting the professional club coaches to accept a 'coaching educator' at the top of the domestic game in the UK would not be an easy one – especially a man who had not played international football himself. As John Huxley remembers,

> Phil was a teacher by trade, and his social and educational background was different to most of the men who played and coached rugby league, who tended to come from the industrial working class in Lancashire and Yorkshire. He'd gained a degree from Loughborough University and he'd started out as a rugby union player, so there were a number of reasons for suspicion, or superstition, when Phil was appointed as the national director of coaching.
>
> If you went along to coaching sessions regularly, as I did, you would also notice a big difference in the way Phil and most of the other coaches went about their business. Where most of the coaches would emphasise a loose mixture of lapping and semi-opposed games of 'touch', Phil would run very disciplined, highly-organised sessions in which different compartments of the game would be broken down in a scientific manner with detailed attention paid to each area… My impression then was that Phil was a coach ahead of his time, and the only other British coach in the same bracket was probably Vince Karalius.

At a critical juncture, Phil received help from an unexpected but welcome source – Alex Murphy. 'Murph' had a reputation as being a maverick from his playing days. He was also outspoken, which didn't go down too well with the establishment; but he was indisputably one of rugby league's finest ever scrum-halves and his opinions carried a lot of weight.

When he'd first broken into the Great Britain Test side for the 1958 Ashes series in Australia, he was only 19 years old.

> Alex was playing half-back, which meant he had to put the ball into the scrums. The scrums were a heaving contest in those days and Alex got some very specific advice from Percy 'Tommy' Harris, GB's gnarled and fearsome Welsh hooker.

Tommy was confident he could get the better of his opposite number: 'Just you put the ball in straight kid, and I'll win it...' instructed Tommy. So at the first scrum, what did Alex do? He put it straight into the Kangaroo second row and they won the ball. Tommy shot Alex a glance that could have killed, but that was Murph. He wasn't the kind to be ordered around by anyone.

The last thing you'd expect Alex Murphy to be was a bastion of law and order. But when Phil began the process of gaining acceptance for the principle of coach certification and education, he knew he needed support from someone who packed a wallop inside the professional game.

I was nervous driving across the Pennines from Huddersfield to Warrington to staff the first 'Open Course'. In fact nervous would be an understatement. In addition to the amateur coaches and schoolteachers on the course would be several professionals, with big hitters like Billy Benyon (St Helens), Kevin Ashcroft (Leigh), Tony Barrow (Warrington) and Geoff Fletcher (Huyton) among them.

I knew that a number of these coaches were attending reluctantly. Their arms were being twisted by the RFL, which would become one of the first sporting administrations in the country to insist that all its coaches be fully accredited and own a coaching badge.

The press had not been too supportive either. The question had been raised, '*Why should coaches who have won the league or the Challenge Cup now go "back to school", to re-learn what they already know?*', and I knew that some of the attendees had ghosted articles in order to fan the flames in the media. One national daily had that very morning run a cartoon on its back page. I was wearing a teacher's cap and gown and ordering a crestfallen Alex Murphy, complete with his dunce's hat, to stand in the 'naughty corner'!

But I was hoping that Murph would be in my corner today. I'd gotten to know him quite well over the years, and I knew I had his professional respect as a player. He had been the first coach to phone and congratulate me when my appointment as national coaching director was announced, and he'd offered both his own support and that of his club Wigan: 'Look Phil... I know how important this course is for both you and the game in general so I won't cause any trouble. I'll knock the others into shape.'

I'd arrived early, as I always did, to start putting out cones and equipment, when I received a call from Maurice Bamford, who was due to staff the course with me. Maurice was the Great Britain coach at the time and his support added a great deal of weight to the course. Maurice simply said, 'My car's broken down, I doubt I'll be able to get there before lunch.' It felt like a large hole had suddenly opened up in the middle of the stage, and as the auditorium began to fill up I could sense an edge to the atmosphere. A couple of the professionals were pointing at the cartoon in the newspaper, their shoulders pumping up and down with laughter, while the amateurs and schoolteachers looked like they were expecting some fireworks. Meanwhile, Murph was nowhere to be seen.

As the clock ticked down towards the appointed hour and Alex had still not arrived, I thought to myself, 'Bollocks Phil, if you are going down, then go down fighting' as I walked out to the front of the stage. At that moment there was a screech of tyres and a car with 'Wigan Rugby League' on it flashed by. Murph burst in a few minutes later with a breezy 'Morning lads, sorry I'm late but I was called into the club.'

After a brief introduction we got down to business, and almost immediately Geoff Fletcher loudly voiced his disagreement with one of the points I'd made. As good as gold, Murph interjected: 'Geoff, I know we might all not want to be here, but at least give Phil a chance. I for one am expecting to learn something.'

The tension in the room immediately eased, and the professional coaches, particularly when we left the lecture theatre and went outside to start the practical work, set a fine example and even began to enjoy themselves. It was a key moment in gaining acceptance for the whole coach education and qualification process.

Murph had been one of the star speakers at my benefit dinner, which was billed as 'the battle of the world's two best scrum-halves', one from either code, Alex and Gareth Edwards. Both were going to speak about their experiences and then the audience had the chance to vote for the winner. Unfortunately Gareth had been doubled-booked and through no fault of his own had to cry off. After a number of panicked phone calls, we managed to get Fred Trueman, the great Yorkshire and England fast bowler and expert storyteller, to fill in for Gareth.

At the event, Alex was sat on one side, with Fred on the other and me perched in the middle between them. In typical Murph fashion he didn't stand on ceremony, grabbing the microphone from the compere with a 'Sit down fella, it's me they've come to hear!'

Over the next couple of hours Alex had the audience in raptures, he was a great raconteur. I remember Fred Trueman nudging me in the ribs as Alex came to the end of his session, whispering, 'How on earth do I follow that…?' in my ear. But follow it he did, and it was a close-run thing. The 'battle of the scrum-halves' was only decided when Alex once again grabbed the mike:

'See what it says 'ere on this ticket?' he shouted, pointing to an entry stub.

'*Who's the world's greatest scrum-half?* Well I can see only one bloody scrum-half here, so it must be me!'

Seeing the organiser's pockets sprouting with cash he added loudly, 'You can pay me my £750 now…' Alex grabbed all the notes and proceeded to count out his appearance fee quite theatrically. The audience was hushed and didn't know what to think. 'Phil Larder, you are the best centre never to have played for Great Britain so I will give this to you,' he then announced, stuffing the whole wad in my coat pocket as he completed his magic trick!

All attention turned to Fred Trueman, but all we saw was the vapour-trail of his pipe as it followed him out of the fire exit… 'Bloody stingy Yorkshire!' came the cry from one-and-all. But it didn't change the feel-good factor of a completely unexpected and generous gesture from Alex Murphy – the gamekeeper who loved to mug as a poacher, and one of the true greats of rugby league.

* * * * *

It is July 1983, and Phil's eyes are closed. The warm breeze passes over his face, he feels the heavy thrum of the engine beneath him and hears the screaming of seagulls – sometimes closer, sometimes further away. He's struggling to come to terms with the reality of relaxation, as he always does… He chuckles remembering the simplicity of Jack Gibson's advice to Peter Sterling when he was having problems with his kicking game: 'Kick it to the seagulls!' – kick the ball to the part of the field where the birds are in occupation, not the rugby players... and that does relax him. On the ferry from Sydney Harbour to Manly Wharf, the seagulls are your ever-present companions, trawling the wash behind the boat, picking off the scraps the people leave behind. Not all the scraps have been abandoned, and the odd indignant human cry from on deck flies back up at the seagulls hovering overhead. Phil feels a slight stab of guilt, knowing that he's on a mission similar to theirs, picking at the brains of men at the sharp end of rugby league's evolution, pioneers of the game.

He opens his eyes and closes them again, snapshotting the landmarks which will become so familiar over the next 20 years of his comings and goings. Fort Denison, the old penal colony tower that stands guard before Sydney Harbour – several thousand tonnes of Kurraba Point sandstone sinking, inch-by-inch, below the water-line. There is the steel-arched bridge and the giant caterpillar of the Opera House, struggling out of the earth as the ferry makes its final turn into the city wharf. Small colonies of observers watch from it, twitching and pointing as passengers disembark from the boat. One last look up at the sun, feeling the warmth of the country burning into his face. Phil's eldest son Matt lived out in Manly for a year at the turn of the millennium, plying his trade as a plumber and enjoying the lifestyle so much that he and his family seriously considered a permanent move to the other side of the world. If any of the Larder children, Matt or David or Anna had emigrated, there is little doubt that Anne and Phil would have followed them post-haste. Anne still recalls her first crossing on the ferry one summer evening in 2001, after she'd arrived in Manly for the final British & Irish Lions Test against the Wallabies; her eyes filling with tears involuntarily as the boat rocked along rhythmically and somehow, she made a secret connection with all the many stories that until that moment, had only been second-hand. The Larder family pilgrimage always comes back to one place, whether it is in person or travelling through memories – it returns to their spiritual second home, Australia.

Phil met up with the two Franks, Johnson and Stanton in Manly, a beach-front suburb of Sydney on his initial fact-finding mission in the summer of 1983. Frank Johnson played for the Newtown 'Bluebags' club and New South Wales in the later 1940s and early 50s. He was also a Kangaroo on the first tour after the Second World War in 1948, marrying his wife Ruby just before embarkation and pining for her for the next nine months away from home. At the end of his playing career he became a prominent coach and administrator in the game, as one of the founding fathers of the NSWRFL coaching panel in 1962 and the principal force in developing league in the Northern Territory of the country. It was Frank who first introduced Phil to the bounding waves in front of the Manly Pacific hotel, to which he'd return on many future occasions.

In the evening they would walk to the Steyne pub on the corner of the Corso, with its stripped-down wooden pews and floors and its packed homage to Manly league 'greats' on the walls – there would be Max Krilich, the Kangaroo hooker on the recent 'Invincibles' tour, Paul 'Fatty' Vautin [who unexpectedly missed out on the same trip], two present and future Kangaroo coaches in the shape of Frank Stanton and Bobby Fulton, and two of England's own who achieved success down under with the Sea Eagles – second row Malcolm Reilly and loose forward Steve 'Knocker' Norton.

It was at the Steyne that Phil first sat down with Frank Johnson and Frank Stanton, the coach of the unbeaten 1982 Australian side that toured the UK. Their opinions on the state of British rugby league were every bit as bare and forthright as the surroundings, their authority somehow reinforced by the stature of all those former Manly 'greats' from both hemispheres looking down from the walls. The two Franks were speaking as custodians of the game's future, not just as the mouthpiece of Great Britain's greatest international rivals.

> Frank Stanton spoke the thoughts that I'd been thinking. He despaired for the English game and said that he doubted if we would ever close the yawning divide in playing and coaching standards which had been exposed by the 1982 tour.
>
> 'You are your own worst enemies. You are held back by a weak administration, with two governing bodies with conflicting agendas always at war with one another.
>
> 'Your professional game is weak, hamstrung by the selection of outstanding ex-players as coaches at your top clubs, positions which they don't deserve by virtue of coaching experience or depth of knowledge about the game. The coverage you receive in the media is swamped by the overwhelming interest in soccer. The four leading sports-pages in the Sydney news all forefront rugby league; in England you struggle to find one paragraph on the game, even in the middle of a Kangaroo Tour.'

His final summary was just as conclusive:

'Nah…. Phil, you're far better off emigrating from the UK and coming to live out here if you want to coach league. Don't worry, we will find you a good job… and just look at the weather in comparison to what you have to put up with over there!'

The two Franks looked over their beers at me and laughed. I could see that they meant what they said, but beneath the surface humour there was a palpable intensity. I felt they were searching for signs of an understanding – an appreciation of the urgency of the situation, that rugby in the UK was in crisis and had reached a 'tipping point'.

In fact, Phil had found his answer only a week before, in two innocent but connected incidents – a bet that spectacularly misfired, and the shattered face of Ron Willey at the end of the 1983 State-of-Origin series. Ron had helped coach the New South Wales team which had just lost the final game of the series to the Queensland 'Maroons'. When Phil was introduced to him soon after the match, Ron Willey could scarcely look at him, as he struggled to come to terms with the devastating loss. Phil had attended the match himself as a guest of the ARL and endured a different, though thankfully much milder version of the same trauma.

My chaperone for the evening was the Queensland director of coaching Bobby Bax, who like Jack Gibson was into horse racing and sports betting in a big way. On the way to Brisbane from the airport Bobby suggested a diversion to the race-track, where he collected on three of the four bets he placed. I should have taken the hint when he asked for my thoughts on the game that evening. Having watched every single match of the 1982 tour live, and knowing that the core of the Test team was from New South Wales – full-back Greg Brentnall, centre Steve Rogers, wing Eric Grothe, half-backs Brett Kenny and Peter Sterling, and the entire forward pack of Craig Young, Max Krilich, Les Boyd, Wayne Pearce, Rod Reddy and Ray Price – I confidently predicted a victory for the Sky Blues… I could only see one starter from 1982 on the Queensland team, centre Mal Meninga, so how could the best team I'd ever seen possibly lose?

I confidently swallowed the hook Bobby had thrown out: 'I will take New South Wales'.

'That will do me,' Bobby snapped back immediately.

'How much on it?'

'Ten dollars?'

'Hahaha… not too confident then!' said Bobby, reeling me in like a master.

'Of course I am… let's make it 50', I replied, not wishing to look like a man who was afraid to ally mouth and money.

'100 bucks it is!' he replied, throwing out his hand to close the deal – or should I say the trap.

I didn't know two things. Firstly, although eleven of the 'Invincibles' had played for NSW in the first encounter at Lang Park three weeks earlier [which NSW also lost], only six remained that evening; the rest had already been played out of the series by their opponents. Secondly, I completely underestimated the 'Wally Lewis factor'. Lewis had been overlooked on the Kangaroo Tour by Frank Stanton over issues with his weight and had lost his Test place to Paramatta's Brett Kenny. He had languished on the bench and only came on to the field when the battles had already been won. Wally had a point to prove.

Wally Lewis had been a bit-part player in 1982 when by nature he was the conductor of the orchestra, and that was the clarion-call to wake up a rugby league genius. He had altered his lifestyle, trained hard, slimmed down and became totally focused on regaining his place in the starting line-up of the Australian team to play New Zealand, to be selected immediately after State of Origin III. In the game itself he produced a masterclass of first receiver play. His game-management, his tactical kicking, his organisation of the Maroons' attacking play, the variation of his passing – soft 'touch' deliveries to his close support, bullet spin passes to bring those twin towers in the Queensland centres, Mal Meninga and Gene Miles on to the ball, was something to behold. The Blues never had a chance, they were 21-0 behind at half-time and it was 33-0 before they scrambled some late consolation tries to make the final scoreline look better. Wally Lewis was man-of-the-match, an award he won at five of the first ten Origin matches. Lang Park was Wally's stomping ground and Origin was Wally's series. He was indeed the Emperor of Lang Park.

Much chastened, I handed over my $100 to Bobby, and boarded the plane back to Sydney. Even today I find it hard to believe what

I witnessed that night. The cream of a great Australian team, which had cut a swathe through the UK and conceded only one late try in the whole of the Test series, had itself been battered over the three State of Origin games, leaking eleven tries to a Wally Lewis-inspired Queensland.

When the Kangaroos to play New Zealand were announced the following day, only four 'Invincibles' [Kerry Boustead, Eric Grothe, Max Krilich and Ray Price] were in it. The impact on my thinking was profound, and I began to realise that Australia could have selected two or even three different teams to beat Great Britain one year earlier. The quality of performance on the field, and standard of preparation off it was in a different world to what I'd known in the UK.

* * * * *

Frank Stanton had been the coach on the 1982 Kangaroos tour of the UK. It was the third Ashes series he'd coached, after the home and away encounters in 1978/79. On Frank's watch, Great Britain had suffered its first series whitewash since 1911, losing 3-0 in Australia in 1979. Britain only managed to score two tries and 18 points over the course of the three Test matches, and the stats say that the Kangaroos' goal-kicker Mick Cronin could have beaten GB on his own, because he touched down twice and knocked over 24 goals all by himself!

Even more worryingly, the combined attendance for the three matches was only 67,000, less than half of the 134,000 on the previous trip down under in 1974. The contrast with the 1966 and 1970 tours was even more brutal, as both of those had attracted upwards of 165,000 spectators. Financially, the tour represented a loss of over $300,000, and in a coaching sense it was pregnant with symbolism. Coach Eric Ashton had been unable to fly out with the tour party because of an accident to his daughter, and it accurately reflected the 'headless' state of rugby league coaching and preparation in Britain at the time. There was a real concern in Australia that the weakness of the international game would have a negative effect on the capacity of the Sydney-based NSWRFL to compete with its traditional domestic rivals, Aussie Rules and union.

The coach of GB's last Ashes-winning series in 1970, Hull's Johnny Whiteley had been restored for the 1982 tour, as a kind of last bastion of remembered greatness, but in reality there was little that he could do to stem the tide of coaching innovation and cultural change that swept Great Britain away.

The first Test at Boothferry Park in Hull told the story for the rest of the series. The tourists looked fitter, faster and more skilful and above all, they had an unbelievable defence.

> For the first time in my life I was watching the team without the ball and it was their defensive organisation and commitment of the players to it which was the most impressive feature. Great Britain had thrown everything they could at them and they would have scored against a lesser team but the Australians had never looked like cracking even when defending right on their own try-line – and when Great Britain had tried to go around them it was the Australian defence which went forward at speed rather than the British attack.
>
> It was only 10-4 to the Kangaroos at half-time, and when I was chatting to other spectators in the crowd, most were of the opinion that Great Britain still had a chance. I couldn't agree with them and felt we were on to a hiding. My worst fears were justified in the second half when the young Australian team really cut loose and scored a further six tries to win by 40 points to 4 and completely stun the home crowd, who shuffled out of the ground in silence.
>
> There were some unforgettable snapshots from that afternoon at Boothferry Park that are still seared into my memory to this day. The skill of their prop Craig Young taking out two defenders before lobbing a perfect miss pass over a third to put Wayne Pearce away in the build-up to the first Kangaroo try; the brute Mal Meninga knocking away the covering Les Dyl as he scored it – 'He knocks him away like he was a little boy... Get off! Off yer go!' said Murph up in the commentary box; the support play of hooker Max Krilich, sprinting 40 metres late on in the second half to set his wing up with a fingertip transfer, and the sheer pounding power of hairy Eric Grothe down that side-line, all huge thighs and ground-eating stride; the Kangaroos' speed at the play-the-ball, which caused GB to give up penalty after penalty when the defensive line could not reorganise in time, and the textbook left-footed kicking of their ex-Aussie Rules full-back Greg Brentnall, who always looked as if he was demonstrating the model technique for a group of youngsters!

But for me, the scrum-half Peter Sterling epitomised the Kangaroos better than anyone, with his superbly-accurate distribution and right-footed kicking game and his fearless low tackling technique… a blond whirlwind, a human dynamo who never quit until the final whistle.

As a coach, that game opened up a new world of possibilities to me. In particular, the physical fitness of the Australians, and their power into the tackle [on defence] and out of it [on attack] impressed me. Their defence was something else again. Johnny Whitely and his assistant Colin Hutton had devised a repertoire of clever moves off half-back Stevie Nash and loose forward Steve Norton for the match, involving wrap-arounds and options coming short and long, but the Kangaroos' line-speed and consistency in coming up as a single line just devoured them before they even got untracked. Tackles were being made 10 metres, 15 metres upfield, and when we tried to get some offloads off our big ball-carrying props Jeff Grayshon and Trevor Skerrett, they just closed up in the support lanes on either side of them.

After the game the GB scrum-half Steve Nash said, '…it's time for British rugby league to stop living in the past.' He could not have been more right. The general opinion before the tour was that the Kangaroos would be fitter and more powerful than us, but we would be able to give them a lesson in the basic skills. What nonsense that turned out to be! The Australians had a level of skill not seen before in these Isles. Their defence conceded only six tries in 13 games, their attack was exceptional and they won all their matches by an average score of 45-5. If that wasn't total domination in every facet of the game, I didn't know what was.

Phil had already tried to contact Frank Stanton earlier in the tour to sound him out about the possibility of watching a Kangaroo training session. Understandably Stanton has not been too excited by the prospect, as he knew that everything he saw could go straight back to Johnny Whitely and the GB camp. But in between the first and second Tests, the mood on the Australian side had changed. They already knew they would win the Test series at a canter, and the larger picture – the future of rugby league as a global sport – had begun to take precedence. The ARL gave Frank Stanton an unequivocal answer to the question Phil had posed a couple of weeks previously: 'It is vital for international rugby that Great Britain become great again… show him the lot.' Phil received an unexpected phone call from Frank Stanton and travelled up to the Australians' hotel in Leeds, then spent the Thursday and Friday before the second Test at Wigan in the Kangaroos camp.

The results of Phil's two-day visit blew his mind and had a huge impact on the course of his subsequent coaching career in both codes. Before he ever got to see one of the training sessions, he became aware of the enormous amount of background planning that had been funnelled into the tour, and the preparation that was still being carried out as the tour progressed.

Phil had noticed that Frank Stanton always carried a little book around with him, entitled *The Psychology of Coaching*. Psychology was one of the major planks in the Kangaroos' preparation before the tour ever reached British shores, and it even influenced seemingly innocuous items like room allocation. The Grand Final in the Sydney club competition had been bitterly contested by the Manly-Warringah Sea Eagles and the Paramatta Eels, and it was necessary to merge players from the two rival clubs who would provide the bulk of the touring squad into a unified playing force on the field. Therefore Paramatta's John Muggleton found himself sharing a room with Les Boyd of the Sea Eagles, with whom he'd fought a running battle in the Grand Final; likewise the two locks, Paul McCabe and Ray Price, found themselves staring at each other across the bedroom carpet. Elsewhere Stanton undertook some social engineering, pairing Ian Schubert with Eric Grothe. 'Shoey' was an in-your-face extrovert, but Grothe was the opposite, a man who kept his own counsel and was even known as 'the Guru' for the amount of time he spent quietly in meditation! Players were being challenged to face their 'opposite' and forced out into the open, and Stanton used a variation of the same technique out on the field in training:

> 'Our routine was designed to involve players in the day-to-day running of the tour whenever possible… It also seemed a natural progression to give the veteran players some responsibility for running training sessions. Having the rest of the players under the eye of the group leaders allows none of them to "hide" during training.'

Players were not allowed space to 'hide' on or off the field, and the principle was extended to their responses to Test selection. When the choice was close in a particular position, the player who lost out in selection had to confront his disappointment, and the possibility of resentment. Before the tour started, the Canterbury scrum-half Steve Mortimer had been the popular selection for the Tests, but in the event his spot went to Peter Sterling:

> 'Steve Mortimer knows that Peter Sterling has the half-back role on merit, so he accepts he will have to fight hard to get his place back. He can choose to take it like a man, because if he sulks he will become a threat to tour unity. I rely on the respect Steve has for Peter's ability and his faith in his own, in equal measure. First and foremost, he has pride in being part of a very happy tour.'

The 'ply-depth' and scientific basis for video analysis was also taken to a new level both before and during the tour. During the three months of the 1982 NSWRFL season, Stanton had asked his analysts to work out the average tackle counts for each position. This was then used as a baseline for comparison with tackle counts in the games throughout the tour, typed up on a single sheet of paper and posted in sensitive areas at the team base – as the players filed into the medical room for physiotherapy or medical treatment, they couldn't avoid glancing up and noticing the unvarnished truth of their contribution to the defensive side of the last match, for better or worse. Once the tackle count 'gold standard' had been established, analysis began to focus on the statistics used in American football, such as error counts and 'turnover' production.

Video-based analysis during the trip was no less rigorous. When Steve Rogers [the veteran Kangaroo centre and one of the all-time greats] was beaten twice on the outside by Les Dyl for Leeds just ten days before the first Test, there was a prompt reminder that this danger had been underlined before the game. Rogers pointed out that the Leeds stand-off half John Holmes had twice forced him to move inside to respect the threat of a short ball to David Heron, before Dyl was set free on the wider arc on the third occasion. The video analysis of this attacking shape was stored away for future reference, and when Holmes was selected to play for Great Britain in the second Test it formed the basis of the Kangaroos' defensive planning for that match. Significantly, Holmes was not selected for the third Test, and the effectiveness of the Kangaroos' analysis forced the GB selectors to rethink that crucial position for every Test they played. It helped give the Australians the continuity in selection throughout the series that Great Britain never enjoyed.

The tourists also adopted a healthy attitude towards criticism. There was never any attempt made to hide from criticism in the media. All criticisms of the tourists in the media or by opposition coaches were noted, pinned on the wall and used for motivation in the course of the tour. If Stanton couldn't find tools for motivation via the media, he'd even go looking for it in other sports. When no footage of British successes in rugby league could be found, he had the Kangaroos watching film of Ian Botham destroying the 1981 baggy caps at Headingley instead. Criticism within the group was sealed from the outside world. After every match, there would be one hour in which honest opinions and self-criticism were exchanged behind locked doors. Not even the manager Frank Farrington was allowed in, it was just Frank Stanton and the team, no-one else.

In terms of their physical development for elite contact sport and their concentration on defence, the Kangaroos were years ahead of Great Britain:

My first impression out on the training field was how much bigger, yet leaner the players looked compared to ours. Frank explained to me that all the clubs in Australia employed conditioners and that all the players were on carefully controlled weight training programmes. Most of them drove into their clubs early morning and lifted heavy weights before work then returned in the evening for club training. Their diet was rigorously enforced, the players were weighed each week, and those carrying too much fat were heavily fined and forced to do extra conditioning as part of the 'fat club'.

The most striking feature of the training sessions was their simplicity. Their training was so simple, it was almost like watching a session for the under-13s. Four groups of seven worked on honing their basic skills – catching a high ball, falling on the loose ball, picking the ball up when it was first rolling towards the player, then away from him; simple passing drills, with the players at times standing wide, then slowly contracting around the ball.

The coaches' mantra was 'simple but perfect': every pass had to be perfectly directed and carefully weighted and the precision had to be maintained as the speed of the drills rapidly increased. This was the opposite of what was happening in Britain at the time, where games of tig-and-pass, unopposed rugby and work on set-piece moves took precedence over the perfection of fundamental skills.

The second training session, which concentrated on defence, was even more of an eye-opener. This was something entirely new in my experience and the first defensive training session I had ever seen. First of all the players were required to tackle large rubber tubes, which rolled and wobbled unpredictably as the players tried to hunt them down all over the field. Then out came the tackle shields, square stuffed plastic shields which allowed defenders to leave the ground and strike the opponent with little risk of injury to either party. One group held the shields in a line while a second group hit into them. The hitting was extremely disciplined with the players holding a perfect line and accelerating into the shields before forcefully digging into the shield on the same shoulder. Then they trotted back to the mark, re-forming the line quickly and repeating the drill on the other shoulder. The defenders were extremely vocal and their communication skills were highly developed. They talked, listened and reacted together in what rapidly became a moving wall of sound, rising in a crescendo to the 'boom' of contact with the tackle shields…

This was so new to me at the time that I remember reeling along the sideline, trying to get ever closer to the action as I struggled to take it all in. If these were not 'men from another planet' as Alex Murphy had christened them in TV commentary, they were certainly men training and playing well ahead of their time. This was an incredible glimpse of the future and I felt humbled to see it at such close quarters. I was in the debt of the ARL and Frank Stanton in particular in opening the doors for me.

As the reputation of the Kangaroos' innovative training sessions spread like wildfire, a large shoal of coaches from league's oldest rival, rugby union, began to feed from them towards the end of the tour. Phil was duly impressed by Frank Stanton, the man who orchestrated it all, by his ability to take ideas from other sports and transplant them into rugby league and to continually stay abreast of developments in sports psychology, motivation and the acquisition of skill, game analysis and statistics. As Phil was to discover, there was another coach back in Australia who managed this juggling act at least as well as Frank Stanton, and his name was Jack Gibson.

The Kangaroos' tour manager and the Newtown club's chief administrator, Frank Farrington, was as helpful as his namesake and both of them encouraged me to write a report on my observations with a view to presenting it to the Council of the Rugby Football League.

When we shook hands at the end of the tour, Frank Farrington insisted that I visit Sydney early in 1983 in order to spend time with both Peter Corcoran [the director of the Australian Rugby League Coaching Scheme] and Jack Gibson, the coach of the Grand Final winners Paramatta.

They left with my head still buzzing with unanswered questions. Were we keeping up with the modern six-tackle game of league? Were our top coaches keeping abreast of modern sporting developments? Most British clubs were content to appoint top-class players as coaches, without encouraging these players to learn the various techniques of coaching. The job descriptions of player and coach were and are completely different. In Australia they had to qualify through the National Coaching Scheme before they could coach even a reserve grade team. In Britain, clubs tended to appoint star players as coaches because of their experience and charisma, in Australia they only appointed them against the background of a sound coaching education.

I felt that our existing coaching scheme had a lot to answer for. Controlled by BARLA, it had been geared only to grass-roots [amateur] level, and had not embraced the professional game of six-tackle rugby league. The two-tiered administration system had failed completely to connect the amateur with the professional game, whereas in Australia all levels of the game were working together towards one common objective. Grass-roots rugby was the subject of heavy investment by the professional arm of the game, and in return all the top youngsters were funnelled into the top of the professional pyramid in Sydney.

Phil had come across an article by the Australian journalist Bill Mordey in *The Australian Mirror* which clarified just how advanced the ARL was in its structuring of the domestic game. Mordey recorded that:

'A record 307 graduates from Penrith were presented with Grade 3 coaching certificates last Monday night, and the coaches will all be utilised within the 387 teams playing in the district. This development of the juniors is being shown in the first grade side, which had only three imports taking the field last Sunday against Norths. The Penrith club outlaid about $4,000 on the current coaching classes.'

The Australian National Coaching Scheme developed a direct relationship between grass-roots and the professional end of the game, and that in turn ensured competitive standards. If a player at the professional level let go of those standards, there were plenty of men ready to replace him from the junior feeder club ranks.

Recent ex-players had to go through the coach education process before they could become top grade coaches, otherwise teams in the ARL wouldn't employ them – so there was a mutual respect between the scheme and the league and they served each other's needs. At the time Phil submitted his report [February 1983] Steve Rogers had enrolled as a student in the Scheme with a view to moving into coaching two years later.

Coincidentally his son Mat also became a dual-code international and played against England in the 2003 World Cup Final.

Steve Rogers was just starting out on his league career, as a callow but supremely talented 18-year-old, back in 1973. He went to the Grand Final as part of the same Cronulla-Sutherland side as the great British half-back Tommy Bishop. At 5ft 2in Bishop was the ultimate Jekyll-and-Hyde scrum-half – so testy and such a niggler that he once got Noel Kelly sent off in a Test match at Swinton – and at the same time a brilliant ball-player, whose 'classic ball skills were without peer anywhere in the rugby playing world. He carved out running angles for his supports with passes timed so sweetly that even knowledge of his creativity was often of little value to opposition teams.' Bishop had been a success on both sides of the globe, travelling to Australia as captain of both his club St Helens and his country and dragging the new franchise of Cronulla up by its bootstraps after he arrived in 1967. Within six years Cronulla were contesting the Grand Final against mighty Manly-Warringah under the orb of his influence.

By 1980 Tommy Bishop was a fully-qualified 'Australian' coach who was shocked by the decline, or more accurately the absence of coaching/ training standards when he returned to England as the new coach of Workington Town:

'I have an Australian first-class coaching certificate that covers weight training, psychology, nutrition and a lot else besides. I doubt that any other British coach can say that… In fact I don't believe any coaching goes on here, it's pathetic.

'Coaching here seems to consist of tig-and-pass, and British players are mercenaries who are only interested in what they can take out of the game, not what they can put in. Our players must be tied to contracts if our game is to recover from its depression. In Australia, I had a hold over players, they couldn't just walk out on a club like they do over here.

'Success boils down to good coaching and players wanting to make the best of themselves. Wayne Pearce has an eight-mile run before breakfast every day. No British player would do that.'

With its litany of coaches who had never been accredited, there was no real sense of accountability in British rugby league of the early 1980s. The standards were lax and inconsistent. There could be no clearer or more damning appraisal of British rugby league at the time than Tommy Bishop's. It was confirmed when, in the *Adidas World Ratings* published at the end of the Kangaroos' tour, the top five rated stand-off halves were all Australian – Brett Kenny, Wally Lewis, Alan Thompson, Mitchell Cox and Terry Lamb. The last two were uncapped players in the NSWRFL who had never played a Test match.

For Phil Larder, the only solution to the pervasive mediocrity and the intellectual 'fog' of the British rugby league scene was to escape from it entirely. He took up the offer of the two Franks to visit Australia and immerse himself in the rugby culture of the country. In the process he would find himself in the presence of the greatest rugby coaching mind he was ever to encounter in either code – Jack Gibson.

Chapter three

Super-coach and the Australian way

THIS is not 1983, it is one year later, and there is no Peter Corcoran [the ARL's coaching director] to greet Phil Larder at Sydney airport. There is no air-conditioned black limousine to ease him to his destination, with its glossy advertising trim for the Rothman's Foundation and the Australian Rugby League. This time, there is nothing for show.

A battered Chevy 4x4 pulls up, with two occupants. A huge wild-looking black and brown Alsatian sits on the passenger seat alongside the driver, who is regarding the new occupant sullenly over the edge of his horn-rimmed spectacles. Neither appears to welcome strangers.

The man gets out, tall, rugged and trailing the butt of a 'Craven A' cigarette in his left hand. Smoke curls up from it silently as he simply announces, 'Jack Gibson. What's doin'?' The gaze never flinches as Phil takes up the offer of his leathery hand, the size of a shovel. Both the grip and the gaze stay with him a little longer than the greeting demands, until it feels more like an initiation than an introduction.

Where Peter Corcoran small-talked freely on the journey back one year before, in the cabin with Jack and his dog, there is little more than silence. Sentences when they come are terse and clipped, as if they've been torn away unwillingly from some deep meditation. The Alsatian continues to look at Phil as if he has yet to earn his trust, and that it will not be an easy task…

Jack mumbles something about making a detour and stops at the side of the road to pick up a man even bigger than himself, aptly nicknamed 'Tiny'. Even at a strapping 6ft 3in, Jack is dwarfed and the newcomer is shoved unceremoniously into the back of the pick-up with the Alsatian, who barks out a gruff warning.

The truck eventually stops beside a nightclub in the sleazy, downtown area of Sydney. It is early evening and nobody is about. Phil gets out with 'Tiny' and Jack, glad to get away from his canine companion for a few moments.

Tiny advances and bangs a huge fist on the front door. There is the sound of footsteps descending the stairs before a small hatch opens and another giant, presumably one of the club 'heavies' replies,

'Yeah, what do you want?'

'The manager,' replies Tiny in a surprisingly undemanding voice.

'He's not here.' The hatch is slammed shut abruptly and the feet pound back up the stairs.

Tiny knocks again, and the process is repeated a couple of times until the heavy finally loses patience and growls:

'I have told you the manager isn't here. Even if he was here he wouldn't want to see you. Now do me a favour and f**k off before you get hurt.'

Tiny grabs the man by the collar and pulls his face closer to the hatch: 'Do you know who this is?'

For the first time 'Gibbo' steps forward into view. The heavy's attitude changes immediately and he is contrite and deferential. All the air suddenly goes out of him:

'Oh I didn't know it was you Mr Gibson, you should have told me the first time. I'm so sorry, just give me a minute to get the manager.' This time the footsteps ascend the stairs more urgently, and the manager appears to offer both an abject apology and one year's free membership for Jack's teenage son Luke, who had been thrown down the stairs of the club the previous weekend and warned never to return.

Throughout the incident, Jack had not uttered a single word because there was no need to. His reputation preceded him, and it extended far beyond the one he had made for himself in the narrow confines of the NSWRFL.

Jack Gibson lived a double life, and very few people in the world of rugby were admitted into Jack's shadow world. Jack's early career in rugby league had coincided with his association with Joe 'Boss' Taylor, who controlled an underground empire in the seamy side of Sydney –

betting and bookmaking joints and casinos. Jack was quick with his fists and became Taylor's minder and began to run some of his operations for him, including the notorious 'Thommo's two-up', where punters would bet on the outcome of two big brass pennies spun into the air, coming down either 'evens' [both heads or tails] or 'odds' [one tails and the other heads].

Boss Taylor kick-started Jack Gibson's rugby league career when he invested heavily in a 'Celebrity Club' A-grade team in the eastern suburbs of Sydney and Jack began playing in it in the forwards, mostly as a second row. Jack's development as a rugby player and coach, and his interests in the Sydney betting underworld ran hand in hand, to the point where he could walk into 'the Big House' [Paramatta jail] as coach of the Eels in the 80s to be given a standing ovation by the inmates! 'Taylor', the name of Jack's Alsatian, was a secret nod to 'Boss' and Jack's origins as much as it was to Paramatta's young full-back [Paul Taylor] of the time. It was a constant reminder of where he came from, and the grainy half-lit world that his success in rugby grew out of, but that world was seldom revealed in the sunny outdoors of rugby league. As one of his ex-players, Peter Dimond put it, 'He was a mystery man. No-one made any enquiries.'

That old Chevy pick-up that Jack drove to collect Phil Larder from the airport gave up one of the essential clues to both his character and the origin of his success as a rugby league coach. Early in his playing career he had been nicknamed 'Hoot' after Hoot Gibson, an American rodeo champion and pioneer cowboy film actor in the Wild West movies of the 20s, 30s and 40s in Hollywood. Jack loved all things American, and with his coaching hat on he was able to explore and translate developments in other sports successfully to rugby league. He was fascinated by American football or 'gridiron' in particular, and both its practices and its terminology became the principal source of his innovation as a coach in Australian rugby league.

The light bulb was switched on when Jack Gibson was still in the infancy of his coaching career, in charge of the famous St George Dragons club in 1970/71. Terry Fearnley, a playing colleague of Gibson's at Eastern Suburbs, who was later to coach Paramatta, New South Wales and the Kangaroos, takes up the story:

> 'I was down in Melbourne on a sales manager's course for General Motors Holden. I'd retired as a player and hadn't thought of coaching or continuing my involvement in rugby league.

'…We had several lectures to sit through when out of the blue, came a film on motivation by Vince Lombardi. I hadn't heard of him, but I came out of the room that day mesmerised by what I'd seen and determined to become a football coach, not a sales manager!

'I wanted to show the film to Jack… He just grunted when I mentioned it. At the time he was coaching the "red V" [St George] and they were going through a really bad patch, losing something like six games in a row. The Dragons were a big club and the directors were getting uneasy.

'So Jack arrives for training one night with just this Lombardi video under one arm. He gathers the players from all three grade teams together and gets them to watch it. No laps of the oval, no training drills, just the film…. The players were so awestruck that he rewound the reel and let them watch it all over again… The directors of the club were going wild…but for the next seven weeks, St George did not lose a game in any grade, first, second or third. Jack's search for knowledge from America had begun and the rest, as they say, is history.'

The film that changed everything for Jack Gibson as a coach was called *Second Effort* [http://www.historicfilms.com/tapes/15514]. It featured the great Green Bay Packers coach Vince Lombardi, supported by one of his All-Pro offensive linemen Jerry Kramer, offering advice to a travelling salesman [played by actor Ron Masak] who has lost his motivation for the job. The film was made in 1968, at a time when Lombardi's glittering head-coaching career, during which he won three successive Superbowls with the Packers between 1965–67 and five championships overall in the space of eight astonishing years, was coming to an end. There is no doubt that Lombardi was one of the most influential coaching thinker-philosophers of any sporting era, and *Second Effort* went on to achieve extraordinary popularity as a tool on leadership and management courses.

The film begins with Masak giving up on a sale to his prospective buyer, played by Lombardi. 'Why didn't you make the second effort?' asks Lombardi, 'Do you always give up on things that easily?' It is the cue for an explanation of the principles behind the Packers' winning culture:

- The importance of fundamentals [blocking and tackling in American football], and of peak physical conditioning.

'Fatigue makes cowards of us all...' says Lombardi, 'This is what I mean by going back to fundamentals. Every season, every veteran is expected to start the same way a rookie does. It's as though we've never seen him before.'

- Mental toughness. 'Success at anything in this world is 75% mental. In our league, the teams are physically equal, and it's the team that turns up mentally prepared on any given day that wins the ball-game. Mental toughness... is not giving in to yourself. It's a state-of-mind, you might call it "character in action".'

- Discipline and respect. 'You better set your watch 15 minutes early. In this world there's regular time and Lombardi time. Around here if you're ten minutes early for practice you're still late!' says Jerry Kramer.

- Knowing your enemy, and every detail of your job inside out. 'We believe in knowing everything we can about the competition... We want to know all the characteristics of the men on the other team, the pluses and the minuses. Then we put all that information into a computer, so the next time we play that team, we know all there is to know about the opponent.'

Many of these principles would have become second nature to a side like the 1982 Kangaroos. The importance of excellent fundamentals, supreme physical conditioning, accurate analysis of the opponent and high internal standards [Lombardi time] were features writ large in the constitution of that team. But back in late 1971, this was revolutionary thinking in the world of Jack Gibson and Australian rugby league. For Vince Lombardi, it had already become a way of life: 'I don't know how else to live... Unless a man believes in himself and makes a total commitment to his career and puts everything into it – his mind, his body and what we call here his "heart-power", what's life worth to him?'

Gibson was mesmerised by the film, by Lombardi's gift for distilling sporting intelligence into one-liners and the professionalism of all aspects of the Packers' preparation. He immediately introduced 'Lombardi time' for all St George training sessions, events and meetings and replaced the players' traditional pre-match steaks with an energy drink called Sustagen which was being promoted by the Australian fast bowler Dennis Lillee. When he signed to coach the Newtown Bluebags the following season, their name was immediately changed to the Americanised 'Jets', as in *New York Jets*.

A few months later, in March 1972, Jack Gibson and Terry Fearnley decided to fill their off-season with a trip to the US in search of coaching's holy grail. By chance they happened to stop over in Honolulu, and found themselves staying at exactly the same hotel – the Outrigger's Reef above Waikiki beach – where the NFL's annual conference was due to be held. After a swift introductory conversation with one of the organisers, Jack was introduced to Dick Nolan, the head coach of the San Francisco 49ers. Nolan was the coming man of the NFL, having posted three successive winning seasons up until 1972 and advanced the 49ers to the play-offs on each occasion. Like Jack Gibson, Nolan was a relentless over-achiever and self-improver who, as Frank Gifford once said, 'Didn't have the physical talent to do it all. He just willed himself. He was smart. He was tough – as good as there comes in that respect.' Terry Fearnley immediately noticed the affinity between them when they met: 'You could have transposed them, they were that similar.' Neither had made it to the very top as players, and both were making their second effort as coaches. For Jack Gibson it was like looking in the mirror – albeit a slightly distorted one as Jack was looking at 'himself' with the benefit of a far more advanced coaching support system than he enjoyed in rugby league.

Nolan had been a defensive back as a player, and a defensive co-ordinator under Tom Landry at the Dallas Cowboys in the six years leading up to his appointment as head coach of San Francisco, the perennial whipping boys of the NFL. He was primarily a defensive thinker and most of the improvements he had brought to San Francisco were on that side of the ball. As Terry Fearnley recalls, 'Dick invited us to look over his operations in the next few days and we were blown away with their professionalism and resources. A lot of Jack's philosophies emanated from that trip and he formed a lasting friendship with Dick. The thing about Jack was that he was always willing to learn. He was always looking for any little thing to give his team an edge.'

Jack Gibson's recollection of his first visit to a training session at Candlestick Park made a strong impression on Phil Larder on his 1984 visit to Australia:

> At the very first session Jack was introduced to the staff before the players emerged for training. As they trotted out on to the

turf at Candlestick Park they divided themselves into two groups quite naturally. Jack was uncertain which of the two groups he should be watching and assumed that they had been split up into first team and reserves.

It turned out that nothing could have been further from the truth. Dick Nolan came up to Jack and said, 'Those aren't the first team and the reserves… What you're seeing is two first teams, one for offence on the right and the other for defence on the left.' Jack was shocked. Like myself and virtually every other rugby player or coach from either code, he had never seen training designed specifically for defence, so instinctively he went off to the left.

Later that day over lunch, Jack recovered from his surprise sufficiently to ask Nolan about the philosophy and content behind his defensive sessions. Dick Nolan put down his knife and fork and looked thoughtful for a moment:

'Well Jack, in football you have to be able to control your opponent in the areas where he has the ball. If the defensive team did not train to do that they would just be sitting on their asses all day long, and I don't think the offence would like that at all… No they wouldn't like it one little bit.'

Gibbo scratched his head and pushed back his horn-rimmed spectacles on his nose as he did characteristically when deep in thought. American football was a collision sport and as such close to rugby in spirit – closer than soccer or basketball. It had four 'downs' in which the offence had to gain 10 yards or else the ball was turned over, just as rugby league had introduced the four-tackle rule for offensive possession in 1967 [to be modified to six tackles five years later]. But unlike league and union, gridiron employed specialist teams on offence, defence and for punting and kick-off duties. The offence and defence in particular consisted of a completely different set of players, both of which had their 'stars' or standout performers and were valued equally. If anything, the greater value was placed on defence, in line with 'Bear' Bryant's famous maxim, 'Offence sells tickets. Defence wins championships.'

Jack was unequivocal on this point – by far the most important lesson he learned at the 49ers camps was the premium placed on defence and defensive training. As a result he spent most of his time with the defensive coaches watching them train their charges. Every day the 49ers worked on individual and collective techniques: the linemen working first opposite the man, then aligning in a gap between blockers – stunting, shifting or jamming; the linebackers reading the quarterback and coming up to fill in against the run or dropping back into coverage against the pass; defensive backs perfecting their methods in different forms of coverage – bump-and-run, man-to-man or zones. Everything came under the microscope: the positioning of the feet and hands and the importance of body-angle and leverage in contact, the correct reading of opposition 'keys', the pursuit angles on to the ball as a play developed, pass coverage zones and individual responsibilities within those zones.

It was an exciting new world for Jack Gibson, and although much of what he saw was not directly relevant to rugby league he instinctively understood what the 49ers were trying to achieve, and appreciated the detail they introduced to the defensive aspect of the game. He also warmed to the terminology that had been invented to describe that detail.

The defensive coaches hammered home the lesson that the defence was an attacking weapon, able to create 'fumbles' and 'takeaways', or 'sacks' and interceptions: 'We must go forward all the time.' Although technically, only the offence had possession of the ball, both offence and defence were expected to go forward and attack at every opportunity.

Jack said to me, 'Every day, I went back to my hotel with head buzzing with possibilities. I couldn't sleep and would get up in the middle of the night and walk around the room. I'd get out a piece of paper and a pen and plan defensive strategies and training sessions for rugby league based on what I'd seen that day. It was like I was channelling some kind of special energy. I was incredibly stimulated and excited by everything I'd seen, and I realised immediately that it would give my new team [Newtown] a leg-up on the opposition in the season to come.'

I tried to follow Jack's path to the West Coast in 1984, by visiting the Los Angeles Rams' training facility on my fact-finding mission for British rugby league. When I turned up at the stadium and told the Rams' officials who I was and why I'd come, they just looked at me blankly. True to form, the RFL had not even bothered to make a booking for me or inform the Rams of my coming. They told me that the training was scheduled for the other side of town in any case, so I ended up hiring a taxi and getting over there under my own power.

As it happened I didn't get a great deal from the visit – probably due to the ramshackle nature of the planning – and what chiefly impressed me was the ability of their 6ft 4in, 250lb athletes to run around as quickly as our rugby league centres and wingers!

I did have the opportunity to test myself against some of the best collegiate talent the West Coast had to offer however, and that was far more interesting. I was added into a group test of 24 physical education students including an international gymnast and American footballer, a martial arts expert and an outstanding female 400m runner. I was still in my late thirties at the time, only a couple of seasons away from my playing career and I'd kept in shape. The competition started promisingly – I won the 2¼ mile race, came a respectable third in the abdominal endurance test and fourth in the 50 yard dash. So far, so good.

The truth only emerged in the tests to measure upper body strength and flexibility, where I trailed in dead last. In terms of strength and power, I was nowhere compared to these finely-tuned athletes and it left a strong impression on me; furthermore I did not believe any of the professionals currently playing British rugby league would have fared much better than I did. Our physical conditioning for violent contact sport was way behind those benchmark American athletes and there was little point in denying it.

A change in the perception of the importance of defence occurred in the National Football League back in the mid-fifties. The transformation was nowhere more pointed than in the change of fortunes experienced by a rookie taken in the 1956 collegiate draft by the New York Giants. His name was Sam Huff. Huff had been drafted by the Giants in the third round after playing on offence at college, but although he saw a quality athlete, head coach Jim Lee Howell had no real idea where to play him. Caught in positional no man's land and side-lined in pre-season, Huff left camp and headed for the airport. As he was about to board the plane he felt a hand on his shoulder and turned around. It was the Giants' offensive co-ordinator, Vince Lombardi. One imagines that Lombardi delivered a speech to Huff on the value of making the 'second effort' very similar to the one he made to Ron Masak on film so many years later. It clearly had the same revolutionary effect.

Sam Huff returned to camp with Lombardi and was handed over to defensive co-ordinator Tom Landry, who also happened to have future 49ers coach Dick Nolan in his defensive backfield. Eighteen players and coaches were moved into the Concorde Plaza hotel near Yankee Stadium before the start of the regular season, including Landry and Nolan, and it turned out to be a landmark concentration of intellectual property from the defensive point of view. Landry liked his intelligence and athletic ability so much that he decided to both turn Sam Huff into his new middle linebacker, and to design the Giants' defence around him.

As Huff recalls, 'You might say I learned to play middle linebacker while sitting in "the Landry suite" of the hotel.' Landry would call him up and ask him what he was doing. If it sounded anything like nothing [or watching TV], Huff would be invited up to Landry's room to watch some game-film instead: 'Tom had this projector in his apartment, and we'd go over the team we were playing that week, over and over… tendencies, what to look for, keys. I didn't get to finish watching a lot of interesting TV programs that year, but I learned more football in that one season in Tom's apartment than I'd learned throughout high school and college.' [From *Landry: the legend and the legacy* by Bob St John, Thomas Nelson, 2001]

Huff became the first rookie middle linebacker to start an NFL championship game in 1956 and went on to play in six NFL championships and five Pro Bowls. It was the start of a new era of defence and a new breed of middle linebacker – Huff had speed and size but above all, the brain of a diagnostician which enabled him to dissect and disrupt opposition plays before they even materialised on the field. Within two years, at the tender age of 24 years old, Sam Huff found himself on the front cover of *Time* magazine [30 November 1959], and the centre of attention in a 1960 CBS television documentary entitled *The Violent World of Sam Huff*, in which he was wired up to a microphone during an exhibition game. Defence was now in fashion, and it had become at least the equal of offence, attracting just as many high-quality athletes and commanding the same media profile.

In the two decades that followed, the duel was always between the two key tactical brains – the quarterback for the side in possession of the ball, and the middle linebacker for the team without it. The offence would line up with their quarterback barking out calls from underneath his centre. A few yards ahead of him stood the middle linebacker, the quarterback of the defence. He called the defensive signals and he needed a computer-like brain to do it. He had to be aware of where the ball was on the field and how many yards the offence needed for a first down. He had to assess personnel changes made by the opponent as their players trotted on and off the field after each play and the tendencies associated with those changes, as well as the formations and plays associated with each down, first, second or third. He had to know all the defensive fronts and coverages available in every situation. Then, and only then, he had to make his call and ensure that everyone knew what it was. He had to process all this information in less than 30 seconds, *and* react to any last-second changes the quarterback made at the line of scrimmage!

In the course of the 1960s and 70s middle linebackers like Ray Nitschke of the Packers, Joe Schmidt of the Detroit Lions, and later Jack Lambert – captain of the famous Pittsburgh Steelers 'steel curtain' in the 1970s – were to become as celebrated as the Bart Starrs, Johnny Unitases and Roger Staubachs of the American football world. Jack Gibson understood that defence had yet to attain this level of importance in rugby league, and he was determined to balance the account. In the season that followed, his Newtown club were to concede by far the lowest points total in their history [a miserly 10.1 point per game average, featuring a standout 1-0 win over Jack's old adversaries St George!] and begin to set a completely new standard for the sport in Australia.

Suffocating defence became a theme of Jack Gibson's teams, and both Eastern Suburbs [1974–76] and the Paramatta Eels [1981–83] emulated Newtown's achievement, conceding an average of only ten points per game in Gibson's two most successful periods as an NSWRL coach.

> When Jack got back to Sydney, he discussed what he had seen with his coaching staff. They quickly realised that the process of improving the individual tackling skills of the squad and developing their defensive systems would take up valuable coaching time. He said to me: 'There was now far more to do and only the same amount of time in which to do it, so we had to re-plan the off-season preparation very carefully. We also realised the very real danger of over-training, which would leave the players leg-weary and jaded on matchday. That would defeat the objective of what we were doing.'
>
> Jack immediately began the process of introducing the new innovations he'd learned and adapted from Dick Nolan to his

own defensive training sessions. Some of innovations were quite straightforward. Players were instructed to paint 'eye-black' or mascara underneath their eyes to protect them from the glare of bright floodlights; as it also looked like a kind of war-paint it also had an intimidating effect on the opposition. 'Lombardi time' [do everything 15 minutes ahead of time] was introduced for every session or meeting. Fitness was scientifically tested via the 'pinch test', which provided a very accurate estimation of body fat, and a seven-lap run was used to establish players' basic attitude towards conditioning. 'Nautilus' training machines were imported to provide the base for high-intensity weight programmes.

Aids such as tackle bags and tractor tyre inner tubes became an everyday feature of defensive sessions. Players were encouraged not to just hit with the shoulder and drive, but to 'leave the ground' like their American football counterparts as they approached the tackle bags – and they could now do so with the risk of injury greatly reduced. The tractor inner tubes were used to develop flexibility and pursuit skills. Jack believed that it was essential to tackle something that not only moved but also changed direction and as one of players said, 'It was like trying to drown a greased pig.'

The skill of rolling these monsters accurately was even more difficult than tackling them, and I had some interesting experiences when I took the idea back to England and used them on the coach accreditation courses. The inner tubes had to be transferred to each venue, inflated at a local garage and then rolled down the road, and often through the centre of town down to the training field! Furthermore, it was not unusual for the local kids to break into the storage sheds overnight and play with them, so that by the time we started training the next morning the tubes had to be re-inflated at the garage…. It was not long before the district coaches made their displeasure known: 'Bugger this Phil, we are fed up with these bloody tubes, we'd rather be the tackling fodder ourselves.' The inner tubes were ditched and when I phoned Ron Massey – Jack's coaching co-ordinator – to tell him so, he said simply, 'I know Phil, we have done the same.'

Jack also introduced Vince Lombardi's system of weekly individual awards. Lombardi would give out awards to individuals in each area of the team based on their statistical success at sacking the quarterback, defending passes or creating fumbles etc... Gibbo told me that he felt that the awards really helped to increase players' motivation. At the beginning of the week, awards like 'top defender' [based on the tackle count] or 'big hitter' [for the biggest or most important tackle in the game] would be handed out to all three grade teams. The players selected were all immensely proud of their achievements and the young third graders, in particular, were fit to burst having their game performance acknowledged in front of the senior players. The top tacklers from the three grades got to wear the 'top tackler' shirts during each training session in that particular week.

The awards were usually presented by Ron Massey, Jack's right-hand man. I can remember Peter Stirling being interrupted as he was about to get up and give his acceptance speech for one of them by Steve Edge, the club captain. There was a scuffling behind 'Sterlo' and Edge appeared behind him with pads stuffed up his jersey and a big bald wig on his head. This made him look like Ron Massey [who was well-known for being a bit of a 'foodie'] and it provoked howls of laughter after an exceptionally intense training session. It was obvious just how comfortable the players from the three grade squads were in one another's company.

I looked around and caught Jack's eye. He winked at me and I'm sure we were thinking exactly the same thing. Jack believed that the best way to develop the young third graders at the club was to train them alongside the internationals. Looking at Kenny, Sterling and Grothe as they laughed themselves hoarse at Steve Edge's antics, remembering the carnage the three of them had wrought in 1982 against Great Britain and knowing they were all in their early twenties and previously unknown products of the Paramatta third grade team, I could only nod my head in silent agreement.

Jack Gibson was the first to insist that selection and player control should be under the remit of the head coach, rather than club owners or officials. As Bill Parcells once said, 'They want you to cook the dinner; at least they ought to let you shop for some of the groceries. Okay?' The pay-scale was adjusted accordingly so that the salary of the head coach at least equalled that of the top-paid player at the club.

Gibbo was also unafraid to delegate authority and put together his own panel of coaches, which rapidly became a well-oiled professional coaching machine. When you hired Jack, you also hired the best support that money could buy, whether it was in video analysis and coaching co-ordination [Ron Massey], fitness and conditioning [Mick Souter] or medical and physiological welfare [Alf Richards]. This not only generated instinctive trust and family feeling but tended in the long term to create coaching dynasties with real longevity in the given sport. For example, in American football, the New York Giants coach of the 1980s and early 90s Bill Parcells always took Bill Belichick with him as a defensive assistant when he moved clubs. Belichick went on to win four Superbowls of his own as head coach of the New England Patriots in 2001, 2003, 2004 and 2014. Another of Parcells' old coaching panel, Tom Coughlin, returned to the Giants as head coach to win Superbowls in 2007 and 2011, and he's still going strong with the same franchise at 67 years of age.

Likewise, the coach of the reserve-grade side under Jack Gibson at Paramatta, John Monie, took over from the great man when he retired, winning the 1986 Grand Final with the Eels before moving to England and putting together an unprecedented run of four league-and-cup doubles with Wigan. Some of the great Paramatta backs, like Brett Kenny and Steve Ella, went with him, while the loose forward on Gibson's Grand Final-winning Paramatta team of 1982, John Muggleton, successfully adapted Jack's methods to union as the defensive coach of the champion Australian squad in 1999. What one gained, all gained from the collective experience within these groups and they opened up the true meaning of the word 'legacy'.

Ron Massey was a particularly vital component of Jack Gibson's panel. Ray Price once memorably called him 'the gun on Jack's belt'. If 'Mass' would probably not have seen himself that way, he was certainly Jack's eyes and ears – and quite literally as Jack's eyesight began to rapidly deteriorate. Monday mornings were Ron's domain, as he would spend over four or five painstaking hours breaking down game footage from the weekend. He was rugby's first notable video analyst, but he was also far more than that. He was Jack Gibson's coaching counterpoint, the one the players could come to when they were too nervous to ask Gibson for clarification, the one they could make fun of without ever losing the respect for what he did. 'Mass' connected Jack to the players when his own temperament didn't allow him to do it himself, but he was at the same time as far from a 'yes-man' as it's possible to be. He was often positioned on the far side of the ground, away from Gibbo, and that's where he stood psychologically: 'If you want to know about your faults, go and talk to your enemies. They'll tell you. Ron was like "my enemy"…' as Jack once said – but they never had a serious argument.

By the time I returned to Australia for my second visit in 1984/85, Jack had moved over to coach Cronulla. He had a beach-house there so his work was now on his doorstep. Ron Massey had moved with him, and I accompanied Jack and Ron to their 'eyrie' [formerly the press box] at the top of the main stand when the Sharks entertained Penrith Panthers. The elevated position gave them an eagle's eye view of the game and admitted no distractions. Jack sat with Ron Massey on his right, with Jack's lighting up and Mass doing the talking in the course of the game. As I listened, it dawned on me that Ron's rugby league IQ was higher than anyone else I knew, and that he could only be described as a rugby genius. The comments that he made throughout the game were so concise and far-reaching, whether he was identifying a weakness in the opposition's defensive pattern, or the plays that were of the greatest danger to Cronulla, or plotting counters to both.

Ron also had another, more subtle role up there in the press box. On matchdays Jack liked to isolate himself from the team and their families because of his fits of temper, which could blow up as quickly and unexpectedly as a bush fire in the course of the action. It was like watching a pressure-cooker wheezing to release tension as the steam steadily hissed and bubbled out of Jack's ears, and the Craven As were chain-smoked right down to the last layer of the butt.

Jack kept an alarm clock at his side which was timed to go off exactly eight minutes before half-time. This gave him just enough time to regain some emotional equilibrium before going into the changing sheds to address the team, just enough time to chew on a wad of gum to take away the stink of tobacco, and most importantly just enough time for Ron to pick out three simple tactical points to form the basis of Jack's half-time talk.

Nobody would have guessed the contorted anguish that lay behind Jack's amiable amble down to the dressing-room, the relaxed smile and the three crisp points in front of the players – but it was Ron Massey's cool advice at the heart of the rehabilitation! On this occasion the ploy worked [as it usually did], and Cronulla [13-7 down at the half], made the necessary adjustments to win a tight game in the last five minutes...

If there was or is, a more knowledgeable analyst of rugby league football, or a larger or more jovial personality than Ron Massey, I have yet to meet them. The players who teased him so unmercifully in public, never had a bad word to say about him in private… It was Mass who explained to me the educational process of video analysis, how to use match statistics, and how to plot the subsequent player meetings which he co-ordinated throughout the week before a match. He gave me a model for match analysis which I was able to use throughout my coaching career and adapt even when I swapped codes to join England rugby union.

Every match was watched live from above, filmed from the sideline and dissected with forensic precision on tape before Ron would compile his detailed report, noting both the positives and negatives of the team performance and analysing the play of individuals in respect of their skills, decision making and their response to pressure. The report then formed the base for the following week's preparation. Ron was such an intimate part of Jack's success, it is no wonder to me that, as he lay close to death in hospital with the room quarantined from all but the closest relatives, Jack found a way to get in. When the nurse objected 'Only family allowed', Jack just looked at her and replied, 'I am family'.

Increased attention paid to the kicking game was also a product of Gibson's West Coast experience. In gridiron, the action of punting the ball also had its own 'special team' attached to it, with a specialist punter who played no other role in the game than to punt, and a specialist chase team who did not as a rule start on either the offence of the defence. The introduction of the four-tackle rule in 1967, modified to six tackles in the same year that Jack Gibson visited Dick Nolan and the 49ers, moved the game of rugby league far closer to American football than ever in terms of the kicking game. The ability to punt the ball effectively as your set of tackles drew to a close [especially near the opponent's 22] suddenly became a critical factor. Gibson employed an Aussie Rules coach, Peter Phipps, to teach the art of punting, found an outstanding kicker in Johnny Peard to execute it, and so 'the bomb' was born. Holding the ball perpendicularly and applying his boot at the bottom point, Peard could send the ball heavenwards, end over end, and easily match or even surpass the 4.5 second hang-time that was considered mandatory for a good punter in the NFL.

Even full-backs as good as Graham Langlands and Graeme Eadie began to feel the pressure as Peard's bombs tumbled out of the sky with the likes of Jim Porter or Ray Price chasing them, and in two seasons in 1974 and 1975 Eastern Suburbs won 39 out of 44 matches with the 'Bomber' applying the boot and Jack supplying the direction. Gibbo had found an effective way to translate Dick Nolan's principle of controlling the areas of the field in which your opponent has the ball into rugby league practice.

The foundation of the Kangaroos' success in 1982 lay in a jewel Jack Gibson brought back from the West Coast of America – the jewel of psychological preparation. Dick Nolan had introduced him to a book written by two sports psychologists based in San Jose, Professor Thomas Tutko and his research partner Bruce Ogilvie. It was entitled *Problem Athletes and How to Handle Them*. The book was a hot item among NFL coaches at the time, and Ogilvie and Tutko had created a 190-point multiple-choice questionnaire – which was in a constant state of improvement – to assess the characteristics and suitability of their players for professional football. The test was called the Athletic Motivational Inventory but that got reduced quickly to 'the Instrument'. It was designed to measure eleven basic personality traits: drive, self-confidence, aggressiveness, coach-ability, determination, emotional control, conscientiousness, trust, responsibility, leadership and mental toughness. 'The Instrument' provided a breakdown of the personality structures most likely to succeed and thus a pathway to the accelerated evolution of a sporting team.

As Tutko put it, 'It hurts us immensely to see a person who has talent not being handled in a way to bring out that talent. To have that person handled correctly, that's our bag.... A winner, in our estimation, is a guy who works up to his potential even if he loses every goddamn game. But he does the best he possibly can.' This was right down Jack's alley. Although the test couldn't tell you whether a player would succeed at playing either professional football or rugby, it could indicate whether he had the desire, leadership and toughness traits to make the attempt. It could also show coaches how to handle certain personality types and how to motivate the team as a group by mapping out the balance of personalities within it.

Gibson had all his players undertake the test. One of them scored a perfect 100%, a feat that had never been matched previously, even in America. His name was Arthur Beetson, and the Instrument prophesied that he would become the ideal captain. With 'meat-pie Artie's' reputation for laziness and over-eating it seemed like an unlikely solution, but Gibbo promoted Arthur to the Eastern Suburbs captaincy in 1974 on the back of his test result and he never looked back, becoming a captain of both his state [Queensland] and his country thereafter. Although coaches in both sports often ridiculed Ogilvie and Tutko's methodology, Jack Gibson knew its value and how it had helped cement, in a small but significant way, a lifetime relationship between himself and Artie Beetson – to the point where big Artie saw Jack as a coach, a father and a brother, all rolled into one. And when Frank Stanton later swept across Great Britain with his team of 1982 Invincibles, his constant companion was a book called *The Psychology of Coaching* – written by none other than Thomas A. Tutko of San Jose State University...

By the time he left Australia, Phil had understood what made Jack Gibson a 'super-coach', and he had even gained Taylor's acceptance after taking him down to Cronulla beach for some vigorous walks in the early morning. He also left the country with a peculiar reminder of Jack Gibson's double life:

> I packed my bags and began the journey back to the UK with many thoughts in my head... Jack had said to me, 'Coaches coach what they couldn't do. I couldn't play the game clean, I wasn't disciplined as a player so therefore I demand it of my teams...' and that had penetrated me at some level. I could already feel my coaching life being pulled in that direction. Another of Tutko and Ogilvie's revelations was that coaches were typically far more driven personalities than their players, and I wanted the teams I coached to achieve the defensive excellence I hadn't been able to deliver as a player. That, if you like, was going to be my 'second effort'.
>
> I was woken from my reverie by the drive back to the airport. After checking out of the hotel, I found myself with some time on my hands before the flight was due to depart from Sydney airport. So I thought I'd fill my last few hours in the city with buying last-minute presents for Anne and my young family. Gibbo happened to own a large department store and he'd given me a 15% voucher on any purchases I made in-house.
>
> Peter Corcoran and his wife Chris were waiting to pick me up outside the store as I emerged happily with my bargains and I could see the frowns on their faces. Frank Stanton wanted to see me off at the airport and he was seated in the back with a smirk of amusement on his face.
>
> 'So Phil, did you buy much?' Frank asked jauntily.

'Not much Frank,' I replied. 'I've already bought most of my presents, so I've just been rooting about.'

Frank could contain himself no longer and let out a howl of laughter, but there was only an embarrassing – and embarrassed – silence from the front.

Frank leaned over to the passenger seat in the front with a mischievous grin:

'Phil, you do know that Gibbo's store is right in the middle of the red light district, don't you?'

I slowly began to put two and two together with Frank's promptings. In Lancashire, 'rooting about' means 'window-shopping' but in Australia the meaning is entirely different... I looked across at Peter's pale, taut face – looking straight forward through the windscreen and not deviating an inch – and his white fingers as they dug into the steering wheel with ever-increasing force. Frank began to bob up and down with barely-contained glee... Looking out of the window in a desperate attempt to avoid catching his eye, I spotted some scantily-clad girls and lurid bar signs speeding past in the opposite direction. I'd been 'rooting about' at one of Jack's joints in one of the seediest suburbs of Sydney, King's Cross... Maybe the spirit of Jack Gibson had entered me more deeply than I thought, after all...

* * * * *

Phil Larder made two visits to Australia one year apart, in 1983 and 1984. Although Jack Gibson made the most far-reaching impact on him as a professional coaching personality, in the first instance Phil had gone down under to explore ways of introducing a coach accreditation scheme, and of restructuring the games at all levels [amateur and professional] in the UK. His initial point of contact was Peter Corcoran, the ARL's national director of coaching. After 30 years of playing second fiddle to Great Britain up until the end of the 1950s, Australia began to get its act together with its National Coaching Scheme which commenced in 1960, and Peter Corcoran was at the heart of a revolution that came to fruition in the course of his 17 years 'in office'. By the time of Phil's first visit in 1983, the accreditation scheme was well into its third phase and had generated 7,000 qualified coaches.

Peter Corcoran himself was the opposite of Jack Gibson, an academic who taught at high schools and lectured at university and was well-versed in the theory of education. Very much like Jack Gibson, he knew how to translate theory into working rugby practice. Phil had an immediate experience of the freedom of sporting information on his first day.

> On my first visit, I stayed with the Australian Rugby League's director of coaching, Peter Corcoran, who could not have been more hospitable or helpful. Openness and freedom of exchange was a core principle of behaviour in Australian sport.
>
> Imagine my astonishment when, on my very first morning in Australia, Peter and I walked into the Rothman's National Sport Foundation in Sydney and I found myself looking directly at Dick Marks, the director of coaching for the Australian Rugby Union! Dick's office was opposite Peter's and he immediately came over to us, sat on Peter's desk and started chatting about the 'Auckland training grids' which he'd observed being used on the recent Wallabies' tour of New Zealand.
>
> The Rothman's building houses many of Australia's major sports, such as cricket, track and field, soccer and swimming and it turned out that such exchanges of information between the various sporting educators were not only extremely common but essential to its operation. The sharing of information between sports was a basic principle, and I had no doubt that the success of the 1982 Kangaroos for example, strongly impacted on the grand slam-winning Wallabies two years later.
>
> Australians are eager to share because they see the wider picture of international sport and want to be the dominant world force is as many different sports as possible. With us, the dominant emotion is not generosity but fear and suspicion. If we had enjoyed the same regular exchanges on this side of the globe, the defence structures in English RU would have been developed a full decade before I was formally contracted in 1997. Who knows what England would have been able to achieve? Unfortunately in England we are afraid that sharing information will lead to another sport becoming more successful and popular than our own, and when I proposed a similar open exchange to Don Rutherford, the technical director of the RFU on my return I was firmly rebuffed – not by Don and his staff coaches but by the administrative arm of the RFU.

In 1983 Peter Corcoran was battling to spread the word of his Modified Games Program, which he'd introduced one year earlier. Children aged 6 to 9 would play 'Mini footy' while those between 10 and 12 moved on to 'Mod league'. It was Peter's task to convince junior clubs and coaches to adopt the new games as part of a national movement to adapt the laws of major sports to make them suitable for children.

Corcoran reduced the size of the field, the ball, the goalposts and the teams, so that there were now only three forwards, one half-back and four backs per side in Mini footy, and 11 players [13 minus the loose forward and full-back] in Mod league. There was no kicking allowed in general play, and the aim of the exercise could be summarised as 'enjoyment-in-handling'. Defenders could not move forward until the ball had been handled by the first receiver, and the attacking team turned over the ball if either its acting half-back or first receiver were caught in possession. This encouraged the development of chain passing and ensured that physically larger children could not simply step into acting half and run away from everyone else in a classic cartoon under-age scenario! Additionally, tackling above the level of the armpits was forbidden, and a Code of Conduct and Safe Play was enforced in matches overseen by nationally-accredited coaches, referees and first aid officers.

Both games had been designed on sound educational principles, with the emphasis on groups of youngsters working together as a team – communicating, making friends, developing a more rounded attitude to both winning and losing, improving fitness and gaining confidence in their ball skills whatever their size and physical development. By 1985 both Mini footy and Modified League were the only games of rugby league being played throughout Australia by children under the age of 12. Their ideals were so educationally sound that many other team sports – both in Australia and beyond it – began to copy the same principles and outlook. Peter's work was rightfully acknowledged by the award of the Medal of the Order of Australia, and ensured the long-term growth of rugby league at junior levels – registrations had jumped from 79,000 in 1999 to over 120,000 in 2008.

With the increase in the value of a try to four points [instead of three] and the automatic hand-over to the opposition [instead of a scrum] after six tackles being introduced at the start of the 1983 NSWRL season, Australian rugby league was in a state of rude health. It was attracting new spectators because it was becoming faster and more enjoyable to watch, the rules for junior play had become simpler and more approachable for youngsters and their parents, and it was churning out qualified coaches in their thousands. Above all, at the very highest level of the sport it had generated a coach who, according to Wayne Bennett, 'brought us out of the dark ages into a credible place in sport… He changed the face of our game in relation to how coaches were perceived and how the game was played and approached.'

Australia had achieved a state of almost perfect alignment between higher and lower in the sport of rugby league by 1985. Peter Corcoran's changes to the game at junior level had been accepted and integrated and youngsters were pouring into the mini and mod leagues. The NSWRL had been stabilised as a 13-franchise competition [after Newtown dropped out] with a presence in the Capital Territory [via Canberra Raiders] and a few years later in Queensland – the Brisbane Broncos came into being in 1988. All of those franchises had an established network of satellite clubs in their catchment areas which provided a constant stream of talent up to the top level. All teams from professional down to Mini footy benefited from qualified coaches and support. At the highest level there were professional coaches like Frank Stanton, Bobby Fulton and Laurie Freier, and beyond them Jack Gibson who trawled the globe for innovative practices to improve the game still further. As Jack's new ideas on defence became absorbed into the mainstream, so offences found ways to improve to counter those ideas. It was a very positive dynamic.

Jack had left me with some parting words that were to prove uncomfortably prophetic. He had warned me about the volatile and unpredictable nature of coaching as a profession: 'Phil, there are only two types of coaches, those who have been sacked and those who are waiting to be sacked, so making a move into full-time coaching is a giant step that demands careful thought. Make sure that you have a thick skin, can handle the pressure, and afford to be out of a job for some time before you put that coach's hat on again.'

As the next phase of my career began over the next 12 years or so, I would learn the bittersweet truth of those words, especially as I embarked on the transition into a sport whose frontier with rugby league was supposed to be an impenetrable iron curtain that never would, or could be broken down.

Chapter four

More pricks than kicks

P HIL Larder's worldwide trawl for the latest and best-informed intellectual property steadily bore fruit in both domestic and international competition. From 1986 to 2001, Great Britain advanced to the point where they could consistently take one of the Tests off the Kangaroos in a three-match series. Without ever really threatening to overturn the world order in rugby league, they were at least competitive again and could take the field on equal terms, knowing they had the respect of the opposition.

After a spell as assistant to two national coaches, first Maurice Bamford and then Malcolm Reilly between 1985 and 1992, while he was still primarily employed as the director of coaching, Phil took over the reins as national head coach for two years in 1995/96. He dipped his toe into coaching waters in the volatile club game with first Widnes, then second division Keighley and finally Sheffield Eagles.

It is never easy making the big decisions in life. It is never black and white. Listing the points for and the points against, but you are always thrown back on yourself. Should I leave my comfort zone, the place and people I've loved, for that new and exciting challenge, the huge step into the dark? Do I think this through logically and let my brain make the decision or do I follow my gut instinct and let my heart lead the way?

It is a nightmare of sleepless nights, of tossing and turning between 'yes' and 'no', your head buzzing itself to the point of exhaustion before finally letting you drop into unconsciousness.

You are on the edge of a cliff trying to pick up the courage to jump. Maybe someone takes the initiative for you and kicks you over the edge – or if you're lucky, throws a rope around you before gently letting you down.

In the five years between 1992 and 1997, I experienced many more kicks than gentle descents, and the final boot from the Sheffield Eagles propelled me clean over the cliff edge into the unknown of coaching in the rival rugby code.

The Eagles sacked me after only ten games in charge. From the first day I walked into the club, I realised that I had made a huge mistake. I had been negotiating with the Huddersfield Giants for several weeks and was about to sign on the dotted line, when one evening after a Great Britain training session, I was approached by Gary Hetherington. Gary had not only founded the Eagles on the fringes of rugby league heartland but had taken them all the way into BSkyB's Super League. It shocked me when he reported the highly-confidential 'news' that he was about to leave Sheffield and take over at the Leeds Rhinos. It turned out that Gary wanted me to replace him as head coach of the Eagles. In retrospect, it was not so surprising. Despite the Eagles' rapid rise to the dizzy heights of Super League, the club had never captured the imagination of the soccer-mad Sheffield public and its core support-base was minimal. In contrast, Leeds had always been one of the leading clubs in the game with a solid infrastructure, a large spectator base and an international-quality ground.

Gary was 'Mr Sheffield Eagles'. Probably the first great salesman and marketer of the game in the professional era, he had built the nest and nurtured the fledgling; now he was about to be seated at the high table. Not only was he head coach at Eagles, he was also chief executive, chairman of the board, council representative and probably head bottle washer as well!

I was flattered by his offer but was determined to sign for the Giants the following day, but Gary was like a dog with a bone – he would not let it go:

'I've hand-picked the board of directors at the Eagles, Phil. The club is commercially sound and it will continue to grow.

'They won't interfere on rugby matters Phil, they will give you total co-operation and you will be in a full-time professional environment. You'll be able to train during the day, whereas the

Giants are part-time and you'd only be able to train them in the evenings.

'Look what happened to you at Keighley. You achieved everything you could possibly have done. You finished top of Division 2 by a country mile, entered the play-offs and beat the Giants in the Grand Final and the RFL in their wisdom still blocked your entry to the top division.'

Gary had touched a nerve – I still hadn't come to terms with Keighley's exclusion from the newly-formed Super League in 1996.

'Look, Gary,' I replied, 'I am set on joining the Giants. The decision by the RFL to deny promotion was because of the BSkyB sponsorship, the creation of Super League and the reduction of teams in the top division. That was a one-off and I can't see it happening again.'

'Don't be too sure,' he said. 'I am on the RFL Council and we are already discussing ring-fencing the Super League, and dispensing with promotion and relegation altogether.'

That news was worrying because I had resigned from my position as director of coaching, confident in the knowledge that I would be given the chance to coach at the very highest level of rugby league in the UK. After talking to Gary Hetherington, it appeared that Huddersfield might be no better off than Keighley, stuck in the second tier of the [semi-] professional game with no hope of promotion.

The attack on Phil Larder's intent to join Huddersfield was immediate and two-pronged. Maurice Lindsay, the chief executive of the RFL, was obviously aware of Hetherington's approach that evening, and with Phil caught between stools, Gary Hetherington called Maurice Lindsay up on his mobile to close the deal. Hetherington handed over the phone and Phil heard the CEO's voice on the other end of it. Lindsay told him not to worry: 'You haven't signed anything with the Giants or even shaken hands, so it's not a done deal.' He went on to explain the necessity of Phil Larder's presence in Super League to monitor the performances of the Great Britain squad more closely. Hetherington then chipped in that Leeds Rhinos would offer him their head coaching role in due course after a couple of seasons at Sheffield. That was the final prick that prompted Phil Larder over the cliff edge, and into a very dark three months with the Eagles.

It was a time when the sport in the UK was in a state of upheaval due to a media war on the far side of the globe involving Rupert Murdoch and the ARL. One of Murdoch's weapons in this war would turn out to be his willingness to inject cash into rugby league in the UK in return for exclusive broadcasting rights. This cash injection was huge, to the tune of £87m for five seasons between 1995 and 2000. Sky almost certainly over-valued the market in their desire to get a broadcasting foothold in rugby league, because in the round of negotiations a few years later they paid out far less for much the same product. For example, Sky agreed a payment of only £45m for the five seasons between 2004 and 2008, almost half of what they were prepared to outlay in 1995. This cash-rich shower prompted the appearance of what could be called rugby league 'venture capitalists' like Gary Hetherington in the mid-1990s, entrepreneurs who saw an opportunity to develop a modern RL franchise business with the kind of marketing bells and whistles that would be attractive to a television broadcaster. Although Sheffield Eagles had been formed in the decade before Super League began, it quickly became an object lesson on what can go wrong when marketing ambition exceeds a club's roots in the actual community it is supposed to represent.

It dawned on Phil Larder that he had actually been railroaded into a no-win situation:

> Gary Hetherington didn't tell me that Leeds had designs on some of our key players, like the halves Ryan Sheridan and Dean Lawford and our loose forward Anthony Farrell. They held out at Sheffield and waited for Gary to pick them up later in the same season. The other plan that Gary had put into place was aimed at recruiting players from the clubs who were to lose their franchise in the Australian NRL, but they were not available until two weeks before our season started, after having just completed a strenuous season in the ARL. When given a choice between joining Leeds or Sheffield, most understandably opted to play at Headingley with the Rhinos.
>
> Unlike the Eagles, I had been able to research Huddersfield Giants very thoroughly and knew all the relevant facts about them. In hindsight I should have stuck by my original judgement rather than accepting the unsubstantiated pleas of Messrs Hetherington and Lindsay. Everything in the Eagles' set-up was a hand-to-mouth exercise – for example having only six players

signed up at the start of pre-season training, and three of those were scrum-halves! – and all the surprises were of the unwelcome variety…

At my previous clubs Widnes and Keighley, I had been able to take a long look at players and sort the wheat from the chaff in pre-season. I knew the players' strengths and weaknesses and I had identified a captain and the team leaders, and was already a long way down the road to generating team spirit and a strong work ethic. The players also had the benefit of knowing me, they understood when they could relax and have a laugh, but also knew when they had to dig in and tough it out.

The lack of a proper pre-season also meant that I was unable to apply the rigorous standards of physical conditioning which I always demanded from my players. As a qualified PE teacher I attempted to produce the fittest team in the competition capable of working harder than the opposition, so that we could continuously overload an attacking area and create more players around the ball. Psychologically, you can also learn far more about your players by their reactions when they are exhausted, about who is prepared to make that 'second effort' when it hurts the most, and likewise who is unwilling to go that extra mile when the heat is really on.

By the first game of the season both Widnes and Keighley had been raring to go, but as the start of the 1997 season was rapidly approaching Sheffield Eagles were nowhere near. We only managed to win three out of the ten games in which I was in charge before I was sacked. I recalled Jack Gibson's warning that there are only two kinds of coaches, those who were sacked and those who are waiting to be sacked, and the fact that one of those who had failed to support me in the boardroom was none other than my assistant coach John Kear left a particularly bitter aftertaste. The club and playing squad, including the coaching staff, have to develop the close-knit bond of a family if they are to succeed, and to see this bond being ripped apart by someone who should have been one of my staunchest supporters was gut-wrenching. It went against all the principles I'd lived and coached by and it was my greatest disappointment during my short involvement with the club.

It was no consolation to me that I was the 11th out of 12 Super League head coaches to get the proverbial bullet before the season was only one third complete. Looking back on it, the absence of Dennis McHugh, the English Schools under-16 coach who had been my right hand man at both Widnes and Keighley Cougars, was crucial. Not only was Dennis an excellent coach in his own right, he was also a superb complement to me in pressure situations. He had strong opinions and was never afraid to voice them, but when I made a decision, he would support me completely even if he did not agree. I trusted him implicitly and was disappointed when he was unable to join me at Sheffield. Trust is essential and without Dennis, I didn't have enough support around me.

I suppose the chairman sacked me in a relatively pleasant way. He did make me laugh when he showed me a letter from a member of the board of directors which he claimed had tipped the balance against me. This director, who was in charge of the transport in the city, had listed a set of grievances against me including a tough training programme and harsh words to a couple of players with low matchday involvements. He compared my job to that of the employee who created bus timetables for him! Having only recently arranged for the Great Britain RL squad to spend a week training with the Special Boat Squadron in Poole, it became obvious that we were living and functioning on two completely different planets.

When all is said and done I was not able to create the same combination of winning and entertaining rugby I'd been able to produce at Widnes and Keighley. However, any debt owed by the Larder family to the Eagles has been paid back with interest by my son David, who joined the Eagles as assistant coach in 2012 – they went on to win the Championship Grand Final for the first time in the club's history that year, then repeated the feat the following season.

The true position of the Sheffield Eagles in the new marketplace was not revealed until a few seasons afterwards. An average home crowd of 4,200 in 1997 rose only to 4,400 in the Challenge Cup-winning season one year later, then dropped away to 3,500 in 1999. The Eagles' financial struggles became acute to the point where the club was asked to merge with Huddersfield Giants in late 1999. The merger was a predictable disaster, and with the new owner Paul Thompson withdrawing his support the future for Sheffield Eagles only contained one possibility. While Huddersfield have done better than survive, finishing top of the regular season Super League table in 2013 with average home attendances growing to over 9,000 in the current season [2014], Sheffield have dropped back naturally to the semi-professional level which their support base and attendance levels warrant.

Maybe the whirligig of time did indeed bring in its revenges. The coach of the newly-merged Huddersfield–Sheffield club back in 1999, John Kear, found himself in a similar situation to Phil Larder, one in which the scenario which had been painted by the marketeers failed utterly to materialise. Kear had only eleven full-time Sheffield-based players to work with after the unholy 'Shuddersfield' union, and all training and matches rapidly devolved towards Huddersfield and the Alfred McAlpine stadium after a couple of half-hearted experiments at Bramall Lane. By July 2000 Kear was gone and the Sheffield element in the merger – plus all the work and money that Gary Hetherington had poured into the club – had vanished without a trace. Whether John Kear and Gary Hetherington reaped exactly what they'd sowed in the Sheffield Eagles environment perhaps only they will know, but the conclusion that the marketing of Sheffield as a RL entity wrote cheques its support base was never likely to cash, is now recorded in indelible ink.

The underlying irony was that Phil Larder had just arrived at Sheffield from another club that had both the entrepreneurial spirit and a root in its local community, the Keighley Cougars – but had still been scuppered by the 'Christmas Sales' gate-crash towards Super League and a summer season.

> I chose to join Keighley Cougars after learning that Hull FC had similar financial issues to Widnes, the club I was leaving. Keighley were only second division but I am not ashamed to admit I was seduced by 'Cougarmania'. The driving force of the club, directors Mick O'Neill and Mike Smith, drove all the way to Widnes and telephoned me from a phone-box just outside the ground and they just wouldn't take 'no' for an answer! Who could resist such contagious enthusiasm?
>
> I liked the fact that they were selling the game within the local community and had appointed Mary Calvert as an advisor to do just that, creating the 'Cougar classroom' for schoolchildren and transporting over 1,100 kids from Cougar Park to Wembley in a long, winding snake of coaches to watch the Test match against Australia in 1994. Mary was also responsible for launching a drug education programme called 'Project Six' in the local area.

Meanwhile I'd been promised a £100K war-chest to buy new players and I liked that as well. I was able to bring in six new players and they formed the nucleus of an outstanding team.

It is hard to over-estimate what Mick O'Neill and Mike Smith achieved in dragging the average home attendance up from a paltry 350 in 1989 to over 4,000 in 1995, with the sell-out point of 6,500 at Lawkholme Lane [or Cougar Park in Keighley's brave new world] often being reached in the glory years of Cougarmania between 1994 and 1996. Every financial challenge, whether it was the refurbishment of the 'Hard Knock Café' or the provision of new pitch drainage and resurfacing or the building of a new stand to replace the old 'Scrattin' Shed' was addressed with a creative fund-raising strategy. The directors committed themselves to each improvement more in the hope that they would find a way to finance it, rather than the absolute knowledge that the money was already available. When the local Bradford Metropolitan council was asked to provide a £150K grant towards the cost of upgrading the ground in 1994, it refused on the basis that the club was 'technically insolvent'; new director David Bailey was surprised to find that the office telephone line had been cut off and had to scuttle down to the town centre to pay off the outstanding bill of £900. Phil himself went into the office one day only to find the computer screens blank because the electric bill hadn't been paid! Smith and O'Neill's vision of both the game in general and the club's future in particular, was both intoxicating and frequently prophetic, especially in their support of the concept of summer rugby and their insistence on attracting youngsters to grow the support base, but the financial foundations were always shifting beneath their feet – much like the poorly-drained 'sea of sand' Cougar Park beach-pitch upon which the players were required to perform.

Keighley needed to be a club in the very top echelon of the game in order to justify the marketing effort and recoup the huge investments of time and money that were being made, but the progress towards Super League was travelling even faster than the club's own development. The 'Framing the Future' document produced by the RFL committee recommended only a one team promotion from Division 2, and other qualification criteria like a 10,000 minimum ground capacity for future Premiership sides moved the goalposts ever further away from ambitious clubs like Keighley. The faster Messrs Smith and O'Neill chased the shadow of the top-drawer rugby league they were seeking, the further it seemed to recede into the distance.

But Mike Smith and Mick O'Neill ploughed on regardless. On 4 April 1995, *The Keighley News* proclaimed 'The Eagle has landed'. Daryl Powell, a Great Britain international and a very big name had been signed for £130,000, four times more than the club's previous record signing, and Mick O'Neill said he could still feel his hands shaking as the ink dried on the paper.

On the same day, league CEO Maurice Lindsay was in talks with Rupert Murdoch's BskyB, negotiating a TV package for a European Super League and summer rugby. The plan, which featured some ludicrous club mergers and franchises based in London, France and South Wales, was rushed through at unseemly speed, and Keighley were shut out of it completely. Although the original plan was later modified to include a further two divisions below the Super League itself, and promotion and relegation between all three divisions, Keighley's status remained the same.

> The rugby league bye-laws stated that the two teams finishing at the top of the second division table at the end of the season would be automatically promoted. This was in black and white, writ large in tablets of stone… or so we thought.
>
> With only four games left to play the Cougars were in an unassailable position, not only at the top of the league, but guaranteed to finish in a promotion place even if they were to lose their remaining four games. I had a meeting with the board and they assured me that we could afford to go full-time as soon as we were promoted, so we drew up a shortlist of players we wanted to keep and those we wanted to buy on that basis. It came as a surprise to learn that Sheffield Eagles were prepared to sell Daryl Powell. Daryl, a Great Britain international captain, had great leadership qualities and could play in several positions and his signing made a strong statement of intent that Cougars meant business in the top division the following season. He cost the club £130K, nearly four times more than the previous record signing Nick Pinkney, and it took Mick O'Neill several days to calm down. He looked glazed from a heady cocktail of euphoria and anxiety at just how quickly events were moving forward.
>
> The remainder of the season was a roller-coaster ride; we won our four remaining fixtures, scoring over 100 points against bottom club Highfield in a game where more than 4,000 Cougar

supporters travelled en masse across the Pennines to provide the bulk of the crowd; finished top of the league, won through to the final of the play-offs, incidentally smashing London Broncos on the way, and then beat Huddersfield Giants convincingly in the Championship Final at Old Trafford.

On the coach trip back to the official celebrations at Cougar Park, I was sitting with my wife Anne, and Mick O'Neill and Mike Smith were both at the front of the coach listening to the radio. Suddenly there was a shout and I saw a glass of champagne being flung at one of the bus windows. It broke with a sharp jangle and I watched as the bubbles dripped down the glass. Then there was silence. At that moment I knew that the party was over.

It transpired that RFL's CEO Maurice Lindsay had signed a contract with BSkyB to launch Super League the following season, a league from which Keighley were to be excluded, despite winning the Championship and finishing ahead of the London Broncos, for whom a place at the new top table had been arbitrarily reserved.

Let's get the story straight. The reduction of the number of clubs in a Super League had to occur, but to do it without any warning or time to prepare was madness. The refusal to promote Keighley Cougars when they had satisfied all the criteria laid down in RFL's own rules made no sense to me either, while the decision to promote a side [London Broncos] who had finished below them made even less.

Surely promotion and relegation should have taken place at the end of the season as normal so that the bye-laws of the game were honoured? Surely Super League should have been introduced the following season with all the clubs fully prepared for what was to occur?

I felt the RFL lost a lot of credibility with its heavy-handed attitude. But the big bucks were on offer from BSkyB, and they dutifully jumped through every hoop to get them...

Within 30 months the Cougarmania bubble had burst, Mick O'Neill and Mike Smith had gone, Phil Larder had resigned after not being paid and Mary Calvert and the community programme had disappeared from the club's orbit. The circle was completed when nine of Keighley's top players, including Daryl Powell and Phil Larder's own son David, were sold for a pittance of £25,000 in 1997. When it came time for

Keighley to cash in its most basic assets, the players, it found that they were worth next to nothing. The club was over a barrel and simply had to offload the big contracts involved. The buyer? – none other than Gary Hetherington, CEO of the Leeds Rhinos, the man who left Phil with the Sheffield Eagles' 'hot potato'.

For Phil Larder, broadly the same coaching experience had been repeating itself with monotonous regularity, whether it was at Widnes, Keighley or Sheffield.

At the beginning of 1993, I had taken my first club Widnes from mid-table into the top four play-offs of division one despite them having huge financial problems. The club had realised their deficiencies early in the season and they had taken the drastic step of halving the players' wages. The majority of the squad were not earning much more than £20,000 at that time – when halved it was hardly a living wage, particularly for those players with a young family to support and with wives unable to work because of it.

The situation was serious and there was little doubt in my mind that these financial worries could quite easily have knocked all the enthusiasm out of the team and be a major distraction in winning rugby matches. Creating time for the players to discuss their financial problems, and moving a 'clear-the-air' meeting away from their place of work [Naughton Park] to the nearby Hillcrest hotel certainly helped them to focus on winning rugby matches. With the benefit of some strong leaders, particularly the brothers Paul and David Hulme, the support of the people in the town on matchdays and a change of attacking strategy, we were able to climb away from the bottom half of the table. After losing to Hull early in January 1993, we put an incredible 14-match unbeaten run together which took us all the way to second place in the Championship and a Challenge Cup semi-final with Leeds by the end of March.

The match was played at Central Park, the home of Wigan, and their coach John Monie had allowed me and my coaching staff to use his box directly on halfway and high up in the stand. I felt like Ron Massey and Jack Gibson up in their eyrie, and I had the best view in the house as we utterly destroyed the high-spending Leeds outfit with a fast brand of attacking rugby league, scoring seven tries on our way to a 39-4 win. Although we lost a tense, nerve-wracking final to Monie's Wigan on May Day, I was understandably pleased with what had been achieved from unpromising beginnings back in the summer of the previous year, and felt that with a couple of signings in key areas Widnes would have a realistic chance of knocking Wigan off the top of the tree next season.

All my hopes were dashed upon receiving a telephone call whilst on my annual family holiday from our Welsh star Jonathan Davies. 'Jiffy' sadly announced that he had been offered to our rivals Warrington because Widnes could no longer pay his contract, and that other key players were likely to follow him out of Naughton Park in the near future. Another four internationals did indeed leave the club, and two more were lost to retirement. Despite all the best efforts of the chairman Jim Mills to plug all the leaks – and Jim had always been good to me – he could not create money where there was none. If Widnes had not taken the decisions they did, they would have ceased to exist as a professional entity.

But my three experiences at Widnes, Keighley and Sheffield left some scars. After a while I became all too familiar with the pattern emerging – the pattern of a club biting off more than it could chew financially, or aspiring to a status it couldn't realistically hope to attain in a cash-poor sport that would inevitably bow to the needs of pay-to-view TV. The real casualties were the players and the coaches – players who never knew where they might be playing the next week, or whether the money would be in their bank accounts to pay the mortgage; coaches who could never build a team because the rug was always being pulled from underneath their feet, coaches who either had already been sacked or were in the next room waiting for their turn, listening to the protestations of those who were already going...

I loved my time as a league club coach – especially at Keighley – but it was a volatile time. The insecurity of the job, and the frustration of having everything you were trying to build knocked down by circumstances beyond your control really got to me... I felt I was in a coaching free-fall and couldn't see how my dreams were ever going to be fulfilled in league, and so I started to look over the fence, where there happened to be plenty of people waiting to tell me just how much greener the grass was growing in league's ancient sister sport, rugby union.

* * * * *

The rope was thrown round me by Fran Cotton when he returned home after managing the British & Irish Lions series win in South Africa in 1997, and I was gently pulled down the cliff-face by Clive Woodward when he was appointed England coach a few months later.

My interest in rugby union had first been sparked by a chat with John Bentley and Allan Bateman after Great Britain RL training one Friday evening. Along with my two assistants Clive Griffiths and Gary Hetherington, I was preparing the team for the upcoming tour to Papua New Guinea, Fiji and New Zealand.

John and Allan were two of several ex-international rugby union players in the squad. They never lost the chance to remind me of the rumours that union was about to embrace professionalism imminently, that the players selected to tour South Africa with the British & Irish Lions would be well paid, and that they fully intended to cry off the league tour and rejoin union as soon as it happened.

'But don't you prefer playing league?' I asked plaintively.

'Of course we do', Allan replied.

'As backs we see much more of the ball and therefore our involvements are far higher. But international rugby union is huge. Every game in the Five Nations is a sell-out, there's blanket coverage in the media, and there are regular tours to Australia, South Africa and New Zealand.'

'Phil, you would love it,' said Bentus, backing up his mate.

'The international programme, there's just no comparison with league. The money being bandied about is far more than what we get… when the game does go professional it will go with a bang.'

The pincer attack continued as my head bobbed between Allan and Bentus.

'Union would need coaches as well,' added Allan meaningfully.

'It won't be just players that will be approached. Hard-nosed coaches like yourself, who are able to bring the intensity and professionalism of rugby league training into union will be prime targets.'

The two players collected their bags and prepared to leave the changing shed.

'Same time next week, then,' said Bentus as he reached the door. He paused and turned round to give me a playful wink.

'League can't even sell out Wembley when they play Australia. Put two teams of monkeys on the field at Twickenham and it would be a full house!'

True to their word, both Allan Bateman and John Bentley resigned from the league squad and joined the 1997 British & Irish Lions tour to South Africa as soon as they had been selected. There was a heavy rugby league influence on the first Lions tour in the professional era, and no less than six of the tourists had a significant RL background – Alan Tait, Scott Gibbs, Scott Quinnell and David Young in addition to Bentley and Bateman. Apart from Quinnell who suffered a tour-ending injury early on, all of them except for Dai Young played in the Tests and Gibbs was justifiably named 'player of the series' for his nuclear physicality in midfield.

Nowhere was the influence of the RL players felt more powerfully than on defence and in defensive training sessions. The captain for the tour was Martin Johnson, and he recalls vividly the first training session:

I was defending in a line with some of the league guys outside me, and my first impression was the sheer volume of noise all around me. In union we were pretty quiet, but the leaguers were the opposite. My personal world suddenly became a sea of screaming and jabbering and finger-pointing and it never stopped. At one point I turned around to John Bentley and said, 'Stop f***ing shouting…. You're doing my eardrums!' Bentus just looked back at me as if I was mad and then started up all over again.

But the league guys knew that the essence of defence is communication, and they knew it on a level far beyond anything we 'pure union' players had ever experienced. It was the first time we had done anything like it, on that 1997 tour…

They knew and recognised moves instinctively which were only just beginning to filter into the union game, like the 'screen' ball, whereby a pass is pulled behind the back of an attacking player. They knew what the threat was and how to deal with it.

They also contributed heavily to the planning for Henry Honiball, who we expected to be playing number 10 for the Springboks in the Test series. Honiball was an atypical South African fly-half, a big man who liked to play flat on the gain-line and bring in two or three other support players around him. In Britain you tended to stay back passively and just wait to see what happened in these kinds of situations, but – prompted by the league boys – we decided on a far more aggressive plan. We were going to shoot our defenders up into that space around Honiball, isolate him and cut off his options to Andre Venter, Gary Teichmann or whoever. We called it 'The Scorpion's tail'. In the first two Tests it worked so well that Honiball began to drop deeper and deeper until he resembled a traditional South African outside-half and lost all of his unique strengths – when he was dropped for the final game we knew the plan had worked…

But it was the first time I had experienced this kind of thinking and preparation, and most of it was a product of the kind of professionalism and intensity the rugby league players brought to our defensive training sessions. That was something totally new.

Ian McGeechan in his post-tour memoir *Heroes All* confirms that apparent gamble of taking players like John Bentley on tour was only skin-deep and largely 'in the mind of the beholder': 'Fran [Cotton, the tour manager] knew him of old and… confirmed that John was a great asset in a large group… Like all the ex-league players he was a real talker on the field, always communicating with those around him, and they all had a magnificent attitude to training. They were very professional in everything they did, which is what I wanted to rub off on all the others. It did.'

The 1997 tour to South Africa accomplished two things in respect of the fledgling professional union game in the UK. It created a thirst for rugby league knowledge and methods, and on a more personal level, it built a bridge between Phil Larder and union via the personality of Fran Cotton. Cotton was in the rare position of being a strong believer in the value of both codes and in that sense he was completely objective about the benefits a coach of Phil Larder's stature might bring with him if he chose to jump ship. The connection between Larder and Cotton was cemented by a message of support Phil had sent at the beginning of the South African adventure.

My wife Anne met me in Singapore at the end of the league tour to Australasia and Papua New Guinea and we took a well-earned holiday in Penang. I posted a good luck card to Fran

Cotton, the Lions manager, in which I'd written 'Defence wins Championships.' All the British Rugby League Lions had signed it. I had no idea at the time how much the card meant, or how prophetic the message would turn out to be. It would influence the rest of my coaching career.

I returned home in time to watch the first Test on TV with my two sons, Matt and David who are both leaguers at heart, even though Matt was by then enjoying the social side of rugby union at Huddersfield YMCA. We were not really looking forward to the game and only really interested in the performance of the ex-league boys – but the three of us found ourselves completely won over by the atmosphere of the occasion and the standard of play.

We were back in our seats in front of the TV again on Tuesday, this time eager to applaud one of the most entertaining games of rugby that we had ever seen in either code. The Lions beat Free State Cheetahs 52-30 and ran the ball at every opportunity. I can still remember John Bentley side-stepping infield to score a vital try. I fully understood, so soon after returning from a hugely disappointing tour, how important this win and performance by the midweek team would be for the Lions, as they prepared for the second Test in Durban that weekend. Without knowing it, I was already hooked and the Lions' victory in Durban the following week only confirmed it.

The power running of former St Helens centre Scott Gibbs was hugely instrumental as he repeatedly bumped off the biggest South African players in attack and defence, flattening the likes of 'Os' du Randt and the heartbeat of the South African psyche with it. Scott Gibbs can tell his grandchildren that he not only prevented England winning the grand slam at Wembley with his last minute try, but was also responsible for the England defensive plan which would account for seven successive victories against the Springboks up to the vital group match in Perth in the 2003 World Cup, securing England an easier passage through to the final!

After the tour Fran Cotton phoned to thank me for the telegram, which he said he had read out to the players as a motivational tool before the first Test. He was most complimentary about the professional attitude, concentration in training and match intensity of the ex-league players, and told me that they had coached the defence on the tour.

There was still a punch-line to come. Fran paused and said with some added emphasis:

'Phil, we are about to appoint a new England coach. I am going to strongly suggest to him that we also appoint someone from league to take control of the defence coaching. Would you be interested?'

The conversation with Allan Bateman and John Bentley had already sparked Phil's interest in union, and all the talk in the media about the need to discover professional standards in the union game had fanned the flames. He went to see David Shaw, an RFU performance director and an old friend from Phil's days at Loughborough University. Shaw, a former Gosforth and England second row, was responsible for setting up the 14 regional academies in England and funnelling both coaching and playing talent at the elite end of the game. He also happened to live in the village of Shelley, only six miles from Phil Larder's home in Huddersfield.

I'd forgotten how bloody tall he was. I'd been used to dealing with league players but David must have been nearly a foot taller. 'Sit down mate' I said, looking up at him, 'you are giving me a crick in the neck.'

He picked up on my interest in union and said he would immediately organise a coaching course for me. As my eldest son Matt was already playing union at Huddersfield YMCA, I joined them in pre-season training.

YMCA was a well-organised club with excellent facilities, and indeed Great Britain training was held there. Kevin McCallion was an approachable, well-organised coach with a successful first team squad which was in the process of climbing up through the league system.

We in league always consider that our game is a much tougher sport than union, but I soon found out the other side of the coin on my fourth visit. After the customary warm-up game of 'tig and pass' Kevin announced, while trying to keep a straight face: 'We are doing contact work tonight so Phil, do you want to drop out?'

I was 52 at the time, so I had an excuse, but you don't, do you?... My pride got the better of me. 'No count me in', I said. 'this is what I've come to learn.'

In hindsight the players were quite gentle with me but boy, was it tough. I was hit from every conceivable angle and the 30-minute session felt like an eternity. In league you get tackled hard but more often than not you can see the tackler coming. This aspect of training wasn't too difficult and I still had the footwork to help me escape most of the heavy blows… It was the breakdown that got to me. I couldn't see the hits coming with my body bent over looking for the ball – then Whack! I'd be blind-sided by a shot into the ribs. I put on a brave face in the bath and in the bar afterwards but I could barely clamber out of bed the following morning. Anne just tossed back her hair and gave me a parting shot: 'Phil you still think you're Peter Pan and nothing's changed.'

The Level 4 course that I attended in Doncaster was most enjoyable, and I loved the experience of being simply a student again, rather than the teacher. My student group was shown a picture of four players in line and we were asked to write down what we saw if we were carrying the ball and running at them. Every one wrote 'four defenders' but I had put down 'five spaces' which really epitomised one of the major differences between the two codes.

They were quick to realise my 'foreign' background when Tony Biscombe, who was later to work with me as head analyst in the England set-up, mischievously asked me how to defend a scrum 15 metres in from the right hand touchline and on the defending 22 metre line. I cleared my throat and started rambling, long enough for Tony to interrupt as the trap closed around me:

'That's fine Phil – but what if the scrum wheels and they attack the short side with an 8-9 pick-up?'

As I scratched my head and ummed and aahed interminably, I heard a ghostly voice – one that might have been speaking for the whole of the Rugby Football Union when it murmured behind me,

'Huh… I told you he was just a leaguer!'

Only a few weeks later, Phil Larder found himself sharing an interview room in Shelley with the newly-appointed England coach Clive Woodward. Despite coming from very different social backgrounds, both men were surprised to find they had much in common. Both had attended Loughborough University [Phil was a few years ahead of Clive] and Woodward had spent some time in Australia playing for the Manly club, the same Manly where the plan for the restoration of British rugby league had been hatched. All the evenings with the two Franks, Stanton and Johnson in the Steyne pub came flooding back as the meeting became charged with specific memories.

The rapport was sealed when Clive Woodward revealed his grand plan for new model England:

> Clive said to me: 'Phil, I am more interested in defeating the three teams from the southern hemisphere than winning the Six Nations. South Africa, Australia and New Zealand are by far the strongest teams in the world at the moment and I want to test myself against them. Do you know that between them, they have won all three World Cups so far? I want England to be the first northern hemisphere nation to win the Rugby World Cup, and I want us to do it playing quality rugby, not by just kicking the ball down the f***ing pitch and running after it.'
>
> I was given several weeks to think it through but deep down the decision had already been made by my meeting with Clive. After being burned by the club game during my tenures with Widnes, Keighley and Sheffield, I knew I wanted the chance to build something to last, and I didn't feel that was going to happen at a club. I much preferred coaching international rugby in any case, and there were far too few internationals in league to make it an interesting full-time job. England on the other hand were guaranteed to be playing at least 12 Test matches each season.
>
> The Lions tour to South Africa had also made a huge impression on me, especially coming hot on the heels of the cash-strapped league tour to Australasia. Each Test match in South Africa was a sell-out, with crowds five or six times bigger than those we were used to in league. The standard of play was far higher than I thought possible from a sport which had only just turned professional. But it was the way that the Lions played which was the deciding factor. I had always thought that union was about scrums and lineouts then kick and rush, but the Lions ran the ball at every opportunity, cut clever angles, off-loaded, supported and played an exciting brand of expansive rugby that I could relate to. When Clive offered me a three-year contract a few days later there was no question I was going to cross my personal Rubicon. I accepted his offer without any hesitation whatsoever.

Chapter five

Tigers, roses and the evolution of a defence

PHIL Larder didn't link up with Clive Woodward and the England training camp until Tuesday 18 November, in between the first two matches of the autumn series against Australia and New Zealand. England scraped a draw against the Wallabies thanks to five Mike Catt penalty goals offsetting two Australian tries, before the rugby circus moved north for the first game against the All Blacks, which was to be played at Old Trafford, the home of Manchester United.

I'd watched Huddersfield YMCA play a mid-morning game and then sat down in the bar afterwards with all the other players and spectators to watch the England match on television. There were a lot of people there, and most had to stand to get a view in the club lounge. I could feel the press of bodies above me, and along with it the urgency of their desire to see the national team give Australia a bit of 'hurry-up'. Sitting there with my pint in one hand, I was just an ordinary punter shouting the odds but over the next week I'd be trying to give guidance to the same small figures in white I now saw scuttling across the television screen... Hard to explain that one to the fellow fans above and all around me!

Australia looked a far more dangerous attacking outfit than England and it was because their attacking patterns and understanding of offence were far in advance of England's defensive patterns and understanding of defence. Their second try was scored directly from a ruck just outside England's 22-metre. Scrum-half George Gregan picked the ball up as it was recycled then ran laterally across field offering the ball out on a plate in front of him. He was being tracked all the way by Lawrence Dallaglio, the first England defender at the side of the ruck, but when Gregan swivelled suddenly to deliver an inside pass to the blind-side winger Ben Tune, there was nobody there to mark the Wallaby wing! Tune was completely 'loose' and scored easily.

I turned to Kevin McCallion, the YMCA coach who was sitting next to me and asked:

'How do you stop that?' I could hear the voices behind me murmuring their displeasure.

'Dallaglio's man,' replied Kevin with some authority.

'I am not so sure… I wouldn't want to leave a player like Gregan to run across the pitch without putting him under immediate pressure, would you?' I responded.

'That's true,' said Kevin, 'perhaps Catt [defending outside Dallaglio] should have stepped in?'

At that moment my son Matt, who had played in the back row for YMCA earlier that morning and had also played stand-off in rugby league, piped up:

'But surely that is what Australia were looking for? – if Catt had stepped in Australia would have had numbers on the outside. Dad, you have emphasised to us at every coaching session you have taken that every defender, wherever they are defending, must have a team-mate protecting their inside shoulder. Well there was no-one inside Dallaglio and therefore he was isolated and vulnerable.'

'That's right,' said Kevin, and I could hear his rugby brain working overtime to find a solution to questions that had not usually been asked of English defensive coaching. More in hope than expectation, he said: 'Perhaps a player from the other side of the ruck should have moved across as soon as Gregan began his run?'

'No, Kev,' Matt replied firmly. 'You could not rely on them getting across quickly enough. If you had to rely on the player from the far side of the ruck coming across when the ball was already in play, the first defender would always be vulnerable to a scrum-half scoot and drop-off, or a 10 attacking him with inside support.'

There, unresolved, the debate rested as Phil left the Huddersfield YMCA clubhouse with everyone's good wishes still ringing in his ears. The support was appreciated but the premonition of the huge amount of work and restructuring ahead weighed equally on his mind. It wasn't until Phil met up with his two sons again at the Smith's Arms on the Sunday of the same week that a chink of light began to appear at the end of a long and formidable tunnel.

His younger son David, or 'Dids' as he was known in the Larder family, was already building a big reputation in league as a player, and it was his lack of exposure to union that allowed him to see the situation with total clarity: 'Dad', he said, 'I don't know much about union but the ruck appears to be the equivalent of the play-the-ball in league, and every league team employs two markers who work together to stop that very same move. The two markers are responsible to defend both left and right, but the markers never split. If the opposition attack to one side, the marker responsible for that side goes across as the first defender and the other marker steps in quickly to protect his inside shoulder. You can't blame Dallaglio, he did the right thing by moving up on Gregan, but you will need a player to defend his inside shoulder to make that defence really water-tight.'

Phil knew from his experience in rugby league that the team that dominated the play-the-ball area tended to be the team that produced the most go-forward in a game. The spark for change had to come from rugby league thinking which was both more advanced and professional in its attitude to that defensive 'zone within a zone'. Defence begins from the inside and Phil Larder wanted an advantage in power, and preferably numbers in that area. And so the 'Guard' system was born in the Huddersfield YMCA clubhouse and the Smith's Arms in Highburton, and within a couple of years every serious international side on the planet would be using a version of it.

I took a leaf out of the league coaching manual by adopting 'double marker' thinking at both sides of the ruck. An extra defender would have to be placed at each side of the breakdown and their function would be to protect the inside shoulder of the first defender. 'Dallaglio' would move forward to pressurise 'Gregan' but there would be an extra defender inside him who would not only tackle 'Tune', but knock him down and knock him down hard.

I realised that the players given this responsibility would be itching to take the initiative and move forward themselves so I came up with the idea of calling them 'Guard' so as to change their mindset. The Guard's function was simply to protect the inside shoulder of the first defender and smash any runner coming inside him. The Guard would position himself as close as possible to the ruck while making sure that he could not be bound into it, and the first defender would take the defensive line forward and be responsible for tackling the first threat, whether it was a close 'hit up' or a scrum-half scoot. Once the Guard had completed his first check on the inside, he was free to assist the first defender and make a double hit.

Although I already had a sense that tying up two extra defenders so close to the ruck would necessarily narrow the width of the defensive line, I was prepared to cross that bridge when I came to it.

Phil first linked up with the England squad on the Monday before the first All Blacks game at Old Trafford. He was the first specialist defensive coach associated with the team. His first task was observation and suggestion rather than full-on involvement out on the training field – that could wait until the following week against South Africa.

My first impression was very positive. The players were well-mannered and immediately made me feel welcome but their body shapes were unlike any other team I had been used to coaching! Meeting second rows like Martin Johnson and Garath Archer reminded me of David Shaw, it was like looking up at a skyscraper and I struggled to make eye contact with them, while the front row forwards seemed to be as broad as they were tall. Where the rule changes in league had bred a uniformity of physique – I remember Johnno commenting when the Brisbane Broncos walked through the foyer of the 2001 Lions' hotel in Queensland that you couldn't tell the forwards from the backs – in union the physical requirements of each position were far more specialised.

It was quite a shock to my system to see all these different shapes and sizes moving around the training facilities and meeting rooms, and the complexity of the task ahead began to dawn on me in a very immediate way. I guess it was my gateway into a game that had a contest for the ball at all its start-points – scrum, lineout, tackle area and restarts – where I had come from a sport that had none at all… Not all defenders in union were as equal as they tend to be in league, that much was certain.

The first training session I observed was taken by the forwards coach John Mitchell. It was long, drawn-out and often barbaric. As an ex-All Black coaching against his own country 'Mitch' was determined to make a statement to the England squad about the level of commitment needed to be successful. I felt he was also trying to tell me that a union coaching environment was just as tough as those I'd experienced in league. Mitch and I had a pint together that evening and I can still remember him saying 'Phil, what you don't understand is how tough the rucks are in union; for players to perform well in an international on Saturday, training must be tougher than the game. They have to understand how tough international rugby is, and that the only way to prepare them is to make training tougher.'

But frankly I felt that this kind of beasting belonged in the coaching stone age. With the advent of full-time professionalism, league training sessions had concentrated more on skill development and decision-making and had tended to become shorter and less brutal. The game itself had become far more physical as the impact of collisions between the ball-carrier and the tackler increased. The opinion of the British Medical Association was that the human body could no longer handle more than one game a week and the RFL had made a concerted effort to remove all midweek fixtures so as to reduce the number of injuries. League coaches had also bought into the messages from sport psychologists emphasising the shorter attention spans involved in the learning process. Prolonged contact sessions were therefore a thing of the past.

Nonetheless, it was hard not to be impressed by the immense power and coordination generated by the scrum sessions and the timing and precision required at the lineouts. Mitch certainly worked the forwards hard and was well respected by them because of it. That was the way in union at that time.

As a leaguer I found the back play easier to observe and critique. Although the England backs ran some quite intricate and complex starter moves, to my eyes they clearly lacked the many options that league teams employed to break down well-organised defences. When the forwards and backs combined as two units for the team run, I understood why. Only Lawrence Dallaglio and Richard Hill appeared to be used as ball-carriers but they simply carried the ball forward and set it up for the backs to use on the next phase. As a result Mike Catt [who was playing at fly-half or first receiver] was always short of options. 'Catty' was brave enough to take the ball up to the line and had the ability to pass long off either hand, but because of the chronic lack of passing options and support runners, he hardly ever varied his line of running.

Moreover, communication was non-existent. The all-important 'small talk' between players as the attack unfolded was completely lacking. No 'I am on your inside' or 'run at his inside shoulder' or 'early ball then support' or 'grubber – there is no sweeper'. When I stood facing the England attack, I knew that New Zealand would find it very easy to read and defend.

Defensively, I was also worried. The flanker Richard Hill had run up to me breathlessly after the team run and said how happy he was at the prospect of working with me on his defence – as he had never been coached in that area before! 'Hilly' turned out to be one of those special players who read the game so well that he instinctively took the correct option in any situation. But at that stage his words were a matter of concern, as was the absence of the diminutive no.7 Neil Back from the run-on side. Neil's work rate, speed to the ball and tackling technique were all so impressive that I couldn't believe he wasn't in the team. If he'd been playing league, 5ft 10in or no 5ft 10in, his name would have been the first on my team-sheet.

The remnants of amateur thinking were not confined to the structuring of selection and training sessions. For Phil, the journey down Stretford Way was second nature, he'd travelled down it so many times as a coach for club and country – just as he took for granted coaching processes which had become routine in league, but were as yet unknown in union. When 1997-vintage England boarded their coach for the journey from their hotel to Old Trafford, it was in an old unmarked maroon 'banger' that wouldn't have been out of place on a school day-trip. There were no legends on the sides of the bus to indicate that this was England and it was a special occasion to represent your country, and none of the spectators lining the road to Old Trafford even looked up from their pints to wonder who might be sitting within it, even when the coach pulled up at the traffic lights. The players squirmed with embarrassment at just how small their stature was perceived to be.

When they entered the 'home' dressing room, it had been emptied of all the pictures and mission statements associated with Manchester United's success under Alex Ferguson. All the badges and memories of elite sporting success had been stripped away, and there was nothing there to replace them – only the white backgrounds and dirty edges tracking the scent of where that success had been… By contrast the New Zealanders had taken over the away dressing room completely and made it their home. On the outside of the door was a large banner in bold lettering – 'WE ARE THE ALL BLACKS' – and the England players could not avoid passing beneath it on their way to the pitch. Psychologically, it seemed like they were bowing to the All Blacks' yoke before the game had even started. When Phil went inside afterwards to congratulate the Kiwis on their victory, their pennants, pictures and statements of intent were everywhere on the four walls. It was as if they had taken up squatters' rights in England's house, and their sense of national pride left the England players feeling shabby and apologetic in comparison.

The match itself tended to reinforce that impression, particularly in England's amateurish efforts to defend the All Blacks' wide-to-wide patterns on attack. England captain Martin Johnson has a very lucid memory of the second Kiwi try in the 18th minute of the game:

> Phil had given us a motivational speech in the dressing-room before the game, imploring us to 'take them into back streets', into the dark places where New Zealand didn't want to go. Although the speech produced a fair amount of confusion among the boys at the time, I think Phil knew that we couldn't go toe-to-toe with the Blacks purely in terms of skill, so we had to make it a dogfight and drag them down to our level…
>
> But when they got their skills right, there was nothing we could do about it because we just didn't have the organisation. There was a three-man lineout on our 22, Robin Brooke won it quickly and within two passes the ball was in the hands of Frank Bunce in the centre. As he took the tackle the ball squirted out and I went through and tried to dive on it but their scrum-half Justin Marshall managed to get the ball away.

Lying on my back all I could hear was our hooker Richard Cockerill screaming at the top of his lungs for defenders to join him back near touch where the lineout had taken place! 'Cockers' was turning the air blue with swear words and waving his arms about, but as I got up I saw that all our forwards were within 10 yards of me. They had run towards the ball as soon as Bunce made contact and it felt as if a stone had dropped through my stomach: 'F**k me, they're gonna score.' But that's what we did in those days, we all followed the ball automatically and prepared to hit rucks, we didn't drop into defensive channels and mark the width of the field.

The All Blacks had cleverly left their two locks, Robin Brooke and Ian Jones, out in a line with full-back Christian Cullen and wing Jeff Wilson to the near side touch, so when Andrew Mehrtens brought play back towards them our winger Adedayo Adebayo was facing a 4-to-1 overlap which they converted with depressing ease.

New Zealand were way ahead of us in their thinking about the game and they were able to make use of their ball-handling forwards mixed in with the backs. Until Phil arrived we had no idea how to defend because we still thought of forwards and backs as separate units – as forwards we were there to pile into the ruck and win the ball, not think about what the opposition were doing and where they would attack us next. So we always came out second best. It wasn't until we got the chance to work with Phil that we began to understand that we had to get into position to make tackles, communicate with each other and read the play without the ball, just as forwards had to do in rugby league.

Phil Larder saw everything he needed to see at Old Trafford, and the priority as he began hands-on coaching was to improve individual tackling techniques – Phil rated them as no more than 4 out of 10 on the rugby league scale he was used to – develop the defensive understanding of the forwards, and find ways to get quicker and more agile defenders back to the near sideline from set pieces.

I knew that it was going to be a long, hard road. The players were starting near the bottom rung of a very long ladder and when I asked the squad of 26 players, 'How many of you have attended a defensive training session?', only two hands tentatively went up! The improvement of fundamentals takes time and a lot of patience, so I first introduced 'live' defensive sessions, often of no more than 20 minutes' duration, in which each player was expected to make half a dozen high-quality tackles.

I also created a 'litmus test' for individual tackling technique in which each defender had to attempt ten successive tackles on his team-mates [forwards and backs] carrying the ball down a four-metre corridor at speed. It wasn't a conditioning test so the tackler was given time to recover after every attempt. The forward ball-carriers would attempt to knock the tackler out of the way while the backs would try to swerve and step their way through. The results were shocking. The average of the group was only five completed tackles out of ten, with a squad-high of eight and none of the front-rowers managing more than two. Austin Healey, at the time our most evasive runner, ran down the channel eight times and was not tackled once, which pleased him but depressed me no end.

On the organisational front, I began to devise a series of small-sided games for every rugby union defensive scenario. We started with the issues defenders faced from scrums, lineouts, restarts and around the tackle area. Then we moved on to drills that covered turnovers and kick chase. Most had to be modified to cover every quarter of the field. The more I taught, the more I found myself learning about rugby union itself – an ideal teaching situation! I'd suggest a solution and the players might say, 'No that's a league answer that won't work in union Phil.' I'd ask why, there would be a debate and because we were all learning, the whole educational process would develop at twice its normal speed. It was terrifically stimulating. After every coaching session I would compile notes on the players and assess my own coaching performance. Not knowing the game inside out made me more focused, more self-critical and more of a self-improver than I'd ever been.

Phil soon rediscovered the solid value of his education at Loughborough University. Learning how to teach a number of different sports on the curriculum had shed a new light on his rugby coaching, and Phil had been able to cross-reference ideas successfully during his ten-year stint at Saddleworth School. On several occasions he would return to Loughborough and the superb 'Teaching Games for Understanding' programme developed by Rod Thorpe to re-learn the value of small-sided games, which required players to read and react quickly, communicate with team-mates around them and then combine to outwit their opponents. These games also tended to create an atmosphere of enjoyable improvisation, with players required to think on their feet and use their skills, and that did much to relieve the slog of repetitive defensive routines. Small-sided games had always been the backbone of Phil's coaching in rugby league and they were to prove equally essential to the richness and variety of his routines in the sister code.

Andy Robinson, who was to join the coaching group in 2000, also knew the innate value of the Loughborough exercises:

> Jim Greenwood was our leader and rugby prophet as a coach at Loughborough, and his religion was 'total rugby'. He wrote a book of the same name which is still absolutely current and relevant. He was the spirit of Loughborough off the field, and we did our level best to enact his ideas of a total 15-man game, with every player capable of making decisions on it. Loughborough also gave me a taste for the scientific aspects of rugby union. While I was there I finished a study on the lineout which was subsequently published. I looked at the merits of the counter-movement jump compared to the 'stand-in' and the 'walk-in' jumps. It was all pretty obvious [pre-lifting] stuff in retrospect but it got me thinking about the biomechanical aspects of the game. For example afterwards I found myself comparing the movements of rugby forwards with those of trained gymnasts to see where we could make movement more streamlined and efficient.
>
> But the core of sporting education at Loughborough was really embodied in the 'games for understanding' presented by Dave Bunker, and especially Rod Thorpe. Instead of learning about technique, we were learning about game scenarios in miniature and developing the intellectual muscle that needed to be developed – our game awareness and understanding. For example working on 4-versus-3s and reading body language, and only then deriving the individual techniques or defensive set-ups from that. That's where the real work occurred for me. The teaching of technique was never separate from that overall understanding, and all of it was related to the enjoyment of a game with ball kept predominantly in hand.

The Loughborough influence was germinal to the success of the England team in 2003, as it turned out. Phil had graduated from Loughborough with his DLC in physical education in 1966, and Dave Reddin – who became the national fitness coach at the RFU in November 1997 – had finished his Masters degree in sports science there. In 1998 Dave Alred, who had completed his PhD in *Coaching elite kickers for optimum performance* at Loughborough, joined Woodward's coaching team as both kicking coach and a multi-sport psychologist for athletes performing under pressure. Lineout specialist Simon Hardy was a contemporary of Clive Woodward's there. Andy Robinson finished his PGCE at the university in 1986. When he joined the coaching group in 2000, he not only became the final piece in the World Cup coaching jigsaw, but represented an extraordinary testament to the quality of Loughborough sporting intellect in rugby. The Loughborough background underpinned a coaching group whose aims were intuitively aligned because they shared the same education in the sport.

Clive Woodward had achieved his own PGCE at Loughborough back in 1978. If anything, the Loughborough experience was even more important for Woodward than the other coaches in the group because it represented a very personal release from the negative educational influences in his past. Most of Woodward's formative school years had been spent at HMS *Conway,* a 19th-century corvette and converted 'school ship' which had been towed through the treacherous Menai straits after the end of the Second World War and anchored at Plas Newydd, the estate of the Marquess of Anglesey. The estate offered ample shore establishment and space for surrounding playing fields, with the stable blocks at Plas Newydd becoming the classrooms and wooden huts built for dormitories. It had produced a steady stream of cadets for both the Royal and Merchant navies. The combination of the school's military background and its geographical isolation created a harsh, prison-like atmosphere in which discipline was enforced by ruthless corporal punishment via 'the teaser', a yard-long piece of rope, half an inch wide and with six inches of tight whipping at the end. It was a tough education for a 13-year-old Clive Woodward and one that he did not enjoy. When he ran away from the school for the third time, he was beaten until he submitted to the school's will and never did it again.

According to Woodward, 'the *Conway* years were the darkest years of my life' and they also set the pattern for the years ahead. Clive's professional life and the people in it often became polarised into 'black and white', with a very clear distinction between those who could be trusted and those who could not. Those in the circle of trust were treated with incredible warmth and fellow-feeling, those outside it saw only a closed door, while a third group – those who had been within the circle and then broken trust – risked a reaction as brutal, in mental-emotional terms, as the 'teaser' itself. At the same time, the *Conway* experience would give Clive an insatiable thirst to question the orthodox approach with ideas from outside the frame of orthodox thinking, and an outright resistance to do anything simply because he was told to do it. In future, he would always approach issues from the outside-in, rather than the inside-out, and it would prove to be an invaluable asset when he became head coach of England. Above all, he would develop his ability to create situations where he was in complete control, and his ideas could glide just as effortlessly down the field of a business or sporting endeavour as he had on that far playing pitch at *Conway,* moving the 'ball' this way and that, making magic on the field of rugby administration and leadership without fear of interruption by a higher authority. In future, there was to be no higher authority than Clive Woodward himself.

Where *Conway* was black and represented oppression and resistance, Loughborough was all light and freedom and became a source of liberation. In a sense, it became a counterpoint to, and offered an explanation for, his stormy time on the 'school ship'. The restriction to a single sport had disappeared, and Clive Woodward was free to experiment – to indulge his love of soccer, while pursuing a rugby career and exploring the principles behind other sports like swimming, gymnastics and athletics. There were no limits and the world opened suddenly, like the door to Aladdin's cave. Instead of being beaten for showing a perceived shortcoming, Clive Woodward found himself in an environment where 'weakness' was encouraged, openly admitted and then gently transformed into a strength. As his spiritual overseer at Loughborough Jim Greenwood [quoted in Alison Kervin's excellent biography of Clive Woodward] acknowledged, 'I told him to go out and learn to kick with his left foot and he did. It's impossible for me to tell you how impressed I was with the man – to stand there and admit a genuine weakness and then to learn how to correct it. I was excited just to think how much he might learn from his time at Loughborough.' Twenty-four years later, Loughborough's education would become ultimately, England's gain.

* * * * *

The England rugby team only played 10 to 12 games per year, and that wasn't enough for Phil Larder to continue his own learning process in the new code. To sustain that process he needed to be involved with a team who were playing week-in, week-out. That team turned out to be the Leicester Tigers.

I was desperate to introduce a series of new drills but I had no opportunity to experiment with them and iron out the wrinkles before I introduced them in an international week with England, so I needed some club 'guinea pigs'.

I'd taken two of the Leicester coaches, director of rugby Dean Richards and John Wells, to Hull to watch the Australian Combined High Schools play Great Britain Rugby League in a youth international. After only ten minutes 'Wellsy' was bored with the game and went down to his car to listen to music, but Dean was totally enthralled and talked about signing the young Australian centre Mark Gasnier [who one year later was capped by the Australian Kangaroos].

As a player Dean had been at the top of the game for over a decade but he did not live in the past. He understood that the game was evolving rapidly in the baby steps of the professional era, and he was determined to be at the forefront of any new developments.

So there was a connection already there, and Dean was sufficiently impressed with an early visit I'd paid to Welford Road to contact me immediately after I returned from the Tour of Hell in July 1998. He wanted me to give defensive training sessions at the club on a regular basis. This was exactly the opportunity that I had been looking for. I promised to adopt a low profile at Tigers so as not to antagonise the other Premiership clubs and did not feature on any team photographs or give any interviews. I must have done this pretty well because four years later I was thrown out of the club shop after asking for the staff discount! No-one there had ever heard of me. Fortunately Dorian West came to the rescue and told them that I was his dad.

Dean felt that Tigers had lost out on the 1997/98 Premiership title because their defence wasn't as good as that of the champions Newcastle, who had conceded a niggardly 31 tries in 22 matches, far ahead of everyone else except the runners-up Saracens [36] – while Leicester themselves had allowed 45 tries. So the objective for the following season was to concede fewer tries than

Newcastle, and rely on the truth of the old maxim 'Offence sells tickets, defence wins championships' to do the rest.

Defending in a game of rugby is far more exhausting than attacking – teams will deliberately maintain possession knowing that the defence will eventually tire, lose its shape and gaps will appear. It is, therefore, important to improve a player's ability to overcome this pressure by combining defence and conditioning within the same drill. At Leicester, we would immediately follow a tough, pure fitness session with a tackling and defence drill requiring players to get up off the ground as quickly as possible after hitting a tackle tube, then hit again and repeat the process all the way down the field – in all nine times. At the same time individuals had to remain conscious of their mates on either side who were doing the same thing, so that everyone moved forward in a line together and kept their discipline by communicating with one another constantly.

There were some initial teething problems, as Martin Johnson remembers:

Eric Miller was a talented back-row forward, and I'd gotten to know him on the 1997 Lions tour of South Africa. I was stood next to him on one of Phil's drills but he didn't get the concept. He sprinted away in front of the rest of us and left me well behind as if it was some kind of school sports day. I kept shouting to him, 'Eric, reset and go forward as one f**king line' but he finished 'first' and did a little jig on the goal-line as we finished the drill.

Quite predictably Phil asked us to do it again and I glared at Eric, but exactly the same thing happened on the second attempt, and he saved more time by not tackling the tubes properly. By now I was well and truly f**ked and breathing out of my backside. I grabbed him by the collar and pulled him in close and the words wheezed out of me: 'Eric this is a defensive drill not a f**king race. Which part of Phil's instructions do you not understand? Keep-In-F**king-Line.'

But Phil's session served us mighty well throughout the season. We would build great momentum by 'reloading' off the ground and getting back into our shape quicker than our opponents could recycle ball and organise for the next attacking phase. We just flew upfield with our numbers in the line, carrying away people with and without the ball, we didn't care. Most of the time we never got to the 'out' phase of our 'up & out' defence! It was exhilarating. We'd be flying and sometimes my brother Will [who often defended on my inside] would get the blame if he couldn't keep up. Phil would pick it up with his gimlet eye in the video session and there'd be trouble at the Johnson supper table afterwards!

But I felt that by mid-season, opponents had had enough of our 'D' and I'd frequently hear the cry, 'It's not fair, they've got the England defence coach.' I'd be laughing on the inside, because I knew we had them then.

Phil had been concerned [with both Leicester and England] that his defence was being out-flanked rather too easily once the guards had been effectively tied up around the breakdown, so some more tweaks had to be made.

The first tweak was introduced after our hooker Richard Cockerill admitted that he deliberately pulled the defender on his outside very close because he was not confident of his own ability to handle backs running at him. The rest of the front row confessed that they were doing the same so in training we deliberately experimented with the distance between defenders with the front row involved. Between the Leicester and England environments the improvement was dramatic – the average front row tackle count more than doubled from three up to seven in the space of a season, and we were able to increase the width of the defensive line by almost 15 metres without losing any effectiveness. The tight forwards moreover were now beginning to believe in their own defensive ability and accept responsibility for their own space.

The second tweak was really an organic result of the first. As our [forward] defenders became more confident, they began pushing out with more urgency from the inside. Eventually, from a ruck near the sideline we could align with our last defender as much as 20 metres inside their outside attacker and still be able to slide across comfortably and in position to make a safe tackle when the ball arrived. This slide was fundamental to our success, and as we worked on it the line-speed increased to the point where the defensive line was going forward as quickly on its 'up' as it was on the 'out' across field. The key coaching point was to insist that the defenders started with their outside foot forward to ensure that they went forward first.

The third and final tweak was to give the backfield defence behind our defensive line more responsibility. My success in league, with moving the scrum-half out of the line to a sweeper position about five metres behind it, convinced me that I should do the same in union. Shaun Edwards, Bobby Goulding and Chris Robinson had been particularly successful because they read the game intelligently and were great communicators. They were also well-respected by the rest of the team who therefore obeyed their commands immediately.

At Leicester, Austin Healey had similar reading and communicating abilities. He would know when our spacing was too wide or too narrow, he spotted opposition overloads to either side of the breakdown and he had the authority to make 'trigger' calls on the hoof and know they would be obeyed instantly by the defenders in front of him. He was also proficient at collecting the short grubbers and chips which the opposition either put through the defensive line or over it. This allowed our full-back, usually either Tim Stimpson or Geordan Murphy, to drop deeper and work the 'pendulum' with the wingers.

With the scrum-half in behind the defence, the open-side winger is free to move up flat into the line as soon as his side of the field comes under attack. Once he shifts up, it releases the full-back to move across in order to cover the space behind the winger against the kick. His role is in turn fulfilled by the blind side wing playing as the 'acting full-back'. The effect is of three players swinging like a giant pendulum as attacking play moves from one side of the pitch to the other, back and forth.

The keynote at Welford Road was mental and physical toughness, of the kind that ranked prominently in the testing 'instrument' devised by Tutko and Ogilvie and which was so highly prized by Vince Lombardi in his assessment of individuals fit to play for the Green Bay Packers. Just like Lombardi, the Tigers went out and found players who never gave into themselves under pressure and who were always prepared to make that priceless second effort. If any team in the English Premiership exemplified what Lombardi called 'character in action', it was the Leicester Tigers. Phil Larder had found his way into an environment which Jack Gibson [and Lombardi] would have appreciated as near to the coaching ideal. Tigers knew how to bash everyone else at the scrum and contact area, now they wanted to do it on defence too.

That mental toughness was nowhere more apparent than in the Tigers' insatiable appetite for full contact work, preferably at the end of an already gruelling training session. There was no way that Phil's preference for short, sharp sessions was going to erode this particular bastion of Leicester tradition:

> I will always remember the first time I managed to persuade Dean Richards that 'full on' might not be necessary after a hard game the previous weekend. At the end of the customary tackle drills I started dividing the squad into the first XV versus the rest for the final defensive run. Dean had given me the starting team for Saturday's game so I asked them to stand on my right and the others to go to the left.
>
> When I called Darren Garforth's name out, 'the Scaffolder' walked away from both groups and went to stand on his own.
>
> 'Daz, what are you doing?' I said.
>
> He glared at me and then shouted to the other players: 'This league coach has gone soft on us. I am doing contact and I am going full-on. Who wants to join me?'
>
> All the first team immediately went over to join him and full contact is exactly what we did. We played Saracens that weekend and tore them apart.
>
> That was the Leicester Tigers way of doing things. They were essentially self-policing and they used extreme physical pressure at training to sniff out any hint of mental weakness. In 2001 we were to fly out to play Stade Francais in the final of the Heineken Cup in Paris. At the end of my final 'home' session we were doing a run-through of the opposition attacking ploys and the defence had been excellent until Andy Goode missed Leon Lloyd on a fairly straightforward tackle and Leon ambled across to score behind the posts with a big grin on his face.
>
> I was about to have words with Andy when Daz pushed me gently aside and mumbled, 'Leave it to me Phil.' He went over and picked 'Goodey' up by his collar and then shook him about like a rag doll:
>
> 'Listen mate,' he said. 'We have never won this f**king cup and we want it badly… If you don't front up I will personally

throw you over that f**king stand, okay? So pull your finger out now, or you won't be going to France.'

The Leicester way of doing things quickly became the England way of doing things. When Brian Smith would bring over the London Irish first XV to run the attacking patterns Phil expected to be used against England on the next Saturday, tackling would consist of no more than a healthy 'grab' for most of the 20 or so minutes the session lasted. But towards the end both 'Johnno' and Neil Back would chime in 'Full-on for the last ten' and that was the way it had to be – otherwise the Leicester contingent felt undercooked for the challenge to follow.

There was another parallel with rugby league, because in the form of Martin Johnson, Phil Larder recognised the captain he had wanted since the days of coaching Ellery Hanley with Great Britain. Both commanded the respect of the players through their toughness and ability. Both were quiet and did not waste words, and they were both the best players in their positions in the world when they met Phil Larder – although Ellery was in the process of turning his RL world on its head with a move from the backs into the forwards.

I first met Ellery in 1984 when, as a 23-year-old he was selected to play for Europe against Oceania in a game organised to mark the 50th anniversary of rugby league in France. That game was a complete mismatch. All the Australasian players were in pre-season – fit and fresh and available for selection – while the European season was reaching its climax, with clubs reluctant to release their best players. Bradford Northern kindly agreed to release Ellery, while Des Drummond who was playing for second division Leigh, was the only other international made available. Both were on a hiding to nothing.

Des was an established international and well-respected by the Australians in the Oceania team, who were determined to stop him scoring. Every time the ball was passed towards Des out on the right wing the smalltalk from the Australians in the team reached a crescendo of noise and it became obvious that their goal was to 'nil' us. Nothing changed there then.

Ellery was a relative unknown, but with 20 minutes to go he announced his presence on the international stage. Receiving the ball deep in his own half, he rounded Wally Lewis, handed off the Kiwi captain Mark Graham and burst through an attempted tackle by giant Australian centre Gene Miles to score Europe's only try. Later that evening at the reception, I was joined by the great New Zealand coach Graham Lowe and some of his players, among them Paramatta's Ray Price, Wayne Pearce, Dean Bell, and Hugh McGahan. Ellery became the topic of conversation and it became obvious that he had made a big impression on all of these icons of rugby league.

I became assistant coach to Maurice Bamford in 1985 when Great Britain drew a home series with New Zealand. Ellery's powerful running and unique evasive skills caused problems for the Kiwis in all three Tests, and that season he scored 55 tries in 37 appearances for Bradford Northern before transferring to Wigan for a world record fee of £150,000. By this time I was quite close to him but it was still a shock when he phoned to ask my opinion about moving position from centre to loose forward. This, of course, would be a massive step for him, and as I was driving to his house in Headingley to meet him I ran the permutations through my head. He was already the best player in England by some distance, but he had already played wing, he played five-eighth for his club, in the centre for GB, and now he wanted to move into the forwards!

We sat down over a cup of coffee, and Ellery said, 'Phil, I just don't feel involved enough in the centre, I want to be closer to the action. I want to be a leader respected for the number of my involvements and work rate. I want to lead from the front.'

There was no doubt in my mind that he was both fit enough and strong enough to handle the challenges of the new position. His aerobic capacity was remarkably high for someone so big and strong and he was top of the class in all the anaerobic and muscular endurance tests conducted at national level. Set against this was the fact that as a loose forward, he would be faced by physically the strongest part of the defence for the majority of the game. I feared that he might lose some of his explosiveness as a result.

I could see Ellery was adamant and finally said, 'Why not give it a go then?... But be aware that you'll have to be playing loose forward for Wigan regularly before you can be considered in that position for GB. If it doesn't work out, you can always move back again.' Wigan's outstanding coach Graham Lowe approved: 'The more he is in the game, the better it is for us' – and Ellery's move to loose forward proved to be an immediate success. His work rate was incredible and he often topped both the tackle count and number of ball carries, regularly achieving over 50 involvements per game. His effectiveness at making line-breaks and at creating and scoring tries, was undiminished. Under his captaincy Wigan became the most successful club side of the decade and he was made captain of Great Britain in 1988. He was the first to win three Man of Steel Awards as the best player in Great Britain, won the Adidas Gold Boot in 1989 as the world's best rugby league player, was awarded the MBE in 1990 and in 2007 was voted 'the best rugby league player of all time' by the Australian media.

Ellery later explained his success to me, and the real reason behind his change of position. 'At times when I played in the centre I would not be involved and I could feel the adrenalin draining out of me. I lost the edge and the sharpness and I tended to drift out of the game. At loose forward I am in the action all the time, my adrenalin levels are flowing and I feel energised and confident, ready to explode.' He was a true warrior, and they are always found in the thick of the action.

It was Ellery, more than anyone, who enabled me to under-stand that what propelled an athlete to the very top of the sporting mountain was not only his physical ability but also – and more importantly – what was in between his ears. He forced himself to train harder than any other player in the game, he controlled his diet and respected his body – avoiding alcohol and cigarettes and ensuring he had plenty of sleep. He forced himself through the pain barrier and was utterly determined that no-one would ever get the better of him. He was exceptionally tough, regularly putting his body on the line and handling the intense pressure of expectation upon him. He was just like Martin Johnson, Neil Back and Jonny Wilkinson. All of them had that mental toughness which enabled them to produce their best under pressure on the field and drove them to redefine their limits off it.

On the Kangaroos' tour of Great Britain in 1990, it was Hanley who spoke before the first match of the three-game Test series at Wembley. Australia had already reeled off convincing wins in the opening five games of the tour, including victories over the top three clubs in England at that time – Wigan, St Helens and Leeds. The media were predicting a heavy loss and the Great Britain players knew it.

Ellery Hanley started speaking very quietly and it took the other players a while to realise that the captain was giving his pre-match address. At first he was being drowned out and the people could not hear him. Finally the dressing room settled into silence.

'Today', he said, 'I am going to give everything that I have. I am going to tackle everything that moves, I am going to hunt their ball-carriers and destroy their attacks.

'All I ask is for you to be in line at my side. Let us defend together with plenty of talk. I want to hear who is on my inside, and I will talk to who is on my outside.

'I am going to carry the ball more than I have ever done before. If I call for it, give it me. I want you to be with me and support. I will make at least four line-breaks, and if you support me we will score and win the game.'

Ellery Hanley did everything he said he would, topping the tackle count and making three clear line-breaks which resulted in tries for wingers Martin Offiah and Paul Eastwood. His performance in GB's 19-12 victory was inspiring and earned him the 'man of the match' award.

It was the first time that I had heard a captain say '*I* am going to do this' rather than the usual '*We* will do this' and the effect was extraordinary. Ellery was accepting responsibility in the most fundamental [and prophetic] way.

I did not hear this unique tone of voice again until Martin Johnson gathered all the forwards around him at Old Trafford in 1997. It provoked a feeling of déjà vu in me when he predicted his own performance with a Hanley-like foresight:

'I am going to do something special today. I can feel it deep inside of me. It is going to come out when I hear the whistle and I am going to explode into every ruck. Follow me, and let's create mayhem together.'

Although we lost the match the effort and commitment was unquestionable and Johnno was in the thick of the action at every point, doing what he said he would do. That is when I understood we had the right man in place to lead us to success on the field.

The other aspect of Martin Johnson's captaincy which was extraordinary was his ability to maintain the 'big picture' in a game when his head ended up buried in every ruck and the physical demands of his position were so high. As coaches, Phil and Dean and John Wells would have their three points for the second half ready à la Jack Gibson, but Johnno would cover them all in his half-time team talk anyway! Phil and Dean and Wellsy lost count of the number of times when they simply looked at each other, threw down their clipboards and shrugged their shoulders.

* * * * *

I am sitting in the lobby of the Leicester Marriott hotel. Outside it is a beautiful late-winter morning, and the brilliant sun sits in a cloudless sky. The thick carpet of snow is already beginning to thaw, but for now it faithfully continues to reflect the sun, flooding the hotel atrium with steady streams of light.

Somehow it seems less of a surprise when Neil Back digs in his brief-case for a moment before taking out a dense leather-bound book of encyclopaedic proportions. It is dark brown and looks like a bible. Neil reinforces the impression by handling it with a care approaching reverence. On the front in heavy embossed letters it reads, 'The History of the Leicester Tigers'. Time passes, the light continues to flood the lobby as Neil unhurriedly leafs through page after page. He mumbles under his breath, 'There are a lot of mistakes in here…'

At a certain moment he stops and heaves a sigh, as if there is something immoveable, and that cannot be moved inside him. He looks up quickly as if he has just made a discovery: 'Do you know, I've read through it from cover to cover and I still can't find any mention of Phil Larder? It's like he's the invisible man.'

It is a matter of deep regret to Neil Back that Phil Larder has never received the credit he was due for turning Leicester in to a championship-winning side between 1998 and 2002, almost halving the Tigers' try concessions in those years. That is the weight inside of him. Does his regret extend to Phil Larder's career with England, where the mythology of World Cup success in 2003 has never nodded more than occasionally to the achievements of 'the invisible man' – the architect of the outstanding defence in world rugby over exactly the same period? Another sigh says 'Yes.' The sun shone just as brilliantly on England in 2003 but the 'book' of its success is just as incomplete as the Tigers' bible. Phil's experience in the club shop at Welford Road, when 'Nobby' West had to get him his discount by pretending Phil was his dad, has somehow become symbolic.

Both Phil and Neil know what it is like to wear the cloak of invisibility. When they both entered the new England squad environment in 1997, there was a mutual recognition. Phil saw Neil Back's potential value as one of the key leaders in the team immediately, even though 'Backy' had not been afforded this recognition by previous England coaches:

The selection of the number 7 shows you how a side is going to play, it is one of the selections which influences the choice of playing style directly. Andy Robinson was one of my contemporaries and he was the same kind of size as me. Alongside Peter Winterbottom and Gary Rees, I really rated 'Robbo' as one of my toughest opponents, and he had moved ahead of them as my main rival for the spot in the national side between 1990 and 1995. In hindsight I should have known better and heeded the warning. Robbo only won eight caps for England in the seven years between 1988 and 1995 when he should have had many more.

But at that stage of my career, I didn't think my size would matter. I'd scored three tries for England under-21s in Romania with the national coach Geoff Cooke watching from the stands. A few days later, some of the lads told me they'd overheard a conversation in which Geoff Cooke had said that I was 'too small' for Test rugby. I didn't believe it, because I was sure Mr Cooke would have said it to my face if that was really on his mind. In the event, I saw him coming the other way while I was walking back to the team hotel. Immediately I tried to think of something to say, but as he passed me by he did the most remarkable thing – nothing at all. He simply looked past me as if I didn't exist and walked on without a word. He didn't say, 'Back, you're too small to play international rugby', he just ignored me. It was the kind of treatment a new player could expect in that era – when you walked into the team room, the senior players would look up briefly and then retire behind the screen of newspapers and cigarette smoke without so much as a 'Hello.' It was at that moment I learned it was possible to become invisible, whatever you did on the field and however good either you or other commentators on the game felt you were. I even wrote a letter to Jack Rowell in 1997 asking what areas of my game he wanted me to improve in order to enhance my prospects of being picked.

Incredibly, I never even received a reply. Thankfully he left the post in July that year to be replaced by Clive Woodward in the November.

Although I won a number of caps before then, I never considered my Test career had started until my selection for the second Test against the All Blacks at Twickenham in 1997. It was the first time I felt I was trusted and the coaching staff were fully prepared to invest their faith in me. I found out later that a key to my selection was the presence of Phil Larder in the new coaching group. Clive Woodward had asked him who he thought should be automatic selections. Phil had replied, 'Backy... He's got the highest standard of conditioning, he's the best tackler in the squad and he's the only one who could play league right away.'

Funnily enough, five years earlier the head coach [and later CEO] of Sheffield Eagles, Gary Hetherington, had tried to recruit me but I was determined to succeed in union. My selection also fitted Clive's vision of how England would play the game, with a risk-reward attack featuring two flat receivers and a wide attacking alignment in which my natural support lines would be of most use. But I have Phil to thank for having the kind of open rugby mind that saw footballers before it saw gym athletes, and selected on what it saw rather than through the lens of inbuilt prejudice about the game of rugby union.

Although they had fine records, I think this is why Geoff Cooke and Jack Rowell ultimately came to grief at the very highest level as England coaches. They wanted big blokes playing at number 7 – Ben Clarke, Steve Ojomoh and even a young Lawrence Dallaglio – and in my opinion it set the development of English rugby back years. I had spent most of my rugby life training with the backs, learning how to play the linking role between backs and forwards in attack until it became second nature. I wonder how many of those players, or for that matter the no.7s in the Premiership today, could say the same?

Don't get me wrong – all of Lawrence, Ben and Steve were great players, but they were all natural number 8s, big powerful men of 6ft 4in and 16 stones plus – none had the skill-sets of a true number 7. In global terms, it restricted England to being a bully in its own backyard. A very good bully it has to be said, but in my opinion Cooke and Rowell were content with dominating the Six Nations rather than competing with, and beating the likes of Australia, South Africa and the All Blacks. Ultimately, that is why we came so badly unstuck against New Zealand in the 1995 semi-final. We had no pace in the back-row to match the likes of Josh Kronfeld and Zinzan Brooke, and that was that once the Blacks started moving the ball wide. We had no-one who could compete in that department of the game. Fortunately Phil Larder and Clive Woodward had a very different mindset in terms of what they thought an England team could be, and it certainly affected their view of what a Neil Back could contribute.

Neil Back also found an uncanny, but very concrete echo in Phil Larder's teaching of individual tackling techniques. It replayed one of his most positive early learning experiences, of the coach he had trusted most as a youngster growing up, Jack Carnell:

> He was just 'Uncle Jack' to me, a salt-of-the-earth type who gave far more to rugby than he ever took from it. Jack was the living heartbeat of our local club Earlsdon. He had a huge bank of experience and knowledge, and would spend hours helping me, my brothers and the other players learn about the game. It was Jack who gave me my first tackling lessons and laid the groundwork for my technique in that area – which in time became the rock on which my career in rugby would be built.
>
> Jack would first kneel down on the ground to bring himself down to my level so that we were looking at each other eye to eye. When I hit him, he would always react as if he'd been mortally wounded and fall back on the earth, and I would laugh as if I'd really done it all by myself. As soon as Jack knew I was engaged, he would teach me the fundamentals of technique – 'Head, hands and feet.' Get your angle right, get your head, arms and feet in the correct positions and the ball-carrier would have to fall. Jack's basic advice on tackling was so close to Phil Larder's when he first joined the England set-up, I could scarcely believe it! For me, it really was like comfort food – a case of déjà vu and it took me back to some of my happiest root memories in the game.

The selection of the right number 7 to do the job England wanted was critical, and it was the result of Phil Larder's ability to see Neil Back's value, ironically, in cross-code terms:

Clive had already determined that the most vital part of an international coach's job is selecting the right players, and he asked me who I would pick if England's union team were to play league. I replied without any hesitation, 'Neil Back.'

'Backy' had impressed me with both his attitude and work rate. His concentration and commitment were immense and he appeared to read the game faster than the other players, so he was invariably around the ball and into the tackle before them. I had also been hugely impressed with his tackling during Mitch's contact session.

Clive told me that previous England coaches had considered that he was too small for international football, so I went through my mental check-list:

'Does his lack of height inhibit what he is expected to do in the set piece?' Clive shook his head and said:

'Well… Backy will obviously not be used as a jumper.'

'In that case his speed off the mark will be a great asset to us on defence from both lineouts and scrums. Backy is certainly short but he is big where it counts, in strength and heart.'

As a result of this conversation, Backy became an England regular and formed a tremendous partnership with Lawrence Dallaglio and Richard Hill in the back row. A little later I made him 'defensive captain', a role that he filled with both enthusiasm and knowledge. He became the most instrumental of all in helping me to make England's defence the best in the world.

The effect of Larder and Woodward's commitment to Neil Back was even more profound in terms of its impact on England's playing style. It had the effect of moving England away from the type of game that had always been associated with them after Peter Winterbottom's retirement in 1993 – a game of physical domination of the set piece backed up typically by a huge back-row. Winterbottom was the last genuine open-side flanker to get a prolonged chance in the England side until Clive Woodward took charge in 1997. Although they were frequently acrimonious opponents on the field, Neil Back and Andy Robinson were in fact in the same boat as number 7s who were rated too small to be effective in the Cooke/Rowell era.

Andy Robinson recalls his playing days and the cloak of invisibility with a laugh now, although he wasn't laughing at the time:

I had played against South Africa in November 1995, after they had won the World Cup in the summer. I thought, 'This is my big chance' as I'd been omitted from the squad for the World Cup. Lawrence Dallaglio was on the bench. I touched the ball 25 times in the game, because that was my function as a link player. But we lost the match 24-14 and a couple of weeks later against Samoa, Lawrence was promoted to the starting side. Jack Rowell came up and asked me whether I would mind coaching him on how to play number 7 in the build-up to the game! It brought the trained teacher out of me of course, but that was probably the only part of the experience I enjoyed.

When I first joined the England coaching group in 2000, we already had three number 7s on the pitch. Lawrence had been shifted to his natural position at no.8, Richard Hill was playing blind-side and Neil was on the open-side. So there were three guys who had all had experience of number 7 and knew how to play the position to international standard. That was a huge advantage in terms of support play, our work at the breakdown and the speed of our defence around the field – and it was quite the opposite of England teams of previous eras who had tended to prefer three number 8s in the back-row.

For Neil Back, the old memories of a bitter opponent on the field quickly evaporated in the shared realisation that they had both been at the rough end of the England selection process as players:

'Robbo' and I had had the odd bust-up as players, particularly during one tempestuous match between Leicester and Bath in 1992. There was a lot of quite edgy banter swirling about. I called him a 'has-been' and he replied 'Better a has-been than a never-was' – to which I couldn't think of an adequate reply as I trotted across the field as I hadn't been capped at the time.

When Robbo became England coach in 2000 I thought, 'Now this is going to get interesting' as I was already established in the side.

But in the event, he was good as gold. He took me aside and explained that he wanted a 'fetcher' in the team and that he enjoyed my play as a natural link with the backs. Maybe he saw something of himself and his lost England caps in me, I don't know. But I know I went away from the meeting with him that day feeling as positive about playing for England as I ever had done. I knew my talents would not be wasted on Robbo's watch.

And so a key axis in the England World Cup side was consolidated. Two natural number 7s whose abilities had previously been neglected, one now a coach, the other still a player, seeing the resemblance in one another – 'mon semblable, mon frère'. Above all, a rugby league coach who backed his perception of ability over size and was prepared to design his new defensive system around the smallest player in the team, and back it to the hilt.

* * * * *

The player with whom Phil formed the closest and most enduring bond of all was the Tigers' centre Will Greenwood. Maybe Phil saw something of himself in Will, because he played in the centre – and just like Phil his eyes lit up at the prospect of playing with ball in hand, but dimmed just as quickly when he had to defend without it.

When I first met Will, he was a tall willowy centre playing for Leicester Tigers. I grew really fond of him because of his determination to improve every aspect of his game, his desire to push the boundaries. He had already toured with the British & Irish Lions in 1997 and was an outstanding attacking centre with a deep understanding of the game. He had the ability to read the opposing defence and make quick decisions, which helped us to select the correct tactical options in attack. He excelled at diagnosing the defensive formation and feeding that information back to Jonny Wilkinson, thus allowing Wilko to concentrate on receiving the pass from the set piece or the base of the ruck. Although he was no Jeremy Guscott, Will could use his height and long running angles to escape from the clutches of would-be tacklers, and offload in contact.

Unfortunately Will Greenwood was not the finished article, far from it. He was nowhere near as interested in the game when the opposition had the ball. Both Clive and I knew that Will was a class act and that it was down to me to improve his defensive qualities, in order to make the most of a player who we both realised could become a key ingredient in England's success.

I had many discussions with him in those early days without much success. He was polite and charming with a quick wit. Good fun to talk to but not easy to convince. 'Phil, I am an attacking centre', he would say, 'and I don't particularly like tackling.'

'A bit of me in him,' I thought. I realised I could now give him the coaching that I craved, but never received in my league career.

The turning point was a video session in which our video analyst Tony Biscombe added a special camera, focusing on Will's reactions to the flow of the training session proper. The main feed was the training game, but up in the top left-hand corner you could see Will's face changing like the weather as he first attacked with the ball, then defended without it. When he received the ball his face lit up and became alive with an awareness of possibilities, when he carried it up there was a look of steely determination. But when the opposition had the ball, it was as if the only light in the house had just been switched off. He became the invisible man. A look of apathy appeared on his face and his body language, which had been upright, tense and full of energy before, had changed completely. This happened as regular as clockwork throughout the session.

I showed him the film afterwards and asked, 'What were you thinking here, what was your level of concentration?'

I finally got the straight answer I'd been looking for all along.

'Phil it's bloody obvious', he replied. 'I'm 100% when I have the ball and then it drops to 0% when I have to bloody tackle'.

'Why?' I asked. 'Is it a matter of courage?'

Will thought for a while. 'No, definitely not,' he replied.

'It takes as much courage to carry the ball in hard as it does to make a tackle… No, it's a matter of technique. When I have the ball I am comfortable. I don't have to think about what to do because everything comes naturally to me. With tackling it's different. I get my body in the wrong position and I have to think carefully about what to do, and by that time they are often past me.'

'How can we sort that out?' I asked.

'With practice, I suppose…' came the answer.

'Okay' I said, 'let's follow Dave Aldred's dictum of *little and often*. Aim to make four perfect tackles at every training session and believe me, within six or seven weeks everything will come to you naturally. When you are out there in the middle you will automatically move into the right position and tackling will begin to become easy for you. Will, I will give you 100% commitment, but I expect 100% from you in return.'

'Okay, big man,' he said, looking down at me.

'Let's do it.'

The England fitness and conditioning guru, Dave 'Otis' Reddin, has a similar memory: 'Will Greenwood was way off the pace when I first started working with the squad. The training the players did at their clubs did not approach the standard we required, so we relied on the players employing their own private fitness trainers and doing the extra work themselves. I was able to take charge of the London group at 6am, before breakfast.

'The training was nasty, as tough as you could imagine. At first Will really struggled and could only handle weights that some of the others were using as a warm-up. His determination to keep going with the banter of the other boys ringing in his ears, and the standard that he eventually attained, is a great credit to him.'

Will Greenwood's insecurity over his tackling technique was related to anxiety over its physical foundation, the strength of his shoulder joints:

When I first met Phil at Welford Road, he left a curious impression on me, he loved to join the training run with the players and he'd appear with a perfect all-body sun-tan, shorts that were a couple of sizes too tight for him and his silvery hair gently wafting in the breeze as we did the warm-up. He was competitive too, he'd try to push the pace on and challenge some of the boys.

In my early rugby career I was known as 'twig man'. Although I loved to mix it up physically with the biggest and the best of them, my body was not slow in telling me what I could and I could not do. My first shoulder operation was at the age of 20, back in 1993, after a game against Oxford University at Iffley Road. Audley Lumsden stepped inside my flailing arm and that was that. I can still remember the strange sensation of feeling my shoulder joint stretching the skin to what I thought had to be breaking point. Then the pain started, with all the muscles around the joint going into spasms. When the doctor arrived to put it back in, it got even worse – foot under the armpit and pull for all you're worth.

I've had five shoulder reconstructions in all, and though things are now a bit more subtle – they drill into the bone and attach little darts to the socket – you still get to smell the bone burning and feel the drill boring its way in.

It takes a while to get your confidence back whether you're weightlifting in the gym or preparing for that first true contact on a rugby field, wondering whether the next big hit will take you off again... In fact, I don't think you ever forget the truth that it can happen again, there are too many scars that tell you otherwise. Even when I dive into a swimming pool now, there is still a moment of doubt as I hit the water. After the fifth reconstruction, I told myself: 'There has to be a better way of earning a living!'

So that's what Phil Larder had to work with at Leicester and England, and I can't thank him enough for all the effort he put in to make me an international class defender. It is clear to me now that there is no way that I could have played football at that level and survived all the operations if I had not been playing within Phil's defensive system. Me in the blitz? You can forget it. It was the faith I had in Phil's system that enabled me to stop thinking about what might happen when I got that heavy contact on my shoulder. The line-speed, and the support I always knew would be there on my inside helped me forget about Audley Lumsden.

Phil told me what the stats said, that in the course of a whole game I'd be lucky to have the ball in my hands for a total of more than a minute – so what was I going to do for the rest of it? He made me aware of just how important reading the game and running without the ball [especially in defence] really is. He put me in a position where I could enjoy one of my favourite sayings – that the strong take from the weak and the smart take from the strong – on the field. I may not be able to bench-press much more than 110kgs, but with England and Leicester, I never had to...

At the end of my career I felt strongly enough to express my thoughts and send them off in a letter to him:

'I wanted to put down on paper my eternal gratitude for everything you did for me on a rugby field over an eight year period. The skinny little non-tackling Will Greenwood you helped to turn into a man that took the field fearing NO-ONE.'

It's quite ironic that I now coach the Marlow under-11s near my home, with a special focus on defence! I guess Phil would appreciate that.

Will Greenwood dared to push his boundaries, and no more could be required of any player. In the 2003 World Cup Final, this meant swapping over to the most difficult defensive assignment in the backline, in the 13 channel.

Towards the end of regular time at the 2003 World Cup Final, Mike Tindall was replaced by Mike Catt and Will had to move out from inside centre to outside. Outside centre is the hardest position in which to defend because of the spacing involved and the multiple angles available to the attackers. When he saw the replacement being made, the Australia coach Eddie Jones immediately sent a message on to the field for Mat Rogers and Matt Giteau to attack Will at every opportunity. Eddie told us afterwards that he thought it might have been a game-saver for them with the exhaustion of extra time, but Will dug in and tackled and defended as though his very life depended on it. Under the most intense pressure he produced a faultless display.

There was no doubt in my mind that during the 2002/03 season Will had developed into the best inside centre in world rugby, having added improved fitness and a resolute defence to his superb attacking game. But some things never change, and when he wrote me that emotionally-charged letter expressing his gratitude for my help, he still added at the bottom and over the page: 'I STILL HATE TACKLING!'

Meanwhile Leicester's defence rapidly improved, and by Christmas 1998 Phil was happy with its structure and impressed by the squad's commitment and concentration. He knew from talking to players from other clubs during international weeks that Leicester's new model defence was worrying them, both in terms of its ferocity and its organisation. Matt Dawson said that he hated coming to Welford Road [even more than normal]: 'Even the defensive drills you do at the end of the warm-up as it's pissing down with rain are so fierce. They remind me that your defence will be in my face all afternoon and it's not a pleasant feeling.' Matt persuaded the Saints head coach Wayne Smith to invite Phil to Franklin's Gardens and take a session. When he returned months later he was surprised to see how many adjustments they had made. It was the first trickle in what would become a gusher of intellectual property from Phil Larder to All Black coaches past and future. By 2004 Graham Henry would take Phil's defensive system back to his homeland and, after his appointment as New Zealand coach, install it with the All Blacks – a system they still use up to the present day.

> My time at Leicester was invaluable. It gave me access to a talented squad of players who were fiercely competitive, highly motivated and determined to be successful; and a head coach who was flexible and open to new ideas. Through Tigers I was able to devise drills and modified games, test them out and perfect them so that when I introduced them into the England squad they were already fully polished. The fact that so many of the Tigers squad were involved with England [Martin Johnson, Neil Back, Ben Kay, Will Greenwood, Graham Rowntree, Lewis Moody, Dorian West, Martin Corry, Austin Healey, Darren Garforth, Richard Cockerill, Leon Lloyd, Tim Stimpson and Ollie Smith] only enhanced the impact and increased the speed of development.

Leicester duly won the 1998/99 English Premiership, conceding only 34 tries – 30 fewer than their nearest rivals the Northampton Saints and 40 fewer than the league average that year. In the 2000/01 season the figure dropped to 25 tries, then dropped again to a mere 19 in 22 games the following season, as Leicester won the English Premiership for four consecutive seasons with Phil Larder firmly in defensive harness – and not forgetting two consecutive Heineken Cup triumphs in his final two years with the club.

Moreover, two of the invisible 'tigers' of English rugby, Neil Back and Will Greenwood, had their careers resuscitated by the courage in selection and teaching ability of Phil Larder. The era of defensive organisation in rugby union had well and truly arrived, and it created the platform for both their individual success, and the ultimate success at club and national level alike. Leicester and England were now learning what America and Australia had known for many decades in their own chosen contact sports – that it is defence that gets the job done in the high-pressure games, and in the most important tournaments.

Chapter six

A few good men

CLIVE Woodward's background in business and management set the scene for a radical transformation of the traditional coaching structure in rugby union. Woodward had decided against a career in teaching after leaving Loughborough and was not a coaching educator in the traditional sense. He had some experience at both Henley RFC and London Irish, and with the England under-21s set-up, but lacked the deep reservoir of coaching experience of both John Mitchell and Phil Larder. Whereas most of his coaches came from a teaching background, Clive had created and run his own business with great success.

At first Clive had been easing me in gently, asking me to observe the squad rather than dive straight into coaching. Perhaps because I was chafing at the bit after a couple of weeks of observation, I remember my very first coaching session with England in that 1997 autumn series very vividly. It was on the Tuesday before the South Africa Test on 29 November, sandwiched in between the two games we played against New Zealand – the first of which had been the match we lost at Old Trafford, the second where we fought them to a standstill at Twickenham in a 26-all draw.

As we all travelled to the Petersham Hotel in Richmond to prepare for South Africa I decided to concentrate on developing a basic line defence in training, which would include a guard at each side of the ruck and the movement of two faster and more agile players back to the blind side at all lineouts and side-line scrums. That would involve a major reorganisation but what really worried me the most was something much more fundamental – the poor individual tackling skills of the majority of the squad.

I knew that perfection in the basic skill of tackling could not be achieved simply by hitting tackle bags and I'd had several disappointing experiences using those huge tractor inner tubes. The most important aspect of tackling is the quick movement of the feet into position close to the ball-carrier. This is most difficult to achieve when he is running at speed and changing direction, so it has to be practised and perfected in those conditions.

I therefore devised several drills in which contact was minimal but the aim was clear. The players worked in pairs, less than three metres apart and running at half-pace, with a focus on the tackler moving in close before driving his shoulder into the thighs of the ball-carrier. Each pair though had to be far enough away from the others to avoid possible injuries if there was a collision.

I always insisted that the ball-carrier wore a protective contact suit in these drills and at times added a tackle shield so that the tackler could explode freely into the cushion with his shoulder. The shield drills were useful because you could work on foot placement and a strong shoulder contact. That contact was high, hitting a spot just beneath where the ball would be held.

A great deal of work had gone into the thinking process behind the drills, but I was still nervous as it was effectively my first 'audition' in front of the England players, sandwiched in between a forwards session led by John Mitchell and a backs session run by Clive. I was even more apprehensive after witnessing John Mitchell's run, which was crisp, concentrated and full of productive, error-free work. Thankfully things went well and Daz Garforth ran up to me afterwards and wheezed out, 'That was like a breath of fresh air mate!' – although I could seldom detect whether Daz was taking the mickey or not.

Clive ran a decent session to finish the day's work, but the feedback from the players suggested that it did not have quite the same quality and focus as those run by myself and Mitch. Although none of us said anything, I think we all knew it... It was an uncomfortable, silent moment of realisation and it represented a parting of the ways for the future of the England rugby team. Thankfully and to his eternal credit, Clive chose the right fork in the road.

John Mitchell was an ex-All Black who had previous coaching experience at both national level with Ireland and Sale in the English Premiership, so his credentials were self-evident. From then on the drills and work on the field were increasingly to be left with the 'professional teachers' like myself, Dave Alred [who became a natural teacher in sports as diverse as rugby, golf and American football], Phil Keith-Roach, and later, Brian Ashton, Andy Robinson and Simon Hardy. All of us had a teaching background.

Clive had the strength to acknowledge that the value he added was not in player education on the field but in rugby management and leadership off it. It was a courageous step but one in my opinion he had to take. Clive was the opposite of Malcolm Reilly, with whom I'd worked at international level in rugby league. Mal was a top hands-on coach, but Clive was an outstanding manager of coaches, and that derived from his basic background in business.

He said to me, 'There is no single or "correct" way to do this job Phil, every national coach has his own style and his own strengths. I don't have the specialised knowledge to head up each department at the level that we are now operating. I search the world and appoint the best people available to head up each department. It is my job to manage them, get the best out of each one and above all, to make sure that we are all moving forward with our noses pointed in the same direction.'

It was the same strength that Clive Woodward had demonstrated when openly admitting to Jim Greenwood, in front of an audience of fellow students, that he could not kick off his left foot. That moment of self-awareness had been fortified by Clive's experience in business, where his natural role had always been shaped by his ability to get others to work for him, inspired by his self-belief and the range of his ideas.

Where every other team in the forthcoming 1998 Five Nations tournament would be stuck in the traditional format of one 'hands-on' head coach with perhaps a [part-time] assistant or two, Clive Woodward's 'public' acknowledgement created the space for the rapid growth of a raft of outstanding specialists underneath him, all with head coaching credentials of their own. If he hadn't been able to make that acknowledgement, the new coaching structure which so swiftly catapulted England ahead of all their domestic rivals could never have come into being.

Even at its inception in 1997/98, the elite group of coaches included Phil [who had coached the GB rugby league team], John Mitchell [who would within four short years be appointed head coach of New Zealand and lead them to the 2003 World Cup], Brian Ashton [who had been head coach of Ireland between 1996–1998], Dave Alred [who had played in the NFL and went on to coach both elite golfers and rugby kickers at the very highest level of the game] and Dave Reddin [who became head of performance services at both the British Olympic Association and soccer's FA]. These were individuals who were used to demanding their own coaching space and whose presence quietly nudged Clive Woodward 'upstairs' into the leadership/management role that fitted him best. As Andy Robinson comments,

> I went into coaching primarily because I loved teaching. Nothing gave me greater enjoyment than being able to teach a player a new technique on the training field. In the wider aspect, I wanted forwards who could handle the ball and pass in a movement-based game. After all, as a player I'd been coached by another teacher in Brian Ashton at Bath and I'd been strongly influenced by his vision of the game. When I became an international coach I wanted to promote very much the same vision of what the game could be. That's what got me excited about rugby in the first place, and that's still what gets me excited about the game now. I'd already coached with 'Woody' in the England under-21s set-up, so we both knew what we were about. We knew we could work together and we knew that we had compatible views on the game, so both the dynamics were right.
>
> In a sense it was no different to the relationship I now have at Bristol with our head coach Sean Holley. Sean conducts the on-field training sessions himself or delegates them to our other specialists, but I am still present offering observations, and connecting the detail of the sessions to the bigger picture of where I want Bristol RFC to go in the long term as a club. There is a clear differentiation of roles.

Back in 1997, the idea of a manager overseeing a corps of specialist coaches represented a revolution in rugby union thinking, in a sport which was still taking its first baby steps in a new era of professionalism.

There were precedents for it, particularly in the far more mature professional collision sports outside rugby, but Clive Woodward had first encountered the idea when he went out to Australia towards the end of his playing career in 1985. He had played for the Manly club in Sydney, and the 'Manly Oval' where the local club played their games was only a stone's throw away from the Steyne pub where Phil had first discussed a revolution in English rugby league with the two Franks, Stanton and Johnson.

Manly was the club of Alan Jones, who had masterminded the Wallabies' grand slam of the four home nations in 1984 with virtually no experience as a coach in the first-class game [one successful season with Manly in 1983] and no appreciable background as a player. Although he began life as a teacher, his main talents over time have proved to be twofold: the ability to transfer skills from one spectrum to another [from teaching to politics, business and rugby], and the drive to change set perceptions within his sphere of influence, particularly via the media. Both would become keystones in Clive Woodward's approach to the England job.

In the current social media age, Jones would probably be termed a 'key influencer'. He was a speech-writer for ex-prime minister Malcolm Fraser early in his career, and he has hosted a controversial top-rated radio show in Sydney for over 25 years. With his strong business/political background, as a coach Jones looked at the people around him as potential assets in his new venture. After Clive Woodward had broken his jaw playing rugby for Manly, Jones visited him in hospital but his veiled intent only became clear at the end of the conversation, when he invited Woodward to join up with the Wallaby squad, as permitted by the international eligibility rules of the time. Jones had succeeded by delegating to 'knowledgeable others' while keeping strict overall control as chief motivator and organiser: 'I was the first person in world rugby to have an assistant coach', he said – in fact many assistant coaches, depending on the coaching requirement of the moment. The main coaches on the 1984 tour were Alec Evans in the forwards – who went on to become Wales head coach at the 1995 World Cup in South Africa – assisted by Phil Keith-Roach [who was later to become Clive Woodward's scrum guru with England], and the captain Mark Ella in the backs.

Ella had the extraordinary intelligence to function like an on-field coach. He knew the 'flat-line' pattern of back-play that had been developed between himself, his two brothers Gary and Glen and their coach Bob Dwyer at Randwick inside out.

Clive Woodward wasted no time flagging up Alan Jones's influence on his own outlook at his very first press conference as England head coach: 'I spent a lot of my time [in Australia] studying the set-up at Manly and how Alan transferred his skills – not his rugby skills, but his business and political skills – to his job with the Wallabies. He had hardly any track record in rugby before Manly but there's no doubting how well that transference of skills and other life experiences worked out for him and for Australia.'

There is a substantial overlap between Phil Larder and Clive Woodward's rugby sabbaticals in Australia. Both not only thought outside the box, they travelled outside it to discover what new thinking in rugby might really mean. They visited the Australian Institute of Sport and learned from the free cross-fertilisation of ideas that occurred between sports. Rugby union was pulled in under the AIS umbrella in 1988 and within three years the squad were totally professional in attitude – benefiting from the work of fitness and strength consultants, sports psychologists, nutritionists and even three video analysts who broke down footage of all Australia's opponents before the 1991 World Cup! Both Woodward and Larder found a rugby coach in Australia, in Phil's case Jack Gibson and in Clive Woodward's Alan Jones, who provided a practical model for their subsequent careers.

The similarities between Alan Jones and Clive Woodward are too hard to ignore. Whereas Gibson and Larder were both hands-on coaching educators and therefore a 'match', Woodward and Jones excelled as managers of other people's coaching talents. Jones was, like Woodward, a rugby idealist: 'If you aim for the stars, you'll get your feet off the ground. But if you aim for the floor, you won't even get out of bed.' Both Jones and Woodward were mavericks who influenced the establishment basically from a position outside its control. They were both confident and foot-sure when navigating the political rapids within their sport, perhaps because they had made their fortunes in business before becoming union employees.

As a result they did not depend on its remuneration for their future welfare. This gave them a certain freedom to act independently of external authority and insist on 'my way or the highway'. Both understood the value of extended coaching groups and their own principal role as organisers and managers. They found a niche as 'transformational leaders' in a sport which was either still amateur or taking its first baby steps in the professional era. Neither was able successfully to transfer their leadership and management skills effectively to mature professional sports [Jones with Balmain Tigers in Australian rugby league and Woodward with Southampton FC in English soccer].

In October 1998, the image in the mirror became complete when Clive Woodward visited both the Denver Broncos and the local varsity team in Colorado, mimicking Phil's own visit to the LA Rams in Anaheim 14 years earlier and the massive learning curve, mostly derived from the connection with American football, he had experienced with Jack Gibson.

It was here that Woodward learned that defence could be seen as a separate compartment of the game, complete with its own coaches, drills and philosophies – an 'army within an army'. His experience was to all intents and purposes exactly the same as that experienced by Jack Gibson with the San Francisco 49ers back in 1972, and transmitted to Phil Larder in 1983/84. Woodward encountered first-hand, and with the same wide-eyed wonder as Gibbo, the separation of offence and defence and special teams in their own coaching rooms, and the 20-30 coaches employed to ensure the efficiency of each unit and sub-unit of the team. One of the results of the visit was that England began to change mindset more quickly and definitely when they were no longer in possession of the ball.

As Phil says, 'I started to work harder at enabling the players to switch from attack to defence faster than the opposition, so that if we made a handling error or kicked badly then we would be in defensive mode quicker than the opposition could counter-attack. I would have them regrouping so that after say, a handling error, we would be back into our defensive positions by at the latest, third phase.'

As Dave Alred, who had played the role of kicker for the Minnesota Vikings in the NFL remarked, 'The American football understanding of performance under pressure, and the relevance of psychological and biomechanical detail to that performance is in a different universe to anything in British sport.' The amateur *enfant terrible* rugby union was at least 25 years behind American football and 13 years behind rugby league in terms of professionalism, and that was just going by Phil Larder's watch. In true terms, it was probably much, much further behind both its sister collision sports.

The stark realisation of the enormous gap in professional preparation between teams in the US and the UK was in the forefront of Clive Woodward's mind when he returned to Heathrow. It was such a critical wake-up call that he did not wait to get home before ringing Phil Larder:

Clive called me as soon as he landed. 'Phil, I have had a great visit to the Broncos and the penny has dropped. You will be pleasantly surprised at the way I will re-organise training.'

Clive was as good as his word. The amount of training time that I had with the players was almost doubled and all the specialist coaches gradually became full-time. Moreover instead of watching games with Dave Alred from the other side of the ground we began sitting in the coaches' box.

The process evolved to the point where the specialist coaches had complete responsibility for their own area of the game. World Class Performance Standards were then agreed for every area, which were geared to making us the best team in the world. These made us all accountable and we knew that if we did not deliver we would be replaced.

I knew what was expected of me and at last I had adequate time with the players to make the improvements that I wanted. It was demanding but incredibly exciting and for the first time I became confident that we were heading in the right direction.

It was no accident that England began the process of becoming competent professionals by first attending to their defence. They went all the way back to 1972, to Dick Nolan's statement to Jack Gibson: 'You have to be able to control your opponent in the areas where he has the ball.' As Martin Johnson recalls,

I think there was a brief but benign power-struggle among the coaches when the group first came together, with Phil coming out on top... Clive would be shouting 'attack, attack', Dave Alred would be shouting 'kick, kick'. But the guy we really listened to was Phil Larder, so we progressed most quickly as a defensive team.

Clive drifted away from being a hands-on coach throughout 1998, especially after Brian Ashton joined the coaching group in the autumn and after he came back from his trip to the States – and it was Phil who filled the vacuum and became the dominant voice on the training field.

There were a lot of Leicester lads in the squad, and all of them were familiar with Phil's defensive sessions at Welford Road, so we knew what an effective unit we would develop into if we listened to what Phil said. I think it frustrated Clive a little, because he had this dream of us playing 'total rugby' and scoring lots of tries. But as Phil went into everything in more and more detail, we bought into it and we improved much more quickly as a defensive group. We developed a real appetite for playing hard without the ball.

It was very scientific. We began to question what kind of tackles we wanted to make in certain situations – whether to go low or high, to tackle in ones or twos or to gang-tackle. Then we had a decision to make as the ruck formed – whether to contest the tackle ball or pull out into the line. We worked on how to approach certain individuals on the opposition team, whether we wanted to take them side-on or head-on, and whether we wanted to widen or condense our spacing depending on the opposition attack. It made us all think far more about the detail of the way we defended, and as with anything that is completely thought-through, it brought a feeling of security and excitement with it.

We were so confident in our defensive work by the end of 1998, when we beat South Africa by 13-7 in the autumn and kept a clean sheet against Australia in the other game, that our iron curtain had also become our comfort blanket. I think we were prepared to indulge Brian Ashton's more touchy-feely approach in attack simply because we felt so secure on the other side of the ball.

To be fair we had become so used to Phil and the influence he exerted with England that we forgot what an unusual situation it was at that time. On the 2001 Lions for example, Graham Henry was a hands-on head coach and I felt he was genuinely taken aback by how much coaching time Phil demanded and just how independently he operated – much more like an assistant head coach than pure assistant. It was the England way but it took a lot of time and effort for it to become the Lions way.

In his revealing study *White Gold: England's journey to World Cup glory*, Peter Burns also suggests that Clive Woodward brought something else back to England from his playing experience in Australia: the flat back-line principles pioneered by the Randwick club.

The flat back-line was a product of Bob Dwyer's thinking about the game and the three Ella brothers' – Mark, Glen and Gary – natural way of playing it. Dwyer had in fact inherited the attacking method from a player of a much earlier generation, Cyril Towers, who had played for both Randwick and Australia during the 1930s. When Dwyer went up to watch the three Ella brothers playing for Matraville High in the local schools competition, he knew he was watching three youngsters who were intuitively tuned in on the flat back-line wavelength.

The basic principles were twofold and very simple: the backs did not stand deep on attack, and they stood flat and they ran die-straight. The Towers/Dwyer theory was that the attack could not place the defence under pressure until it was under pressure itself, and in order to create that pressure the first two receivers had to engage their opposite numbers before even beginning to think of the pass: 'You cannot push the needle through the cloth until you get the needle very close to it.' If the first two receivers could accomplish their part successfully, it would prevent the defence from drifting on to the two unknown quantities in the attack – the full-back and blind-side winger – and occupying the space they wanted to exploit.

In practice, this tended to produce a very compact back-line which rarely occupied more than half the width of the field before the ball hit the widest attacker. Passes tended to be short and sympathetic, with both defensive centres required to make more frontal tackles than was the norm in the British game. The collisions occurred far earlier and they were far more explosive. Clive Woodward recalls of his time in Australia, 'Every time the opposition had the ball from set-piece, I was having to make a [front-on] tackle – or try to make one… I was run over a lot in my first game [for Manly].'

One of the major bonuses of this compact attacking method was that the first receiver tended to get a lot of second touches off loop plays and offloads. With half of the field to play in, that represented a very dangerous situation when the first receiver was Mark Ella, and Dwyer would often measure the success of the attack by the number of second touches his first receiver managed to get.

However as Dwyer himself points out, the desire to engage the defence flat and early did not equate to a version of 'total rugby': 'I must make it clear that the principles I learned from Cyril Towers applied to one specific area of play – namely, open-side attack by the back-line with the ball in hand… This is just a small part of the game as a whole… and many people have misunderstood it. It actually has little in common with "running rugby" as the term is generally understood.'

Although the flat back-line theory did not really equate to either Jim Greenwood or Brian Ashton's vision of 'total rugby', it did excite Clive Woodward's imagination of how England might bring a new speed and explosiveness to their attack, and move them away from the traditional set-piece mould of English teams of the past. In this sense it was a courageous move of critical importance to the team's development.

The litmus test arrived as early as the second Test against New Zealand in 1997. Before that match Clive Woodward had demanded that his choice at outside-half, Paul Grayson, keep ball in hand and play flat and in the teeth of the All Black defence. Even before half-time England had scored three tries [with Grayson hitting the open-side flat and early for the second score] and built a commanding 23-9 lead. But there was a cost, as Martin Johnson remembers:

> I looked around the changing room at half-time and I knew we had shot our bolt. We were completely knackered and out on our feet. Bodies were slumped over, and heads were hanging, gasping for breath. No-one spoke, not a word. Everything we had, we had already given in that wild first half on the lush Twickenham turf. There were no batteries to be recharged and there was nothing more to drag out of ourselves.
>
> While I've often thought it was naivety on Clive's part to believe that we could sustain the speed and physicality of that approach, in retrospect it was like many of the ideas he dared to implement. We would never have discovered the levels of fitness and conditioning we needed in order to sustain that level of intensity for a full 80 minutes, if we hadn't tried it against the best side in the world then and there. I guess it brought home the truth of what Backy always used to say about Clive: 'Clive's greatest strength is that he is unafraid to make mistakes – and make plenty of them!'
>
> We lost the second half 17-3 and hung on by our fingernails for the draw, 26-26 – just about… If we hadn't had that experience and lived through it from beginning to end, I doubt any of us would have believed the effort and sacrifices necessary to get to the level of the three southern hemisphere big guns. But now we could see that it would all have to begin with defence and conditioning, and that was what got us to the stage where we could concede one try over two games against Australia and South Africa at the end of 1998 – and beat the best team in the world at that time [the Springboks] 13-7 to bring that year to a close.

With Clive looking for the coaches to interact with another in what he called 'cross-boundary team-working' Phil naturally found himself working with England fitness and conditioning coach, Dave 'Otis' Reddin. Although Dave Reddin had been on the fringe of the England operation since the Jack Rowell years, his abilities had never been fully utilised:

After finishing my MSc at Loughborough in 1991, I stayed on and assisted Rex Hazeldine with the RFU project. At that time Geoff Cooke was the coach, but by 1995 I was working with all the England sides. Tom McNabb had just taken up the role of fitness and conditioning with the England senior team and he was already making waves. I remember the veteran lock forward Maurice Colclough walking out of the very first session Tom delivered and never coming back again!... He just retired from international rugby and that was that.

I'd been working with a lot of sports other than rugby and to be honest, my head was still full of textbooks and I needed practical experience by the bucket-load. My big opportunity came when I replaced Martin Dawson at Leicester Tigers after Martin went back to New Zealand in 1996 and in retrospect it couldn't have been better timed, because it was right at the beginning of professionalism in the sport. Bob Dwyer took over at Tigers in 1997 and of course they had been doing things professionally down under for many years before that! I knew that the southern hemisphere was far better prepared for the game to go professional than we were in Europe, so they were well ahead of us in terms of their input from sports science – biomechanics, physiology and psychology especially.

My first contact with Clive Woodward and Andy Robinson occurred when we were all involved in the under-21 set-up. When Clive was appointed England coach, I think Pat Fox was on a part-time contract as the main conditioner. But at Welford Road we quickly moved ahead of the pack with our professional approach to conditioning and a number of the Tigers players became quite critical of Foxy. Clive didn't want any part-timers on his staff anyway, so I was appointed national director of fitness in November 1997, although the post didn't become full-time until 1999.

Although I can understand his larger purpose better in hindsight, I initially felt quite frustrated with Clive who was spending most of his time creating the 'cultural architecture' of the England squad with Humphrey Walters. I even spat out a critical email saying that he should be spending more of his energies getting us on a par with the southern hemisphere in fitness terms and the message was not well-received at all! At least not at first...

But the drawn game against the All Blacks at the end of the 1997 autumn international window proved the point for me. All the boys could feel their limitations when they had been forced to play a southern hemisphere style game at southern hemisphere pace. The conditioning work we had been doing was the same as in the amateur era, there was just more of it – so it was generic rather than specific. To give one example, our fitness testing at St Mary's College had been based on the 3km run – which was won by Mike Catt (backs) and Will Green (forwards). But the fitness results did not in any way relate to the players with the highest number of game involvements, so we knew we had to become more specific, with individually-designed testing, training and nutritional programmes.

I also persuaded Clive to take on Adam Carey, who changed those nutritional programmes from a carbohydrate to a protein intake base. Adam's influence resulted in immediate and noticeable changes for the better, with players able to build strength steadily and handle more demanding strength-and-conditioning sessions. We instigated a 'whatever it takes' approach, asking players to take on personal trainers in addition to the work they were already doing with their clubs, and I began working with a London-based group of players [Lawrence Dallaglio, Dan Luger, Will Greenwood, Jason Leonard and Paul Volley] at 6.30 in the morning!

Perhaps the *coup de grâce* was when I managed to obtain a copy of the All Blacks' testing and fitness results before the 1999 World Cup – they were 'left behind in a hotel room' as the saying goes – and we put our own players through exactly the same testing regime. The results were staggering, we were a country mile behind the New Zealand players, and now I could prove it in black-and-white. The aims of both Phil Larder and myself were both fundamentally aligned, because we wanted to replicate situations in training where players were required to make a tackle or be part of an explosive collision, then get back on their feet faster than the opposition. This also fitted Clive's desire for us to be 'quicker than the opponent' in all areas.

Training now became very tough. I talked to the players and asked them what they felt like after defending their own goal line for fully five minutes with the sequence ending in a turnover for us. Clive would wanted them to take a quick tapped penalty and attack from our own end whilst the opposition was least expecting it. I had to replicate that physical and mental state in training. The programme consisted of 30-second sprints flat out on a bike, immediately followed by downs & ups, then back on the bike to repeat. Joe Worsley was regularly sick, but he got on with it. Will Greenwood's confidence on defence was gradually built up by a combination of Phil's technical advice [which gave him more self-belief as a defender] and my strength and conditioning programme [which gave him more self-belief as a physical specimen]. All the players found it nasty but they all understood what I was doing and they all bought into it.

There is also a fundamental connection between physical and mental fitness, and I do not think it was an accident that the players who were able to work hardest to achieve their objectives in training were also the ones who became leaders in various departments of the team – for example Will Greenwood on attack, Jonny Wilkinson on game management and Neil Back on defence. They were that little more indefatigable and they had that ability to both do all the physical work that was required of them and yet still have that extra intellectual energy to see what was happening in their areas of the game and communicate it to their team-mates. Neil Back always impressed me in that respect – he was driven by a mixture of pride and anger, and if he didn't get to the ruck first or reload off the ground before anyone else, he took it as a personal slight.

The new drive to make England the fittest rugby union team on the planet crystallised at Couran Cove in June 1999. As Dave Reddin explains, 'We really threw the kitchen sink at conditioning. We had a gym in the forest and did lots of running, both aerobic and anaerobic. Players trained from 7.00am in the morning with a conditioning session as well as a rugby session before lunch.

'Mitch thought that although our top guys were very fit, they were being held back by the bottom 20%. As a result we ran the shuttles in groups with that 20% seeded into each group. The group could not finish until the last runner came back.' It was an environment in which a fitness and nutrition nut like Neil Back could be expected to thrive, and thrive he did:

> On the 2001 Lions tour to Australia, I remember when I realised we weren't going to win the Test series – it was the first time I entered the buffet area where the playing and coaching squad ate their meals. As someone who has always been a bit of a freak about nutrition, I thought 'none of these options make any sense'. Sitting beside healthy low-calorie choices would be sausages and onion gravy, high in un-useful fats and low in nutritional value. It was both confused and confusing, and it was one of those little moments when the bigger picture comes home to you.
>
> There was a huge mixture of standards on that tour, and nowhere was it clearer than in two separate, but connected areas of the game: 1. Defensive preparation – where none of the Celtic nations had experienced a defensive coach or a system remotely like Phil Larder's, and 2. The food people put into their bodies and the unsupervised work they were prepared to do to keep themselves in shape.
>
> Although there were players like Brian O'Driscoll, Rob Howley, Dafydd James, and some others who could always be relied on, I understood how far behind England's standards of nutrition and conditioning the Celtic nations were at that time when a group of English players walking back from a 'voluntary' gym session looked into a nearby Hungry Jacks – only to see half-a-dozen fellow tourists tucking into their burger and fries enthusiastically! On a Lions tour you are asked to forget your own identity as 'England', 'Scotland', 'Ireland' and 'Wales' and come together as one. But back in 2001, there was precious little reason for an English player to do this if it meant dropping his optimal standards of fitness and conditioning.
>
> It was all so different to Couran Cove in 1999 with England. South Stradbrooke island – or 'South Straddie' as the Aussies call it – was a long slab of beach and semi-tropical rainforest bound together by mangrove roots on Queensland's Gold Coast. It was the brainchild of the great Australian 10km and marathon runner Ron Clarke. The atmosphere was monastic and the place was completely free of all the usual distractions. There was nothing to think about but yourself and the needs of your body as an athletic machine. I have to admit it was right up my alley.

If the sight of Aboriginal tribes-people using dolphins like sea-bound sheepdogs to herd mullet into their nets near shore was an other-worldly experience, the absolute focus on nutrition and conditioning standards was also in my opinion a new milestone in English rugby.

We'd be up and running by 7.00am each morning, with the day ahead as follows:

A. 7am Protein shake to build muscle.
B. 7.30am Weights or endurance [6 km run through the rainforest]
C. Recovery agent [carbs]
D. 10-12am Rugby training
E. Lunch [always low fat, high protein with a base in complex carbs]
F. Recovery agent
G. 4pm Rugby training

We were knackered and in bed by 9pm every night. Not all the senior pros were quite as happy as me: 'Bloody place. You can't drink, you can only sneak a couple of smokes and you can't get a round of golf. We're all up at 6 and in bed by 9 and it's driving us all mad,' said one. It was four weeks of hell for some but many of them changed body shape quite dramatically over the month we were there. There were fewer complaints after they looked in the mirror at the end of the month.

Neil Back was one of the England players for whom the thirst for the optimal dietary and conditioning input – alongside skills development – became a religion. The impulse sparked by Dave Reddin spread like wildfire, with Backy taking on ex-Tigers scrum-half Darren Grewcock as his fitness advisor and personal trainer. Grewcock had been to Australia and learned all about the Aussie approach to the science of physical and mental preparation over several courses at Sydney University.

It was 'Grewy' who punctured my belief in bleep tests as useful indicators of rugby fitness. He created rugby-related exercises which tested my ability to perform repeated explosive movements in a 360 degree arc, the sort of thing my position demanded – rather than just running at ever-increasing speed between two points. It was Grewy who also persuaded me of the need for items that are taken for granted now, but weren't at the time – simple things like constant fluid intake during training and playing games, and planned recovery sessions after hard exercise. In 1996, I invested in my personal development when I had an enforced six months out of the game and paid him £1,800 of my own money for 24 weeks' concentrated work, and it was worth every penny.

It all reinforced Dave Reddin's saying that 'everyone has the will to win, but few have the will to prepare to win'. Dave's programmes were always tailored to fit time schedules – to build up your body for peak events like the Six Nations or autumn internationals – and targeted the needs of your own individual position so that you developed the parts of your body and mind that most needed it.

After Dave had introduced Dr Adam Carey to the England set-up, it was he who connected me with Roz Kadir, the senior nutritionist at the Centre for Nutritional Medicine in London's Harley Street. Roz changed my diet, replacing carbs and un-useful fats with a higher proportion of protein. So for example, white bread was replaced by brown rice and rye bread, and within six months between May and October 1999 I had trimmed down from around 12% to less than 10% body fat and put on 2-3kgs of lean muscle. It was an eye-opener for someone like me, who always took pride in taking care of my body, to realise that there was so very much more to learn...

The new structure in the England coaching group also created space for the unique contribution that Dave Alred was able to make as both a kicking coach and a performance psychologist. Alred joined the coaching group in 1998 but Phil Larder had known him for far longer than that:

Dave and I go back a long way. I was first introduced to him by Frank Disken [the compere of the Alex Murphy–Gareth Edwards 'shoot-out' at my rugby league benefit dinner!] in 1985 when I was still the national director of coaching and assistant coach to the Great Britain RL team. Dave had recently returned from playing in the NFL as a kicker with the Minnesota Vikings and was looking to make his name as a coach. He had previously played at Bath RFC, but he probably came to league because union was still an amateur game.

My hero. Alan Davies on his way to scoring a try for Great Britain against France, 1956.

Where my coaching began. With the Saddleworth School Under-13 soccer team, 1970.

Oldham RLFC, 1970. I am in the front row, third from left.

Meeting the Oldham greats during my benefit. Alan Davies is talking to Sid Little and John Etty, 1979.

Frank Johnson and his wife Ruby near their home in Manly, 1974.

Peter Corcoran and his wife Chris, 1984.

Australian sport flourishes because all the sports pool their knowledge. Meeting the coaching directors of rugby league, rugby union, soccer and cricket with Kangaroo coach Frank Stanton, 1984.

Jack Gibson and Ron Massey at Cronulla-Sutherland Rugby League in 1985.

My first tour as assistant coach to Malcolm Reilly in 1988. We are about to embark on one of our highly competitive runs.

Recovering after an intense training session in Australia, 1988.

With GB captain Ellery Hanley in Papua New Guinea, 1988.

With Malcolm Reilly and physiotherapist Dave Fevre after beating New Zealand in 1990.

Ellery Hanley captaining GB against the Rest of the World.

Taken in 1992, who said touring in the southern hemisphere was tough?

Malcolm Reilly congratulates Dennis Betts after beating Australia in 1992.

View from Manly Pacific – my favourite hotel, 1992.

GBRL before an international with France. in 1992.

Leading Widnes RL out at Wembley to play Wigan RL in the final of the Challenge Cup, May 1993.

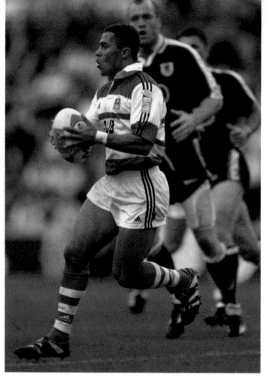

A victory smile with my 17-year-old son Dids after winning the Championship with Keighley Cougars in my first season in charge in 1994-95.

Jason Robinson of Wigan in action during the JJB Super League match against Bradford played at the JJB Stadium, in Wigan, England. Wigan won the match 20-19.

Enjoying Cougarmania with a young fan in 1995.

England preparation at Pennyhill Park. Setting up a ruck defensive drill, 2002.

The brains trust. Clive, Robbo and myself during England preparation, 2002.

The Grand Slam at last. In the dressing room with Clive, Robbo, and Dave Alred after beating Ireland in 2003.

Management in Number One's before the 2003 World Cup.

The England squad for the 2003 World Cup.

Watching filming of Home and Away *on the Thursday before the 2003 World Cup Final, with Matt, Anne, Jay and Dids.*

'Looking quite confident'. Anne with some of the wives before the 2003 World Cup Final.

Clive and I are probably agreeing that this is the best job in the world, despite the serious faces. June, 2003.

Neil Back makes yet another tackle in an outstanding defensive performance against the All Blacks in windy Wellington, prior to the 2003 World Cup.

Bloodied but unbowed. Neil Back, my defensive captain, has again put his head in where it hurts.

The player who made the biggest defensive strides of all while I was England coach – Will Greenwood.

The Colossus. 'Johnno' carries the ball into the heart of the Wallaby defence during the World Cup Final 2003. His leadership made all the difference.

Jonny Wilkinson drops the goal that makes history in extra time.

A proud moment at Buckingham Palace with my daughter Anna after being presented with the MBE by the Queen.

Andy Robinson, myself, Dave Reddin and Dave Alred after we all received the MBE from the Queen.

Ron Massey – the man Jack Gibson could not do without.

Jack Gibson, the Supercoach.

We were all overcome with the welcome we received during the 'open bus' journey through London. Andy Robinson, Clive Woodward, Dave Reddin, Richard Wegrzyk, Richard Smith, Phil Pask and Dave Alred.

I took Dave down to the local ground and he showed me what he could do. I had been rather more than a part-time goal kicker for Oldham RL, and I'd kicked over 100 goals in three consecutive seasons, but it quickly became obvious that Dave was on a far, far higher level to me. I had been surprised by the extent of his flexibility when he warmed up, but that impression quickly evaporated when he started kicking the ball! Although he was smaller than me physically, he quickly demonstrated that he could kick the ball much further than I could. He was more accurate from acute angles, and more consistent and exact with his preparatory routine. His body was like a perfect machine – from the waist up virtually motionless, the bottom half working like a smooth and easy pendulum through the ball. It dawned on me that this was no accident – he always seemed to hit the sweet spot and be accelerating through the ball at the point of contact. Mud or no mud, time and again he picked the ball clean off the top of his 'tee' and sent it fizzing towards the poles. I remember forming the distinct impression that he would be able to do this whatever the weather conditions, come hell or high water. It was as if the external conditions didn't matter.

I had been so impressed by Dave's ability and vision that I had introduced him to Maurice Bamford who was the GB coach at the time. Maurice invited Dave to join us at our training camp at the Lilleshall National Sports Centre where we were preparing to play a three-Test series against New Zealand.

Dave fitted in well and his high spiralling 'bombs' immediately drew the attention of both Maurice and myself. We were like hawks to a hare. For me it was déjà vu, a repeat of Peter Phipps – the Aussie Rules specialist Jack Gibson had recruited to teach the bomb at Paramatta, except that balls were now tumbling out of the slate-grey, rather than a glossy blue sky.

Dave demonstrated what happened when a spiral bomb was kicked high, with a hang time of around four seconds or more. It turned at the top of its apex, and the loss of impetus caused the ball to come down in a circular pattern, drifting and swirling unexpectedly. Henderson Gill was an exciting winger with Wigan RL who was gobby, full of self-confidence and a bit of a showman. He wanted to take Dave's punts on. Maurice and myself still talk about Dave's third kick, which he struck perfectly. It spun high into the sky and then stopped like a 'doodlebug', silently turning over at its apex. 'Gilly' had worked out that the ball would begin to fade away from him as it descended so he took three quick paces forward – but the ball swirled away at the last moment and crashed down on the top of his head, full-on. There was uproar from the rest of the squad and plenty of cat-calls as Gilly trotted after the ball [which was now about 20 metres away] with his distinctive rolling, slightly bow-legged gait, as if to remonstrate with it. When we meet, Maurice and I still remember that moment as clear as daylight and we have a good cackle about it. At the time, we wondered if our kickers had time to master the skill before we played the Kiwis.

Dave was lost to league after that brief but spectacular interlude and we didn't meet again until he linked up with England in 1998, but everything I'd sensed about him in that first meeting came true in the environment Clive built. This particularly applied to his work with Jonny Wilkinson.

Although Jonny was a natural, Dave was able to develop both his kicking skill and the mental attitude that was to make him world-class. Dave also doubled up as our performance psychologist – he would always remind the place-kickers that kicking under pressure was 40% technical and 60% mental – and convinced me that in order to improve a skill, a player has to practise it perfectly and practise it every day. 'It's not "practice makes perfect" Phil', he would say, it's 'only perfect practice makes perfect.'

I certainly understood that concept and had painful memories from my playing career at Oldham to prove it. I had enjoyed one of those perfect days in a cup-tie at Leigh when all the stars were aligned and I had kicked eight goals from eight attempts in the process of helping Oldham through to the next round.

Our next game was at home against league leaders Wigan and it was live on BBC television. I arrived early, as usual, on Tuesday night to practise my kicking before training. The groundsman turned the floodlights on and then came out on to the pitch with me. 'No need to practise your kicking Phil' he said. 'That was perfect on Saturday. Just keep it in your mind and you'll be fine.' Not bad advice that, and I wish that I had taken it, because several people then proceeded to walk on to the pitch and offer comments while I was kicking!

I became distracted, lost my concentration and began to hurry my kicks. I'd completely lost my composure and was unable to regain my winning rhythm, despite another practice session on the Thursday. I kicked only three goals from six attempts against Wigan, and as they beat us by four points I felt responsible for the loss. One week a rooster, the next a feather-duster, as the saying goes.

Dave Alred understood deeply that your mind and body adjust to repetitive practice. If your technique in practice is faulty, or you become distracted by external factors [as I had] then that is exactly what you are learning. You will either be cementing a faulty technique or an open-ness to outside influences that will become more difficult to eradicate in the future. You will repeat the same mistakes under pressure.

'Little and often' is another coaching truism of Dave's which I bought into completely. As soon as I realised that the tackling skills of the England players were poor I put in place a training programme in which every player devoted at least some portion of his time to his tackling technique in every single training session. Each player completed no more than six tackles as perfectly as they could and I would check each tackle later on videotape and discuss them with the appropriate individual.

Dave used the same process with Wilko's kicking. Wilko kicked every day with Dave constantly checking and tweaking his technique. Although both understood the 'often' in 'little and often', I am not sure if either of them understood the 'little' because many of their practices appeared to go on for hours. During our forward planning for the 2003 World Cup, Dave Reddin suggested that when we had an evening kick-off we should train and eat throughout the week at the same time as we would on matchday. The rationale was that the body would adjust and player's energy levels would build towards a natural peak at kick-off time. Otis's suggestion was finally put to bed when Clive spotted one of the potential pitfalls: 'Good idea Otis… but no way are we having floodlights on our training pitch at Pennyhill Park. We struggle to get Wilko in off the field as it is… if there were lights on the pitch he would be out there all night as well as all day!'

Everyone says what a well-mannered young gentleman Jonny Wilkinson is, a true grandma's delight, but I am not so sure. Dave asked Jonny to concentrate on powering the ball through the posts rather than just aiming to bisect them, suggesting that Wilko visualise kicking the ball into the lap of an old lady sitting high in the stand directly behind the posts. So far, so good. Grandma could still field the ball on a good day. But as Jonny became more accurate, the visualisation exercise became much more specific. Now Wilko had to focus on toppling a cup of coffee grandma was holding and knock it clean out of her hands! Suddenly grandma's prospects were not looking so good... So now, if I know of any ladies who are going to watch Jonny play and sitting at either end of the ground, I warn them to pack up their picnics and hide their drinks – because young Jonny is not nearly as nice as he is made out to be... He would be coming after them!

In truth Dave Alred was always far, far more than 'just a kicking coach'. 'They used to call me a "mental coach" – which rather implies that I've recently escaped from an institution...!' he will reply with a laugh, if you ask him about his function in relation to athletes in any sport.

But whatever he does is clearly capable of being transmitted across a wide spectrum of sporting activity, because he has coached elite performers in soccer and golf [Padraig Harrington and Luke Donald] as well as Jonny Wilkinson. In Dave's words:

> I guess the similarity is that I deal with 'one shot, one chance' performers – the guys who are out there on their own with no-one else to blame but themselves, or their technique if something goes wrong in front of 50,000 people.
>
> I studied a range of performance topics while completing my PhD, and exploring baseball provided a useful tool I used to develop goal kicking. I found that the best home run hitters made impact with the ball opposite their centre-of-gravity. So to transfer the concept to kicking, I looked to find a way to remain 'centred' and push that centred mass towards the ball, so that 'all of your body' is kicking the ball. It just happens to be the foot that makes contact. We (Jonny and I) created the process in 2001 after the British Lions' tour of Australia; we looked at how to create more distance off the tee. This involved creating a specific awareness of the power in the core, and then mentally directing that power to the kicking foot. When he begins to clench his hands together he is consolidating the power in his pillar; in the area just behind the navel, and then transfers the stored power to his kicking foot – at the same time being as

stable and strong as possible. You don't need to look at the posts after the kick has been launched when you're in that cocoon of concentration, the crowd will tell you.

The results of both kicking and swinging a golf club are about 80% mental, and the right mentality is only achieved by repeating the same behaviours until they become virtually second nature. A player is constantly working under pressure and needs to practise in an environment that makes his actions and performance accountable. You need to learn to be able to 'love the pressure' and create the same behaviour you're going to have to adopt in a tournament or in a big game in practice. You will have done it many, many times before – that's why I have to see and observe everything the player does. I need to see that consistency of behaviour.

Having had first-hand experience of several different elite disciplines outside the sport of rugby is a great help, because you don't dissolve into the conventional technical aspects of the sport. It prompts you to look at every aspect of the individual – physical, mental and technical – together, looking at everything he or she does from a more holistic point of view. At the same time, you have so many other models from other sports to draw on. If you can get everyone in the individual's coaching group contributing to the same aim, forgetting about results and just committing to a steady curve of improvement, pushing towards those marginal benefits, then you have the right synergy for dramatic progress.

Although Dave Alred had been only a field-goal and extra-point kicker for the Minnesota Vikings, his contribution did not stop at 'goal-kicking coach' for England. Andy Robinson believes his presence was crucial to the improvement of England's kicking game in attack:

Much of our attacking development, especially after Brian Ashton left the coaching group in 2002, occurred through the use of the cross-kick. When we toured New Zealand with the Lions in 2005 and went around the local clubs giving sessions in the 'shake hands' segment of the tour, it was Dave Alred's kicking techniques that interested the Kiwi players and coaches the most, especially the cross-kick. With England, Dave had explained the technical aspects of the cross-kick to Jonny Wilkinson and Paul Grayson, to the point where it became like a forward pass in American football

– it was delivered off the foot that deftly that it looked and felt like a long, flat pass. Our wings Josh Lewsey and Ben Cohen [along with our back-rowers] then began to work very hard to improve their aerial skills on reception of the kicks Jonny or Paul could put over. It effectively became like a forward pass in American football.

For example, in the 2003 grand slam match against Ireland, Paul Grayson came on as a blood replacement for Jonny Wilkinson after 54 minutes when we were only 13-6 ahead and the game was in the balance. His first action was to cross-kick to Ben Cohen on our left. It created a little bit of doubt in Irish minds, and like all defences they reacted to that possibility. So the next time 'Grays' got the ball on the right-hand side, the spacing of the Ireland backs was that much wider. There was a driving lineout and Will Greenwood was able to put Mike Tindall straight through the gap on a short ball in midfield with even Brian O'Driscoll unable to get a hand on him. But it was Ben Cohen's presence out on the far left touchline, out of shot, that interested the Ireland back-line defenders enough to create the gap for Tindall. It was a great example of how the cross-kick could stretch the field and enable us to build the effectiveness of another play off it. It's about building a repertoire and setting up your opponent for a sucker punch. By that stage Ben Cohen had made himself so good in the air on the left wing, and Wilkinson and Grayson were so good at pinging the ball straight across field to him that we just regarded the kick as a forward pass or 'free ball' for us.

England's path to World Cup triumph was paved by the presence in the coaching group of three outstanding innovators who were ahead of anyone else in the world in their areas – Dave Reddin in fitness and conditioning [Otis would still be at the cutting edge in 2012 as performance director for the British Olympic team with his 'shed' housing a myriad of cross-fertilising disciplines under the same roof], Dave Alred in kicking and performance psychology, and Phil Larder in defence; and one man at the top who had the courage to give them their heads and push them to produce their absolute best at all times – Clive Woodward. England were world leaders in these three aspects of preparation by the time the 2003 World Cup rolled around, and that is what gave them the edge they needed to win the tournament.

The group also expanded to include specialists who were more specific, but every bit as important. Phil Keith-Roach, the former

Rosslyn Park hooker, had been taking care of the England scrum since the end of the Jack Rowell era.

Clive had already acquainted me with Phil Keith-Roach – who he'd appointed as the first professional scrum coach of the new era – at our first meeting at Shelley. He must have weighed me up better than I'd appreciated when he said, 'You and "Roachy" will get along like a house on fire.' He was right. When I first met Roachy, he was out coaching a scrum session with his beloved forwards at Wasps' training ground. I trudged over the muddy turf through a thick covering of fog, tracking a shrill voice of encouragement – followed by the inevitable THUMP and the sudden grunts and gasps of effort as the forwards hit the scrum machine for the umpteenth time... When the mists finally cleared, the machine was in steady reverse with a figure sitting cross-legged atop of it. He was dressed in a sweater, jeans and wellies riding on top of the scrum machine like a Roman charioteer. That was my initial sighting of Phil Keith-Roach, and everything I learned about him subsequently lived up to the first impression.

Roachy is an appealing maverick who is great company. He is warm-hearted and polite, but beneath the surface is a wild streak that often launches him into impossible situations full throttle. There are no half-measures with Roachy and the results are frequently spectacular!

On one occasion, he was training out on the athletics track when he spotted a couple of the female members of staff talking to one of the resident art teachers. So Roachy stopped his run and trotted over to them. The art teacher was explaining to his enthralled listeners how he was training for a marathon by taking on three 10k runs per week. The marathon was the toughest athletic assignment on the planet. At this point, Roachy could bear it no longer.

'Tough? Marathon running?? It's nothing compared to a rugby scrum. We have to push two tons of heaving flesh around and the compression forces are staggering... *Then* we have to get up and run after all that...'

Naturally the art teacher disagreed, and within a few minutes Roachy found that he'd agreed to run a marathon [which he'd never done on his life] around the track that very afternoon.

What is more, he finished it too, and showed off his training shoes afterwards… They had fallen apart completely, the soles were flapping off and they looked more like a very scruffy pair of old beach sandals. But Roachy had done his 26 miles and 385 yards in them even though darkness had fallen. Whether the girls were still around is another matter. I have a feeling they were.

Needless to say, Phil was a teacher who had taught at Dulwich College for over 20 years after graduating with his MA in economics from Pembroke College Cambridge – and immediately putting what he had learned to good use by playing real-life Monopoly with the student quarters in the city.

Roachy had a bucketful of coaching 'music' inside him. You could not sit with him without talking and discussing the scrum. Invariably he would have the first three fingers of his right hand nudging into the gaps of the first three fingers of his left hand as he made his point. If he thought you were losing a bit of interest he would have you up on your feet in a one-man scrum steamrolling you across the room. Life was never dull with Roachy around but he was intensely focused on making the England scrum the best it could possibly be. As with most of us at that time, for Phil 'Team England' was not just a job but a way of life.

For Phil Larder, apart from their instant rapport as friends, the introduction to Phil Keith-Roach represented the opportunity to test his selection impulses against a man who had spent the whole of his sporting life in the union code and knew his area of speciality inside out. Keith-Roach recognised that there was work to do on the England scrum when Clive Woodward first took over in 1997:

I felt that we were behind all of New Zealand, South Africa, Australia, France and Argentina at scrum time after the experience of England's 1997 summer tour to Argentina, the four autumn internationals later that year and the first match of the 1998 Five Nations against France in Paris – which we lost 24-17. We had a lot of work to do. At no stage during the two draws and six losses in this period was the England scrum dominant.

Clive's directive was to produce quick scrum ball to fulfil his overall ambition of getting England to play at a speed the opponent could not match, and that in turn afforded us some much-needed time to explore the options in selection. I felt that we were very well covered at loose-head prop and hooker. We had Jason Leonard and Graham Rowntree competing at #1 and Richard Cockerill, Phil Greening and 'Ronnie' Regan competing for the starting berth alongside them. However we were struggling to find the right man at tight-head.

At the same time, New Zealand and Argentina in particular had developed a much more dynamic form of scrummaging which was a world away from our static set pieces. By driving forward immediately on engagement with an instant feed [on what is now known as a 'hit and chase' technique] they provided a superb moving platform for the likes of Justin Marshall and Zinzan Brooke to launch attacks from the scrum base. For the Kiwis the scrum was like a slightly more formal version of the ruck and their interpretation of its value was just as progressive.

England now had two tasks, to develop more power on contact in order to create the same dynamic platform, and to add more personnel to our available pool of scrummagers. The selection process was excellent, way ahead of anything I had experienced before. It included:

1. A rigorous observation process that typically included three live matches per coach on each weekend.
2. Detailed reporting through increasingly sophisticated technology that was being constantly improved.
3. Introduction of a ranking system listing the top ten loose-heads, hookers and tight-heads in a depth chart that was updated on a weekly basis.

Clive set the bar high because he wanted the England rugby team to be the number one ranked team in the world. He demanded the very best from everyone so it was far from being a cosy environment. Everyone was constantly on their toes and looking for small improvements or 'marginal gains'.

The scrum certainly developed between 1997 and the World Cup in 1999 [largely associated with the rise of Phil Vickery at tight-head, who won his first cap against Wales in the 1998 Five Nations] but the curve of improvement between 1999 and 2003 was even steeper. It wasn't a straight-line progression but in retrospect it's easy to recognise it.

Julian White made his Test debut against South Africa on the summer tour in 2000, both Trevor Woodman and Steve Thompson forced their way into the starting line-up during the 2002 season, while David Flatman had been outstanding at loose-head on the 2002 tour to Argentina. With Jason Leonard able to play both sides of the scrum to a consistently high level, by the time we reached the 2003 World Cup I felt that we had three full front-rows who could scrummage against any team in the world and come out on top. This allowed us to both cover injuries effectively and consider the all-round games of the front-rowers in addition to their scrummaging strengths.

England of that era were exceptionally gifted at the core skills of put-in, strike, channelling and base play, at numbers 9, 2 and 8. Nothing was wasted or lost at the scrum base and Lawrence Dallaglio was expert at controlling the ball in tandem with our scrum-halves in that area. We always referred to the England scrum as a 'nine man operation' such was the importance of the scrum-half, and Lol knew exactly when to release, hold or run. The detail in our calling and timing system at scrum-time was recorded on a CD so that the guys could listen to the rhythm in the car as they drove along... Those CDs definitely produced a few smiles along the way, and drew some quizzical looks from other road-users as they saw the players 'jamming' to such a unique soundtrack!

To give feedback and analyse your performances exactly you require the ability to measure your systems. The overriding objective of the scrum was to win your ball and attack the opponents' feed but we wanted a more specific yardstick, so the goal was to produce usable ball from every scrum on our put-in, giving 100% success with no free kicks, penalties or turnovers.

On their ball our aim was to turn over at least 25% of their possession. By 2000 these two goals were being achieved occasionally, from 2001 to 2003 they were being achieved consistently. During the 2003 World Cup itself England achieved both goals in each of the six games leading to the final. In the final we achieved 100% on our feed and turned over 30% of the Wallabies' ball, despite some unusual refereeing decisions by André Watson towards the end of the match!

The new coaching dynamic now demanded that selection in any area of the team was subject to the opinions of more than one coach, and it was here that life became especially interesting. While the two Phils were very much on the same wavelength from a personal point of view, their backgrounds were almost diametrically opposed, with Phil Keith-Roach having grown exclusively out of rugby union and Phil Larder coming from league. Their expectations of what a front-row forwards skill-set could be were therefore very different.

In the early selection meetings all the specialist coaches [and Roachy in particular] were understandably focused on their own area of responsibility. He knew that his job was to select players who would make the set piece strong, and that was his only interest. Perhaps to him it was personal. He was convinced of the impact that the scrum had on every aspect of performance, and that England would struggle to win games if its scrum wasn't dominant.

Initially I disagreed, both because of my rugby league background and my ignorance of the 'ripple effect' that can occur in all departments of the game, and in overall morale, when a team is under severe pressure in the scrum. Generally I believed that while opposition scrum dominance might yield a temporary advantage on first phase and force us to concede some yardage, if I had done my homework on their attack structure, my strong defence would claw that gain back over the next two or three phases of possession. On the occasions when our front-rowers were under pressure in the scrum, I encouraged them to take out their frustration on the opposition by tackling and defending that much harder in open play.

If I was guilty of becoming too blinkered by specialisation, and fighting for the defensive qualities in tight forwards too strongly, it was a fight our full-blooded selection meetings both welcomed and needed… My job description when I first joined the coaching group was after all to find 15 players, teach them how to tackle as individuals and to defend within the rules of a new system. The majority adapted quite quickly. Those that either didn't or couldn't adapt were weeded out.

Moreover, my experience of being a head coach for ten years in my 'previous life' in league always led me to see the wider picture. As England's defence became dominant I became more worried about our ineffectiveness at scoring tries rather than stopping them. I firmly believed that coaches like John Muggleton and myself had begun a mini-revolution that would change the way the game was played. We were to be followed shortly [after 2001] by Mike Ford (Ireland), Clive Griffiths (Wales), Alan Tait (Scotland), Dave Ellis (France) and of course Graham Henry when he returned to New Zealand, so the revolution gained momentum quickly. Soon the team without the ball was the one with the numbers, with an intimidating line of defenders spread across the width of the field and a solid cover defence behind them. Defence had taken over the control of the game.

To regain parity, attacking coaches had to produce 15 players with not only the passing and running skills to worry outstanding defenders, but also the rugby intelligence to quickly reload into the game, take up supporting positions and run intelligent attacking angles off a receiver. Ultimately the onus fell on the tight five forwards to expand their roles and deliver the skills bonus, with or without the ball. If they didn't deliver it, the team that won the ball would not have the skill to use it. They would have to rely on tactical kicking and rolling mauls to win instead, and it was not for that reason I had swapped codes.

The selection dynamic was one based on creative tensions between coaches with overlapping fields of influence, but tensions which were typically resolved by Clive's determination to play a 15-man game. Ultimately the front-row forwards who could run, handle and defend were selected, particularly after Brian Ashton and Andy Robinson were added to the coaching mix.

Our front row for the knockout stages of the World Cup in 2003 was therefore the three best footballers and defenders – Trevor Woodman, Steve Thompson and Phil Vickery – with Jason Leonard filling in on both sides at some critical moments. Vickery was a mountain of a man at 6ft 3in and 264lb, but one who had great balance and agility and 'dancer's feet' that made him hard to beat even in space. He could hit hard & high in the tackle but also bend at the hips and tackle low, and that was a huge asset.

Trevor Woodman on the other side was nowhere near as big as Phil, but he was slightly faster and an even better footballer. He read the game well and was quick to reload, set and go on defence. Even though the two of them were often 'spotted' by the opponent defending together in midfield, they communicated well, trusted one another and combined to defend solidly even when technically mismatched against a back. Steve Thompson, an ex-back-rower, joined the squad in 2002 and proved himself an outstanding short-side defender. 'Thommo' was excellent at standing his ground and refusing to be baited out of position. When he and Richard Hill combined together, it was a case of 'none shall pass' on the short-side.

Jason Leonard retired in 2005 as [deservedly] the most capped forward in the history of the game. Although he had started his career in the amateur era, he was determined that nothing would beat him – certainly not a northerner coming down to the East End holding a tackle shield! When I suggested that he alter his tackling stance, Jason merely smiled and got on with it.

Our other main tight-head, Julian White, presented me with a problem. A huge crag of a man who scrummed like a rampaging rhino, he was too slow in thought and deed to defend in the middle of the field like Woodman and Vickery. But I underestimated his positives – all that was required was a slight change in my own thinking. It dawned on me one Wednesday while I was organising a tackling drill. I asked the players to grab a partner and Lawrence Dallaglio and Julian were left temporarily on their own, so I said:

'Lol, just grab Jules for a minute will you.'

'Sorry Phil, I want to play at the weekend,' he replied with a grin, and didn't move a muscle.

So I thought to myself, 'Phil, are you missing something here?' I'd always thought Julian was a weak defender, but here I had one of our strongest ball-carriers not too comfortable with the thought of running at him. Julian was a formidable opponent as long as the corridor he was defending was narrow, otherwise defenders would either run or step around him. I therefore ensured that he only had to defend a short area, preferably close to the ruck. We would select Julian for 'route one' sides like South Africa, but leave him out for games against Australia and New Zealand who tended to move the ball from one side of the field to the other.

Andy Robinson supports Phil's view of front-row selection:

Although they had to be competent at the core skills of scrummaging, throwing and lifting, we always asked more of our front row. All three of Trevor Woodman, Steve Thompson and Phil Vickery were superb defenders who had the agility and foot-speed to defend a big short-side. They were 10% better – and maybe more than that – around the field than anyone else we had available to us. They were confident handling the ball – I remember Trevor making a break against New Zealand in the 2002 autumn international on our own 22, dummying his way up the field. To have those add-ons builds a huge amount of value into the 15-man game, but Thommo for example had to work with Simon Hardy first of all, to improve his lineout throwing. If he hadn't had that fundamental in place, all the add-ons in the world would not have had a chance to shine in the starting England team of 2002/03.

England were always looking for that vital '10% more' in their tight forwards and the process of selection changed because of it. The same attitude even spread into the 2001 British & Irish Lions selection for the Test series, where all-rounders like Phil Vickery and Scotland's Tom Smith were chosen ahead of more set-piece oriented props like David Young and Darren Morris. Along with fitness, conditioning and nutrition, English attitudes to selection were also ahead of the game, and sometimes uncomfortably so in the summer of 2001.

The scrum also became the backdrop for another important bit of innovative defensive thinking by Phil Larder. Scrum-halves had always prided themselves on their ability to jump around the back of a scrum and disrupt their opposite number at source. Phil however began to introduce the idea of the number 9 dropping off the scrum and becoming a line defender:

My thinking was that on the first phase from a scrum England, with all seven backs all in the defensive line, would be able to stop any opposition in the world from making a break. On the other hand if the England scrum-half was around the back of the scrum and unable to disrupt their possession then clinical passing by teams using their extra man would be difficult to stop. To me it was a no-brainer – why take the risk?

But when I mentioned it to the three stooges [Matt Dawson, Kyran Bracken and Austin Healey] they were incensed. 'Scandalous!' said one, as the other two nodded in agreement: 'You can't do that... typical rugby league thinking! Take that skill away from us and we become ordinary... plodders. We are in this team because we can make a difference.'

All three agreed and spoke as one. That impressed me so I listened. I knew that my knowledge of the scrum was no more than basic, and I had already learned to respect them because they were so intelligent and good at their jobs. All were competitive, determined and focused, fighting one another for the 9 shirt.

It was another example of the creative tension between rugby union and rugby league thinking producing a new innovation in the game. Our agreement was as follows.

1. The scrum-half would read the hit. If our scrum was dominant they would pressure the opposition scrum-half and either make the tackle or disrupt their possession at source.
2. If the scrum hit was neutral or negative for us, our number 9 would immediately drop off and adopt a defensive position in the line. The quality of our scrum was the deciding factor.
3. If the backs felt under undue pressure because of 'special circumstances' – the position of the scrum, the unusual alignment of the opposition backs or one of our backs injured or in the bin, the 9 would [again] adopt a default position in the line.

Despite all the preparation, all the strategic thinking and careful planning can only ever come to fruition in one place – on the field. You need key games where progress is measurable, and concentrated into big 80-minute performances. The second key performance of the Woodward era [after the 26-26 draw with the All Blacks in December 1997] was the 13-7 victory over South Africa, exactly one year later to the day.

At the end of that tumultuous afternoon on Saturday 6 December 1998, there would be a sharp knock on the England changing room door, followed by a voice with a rich, deep South African tone: 'Well done, you've just beaten the best team in the world.' The voice belonged to Nick Mallett, coach of the Springbok side, World Cup holders, winners of the recent Tri-Nations tournament and seeking a record-breaking 18th consecutive Test victory that very afternoon. His words were received in silence.

After being caught cold for South Africa's only try of the game, a score by Pieter Rossouw in the seventh minute after England wing Tony Underwood had suffered an injury on the side of the field where the try was created, England conceded no points for the remaining 73 minutes of the match. Where Martin Johnson had been averaging four tackles per game before Phil Larder took over the defensive coaching, against the Springboks he made 13 – three times as many as his 'amateur' average. The same went for props Jason Leonard and Darren Garforth, with the Scaffolder winning the Man of the Match award. As he clutched his solid gold krugerrand to his chest, Daz said: 'Phil's input has been awesome… he gets us thinking. It's all in the mind, this defence, it's all about organisation. In all my years in rugby I've not encountered any ideas like his.' On the previous weekend, England had shut down a Wallaby side containing attacking talents like George Gregan, Stephen Larkham, Daniel Herbert, Joe Roff and Chris Latham, leaking no tries at all.

Meanwhile England's own try against the Boks was scored via a Mike Catt cross-kick to Dan Luger in the 24th minute, with Luger able to get the ball away in contact for Jerry Guscott to convert. The foundations for future success were in place and never clearer than on that misty afternoon in West London: an unyielding defence based on rugby league organisation, dramatically-improved fitness levels [especially in the tight five], and the kicking game [both in attack and kicking at poles]. Phil Larder, Dave Reddin and Dave Alred – the main builders of the house that Clive designed…

The only other defence on the planet that could rival Phil Larder's was the Wallaby system which had been created by John Muggleton, one of Jack Gibson's students at Paramatta. Muggleton's defence would only give up one try in six World Cup matches in 1999 – and none at all in the knockout rounds. In an interview in *The Guardian* newspaper, Muggleton commented on the improvements Phil Larder had made to England's defence:

> The main thing is structure. It is very hard to find a hole in their defensive line and you are not going to be making easy breaks against them. They adjust better than any other side. Where union forwards will often follow the ball into the breakdown and often leave a hole if you go back the way you came, with England, players are more aware of their role on defence… Phil was always a deep thinker about the game and a good theorist.

Having brought English rugby league into the professional era he seems to be doing the same for rugby union.

It was an eloquent testimony from a man who had been so closely connected in his playing days with Phil Larder's true coaching mentor, Jack Gibson. It was like receiving a letter from home when you are in a foreign country, fighting on the front line.

Chapter seven

Politics, politics, politics… and the 1999 World Cup

C LIVE Woodward took over the coaching reins with the national side at a sensitive moment in the fortunes of the national team, the RFU and the game of rugby union in the northern hemisphere as a whole. The age of professionalism was in its infancy, and in England and Wales especially it had begun with an orgy of investment in the club game from wealthy benefactors. The vast majority of this investment took the form of large, sometime very large salaries for the players themselves. Both England and Wales had failed to establish a system of central contracting of the top players which would have in turn helped to guarantee both the meaningful administrative control of the two governing bodies and their ability to regulate the salary structures within the clubs. By 1998 the club benefactors 'owned' the players because they had primacy of contract with them, and international players in particular were feeling the pressure from two sides – from the club owners who paid their wages and the national teams they yearned to represent. With his experience in rugby league, Phil Larder foresaw that Clive Woodward's capacity to win the political battles off the pitch might prove to be every bit as important as his ability as a head coach on it.

Clive was certainly different to the norm and had the ability to attack problems from a completely different angle that was both invigorating and inspiring. He could certainly think outside the square and although some of his ideas were bizarre, others opened up opportunities that showed us a completely new way of looking at things.

He was hugely ambitious and determined. He was not an England coach who would merely be content to win the grand slam. He aimed much, much higher, he wanted to take on the whole world and beat it. He had impressed me at our first meeting in Shelley when he'd talked about being measured by our results against the southern hemisphere, and his overriding goal of winning the World Cup. It was quite obvious now that these were not merely empty words. He meant what he said and there would be no half-measures. However, from my experiences as a head coach in League I knew that he would have many difficult and complicated battles to win away from the training field if our ambitions were to be realised.

Steve Holdstock, the ex-Nottingham wing and work colleague of Clive Woodward's at Rank Xerox, saw him as someone with 'the balls to do things differently', even if that sometimes involved some very sudden changes of course; as a leader who inspired loyalty and was expert at 'getting people to want to work for him'. The ballsy, confrontational side had appeared while Woodward was still coach of Henley RFC in Oxfordshire. A BBC *Rugby Special* crew had been despatched to discover the secret of Henley's two promotions in four seasons, the second to the National Leagues, under Woodward's stewardship between 1990 and 1994. The programme's audience found him ready with felt pen and trademark flip chart in one of the rooms in Henley's modest clubhouse, not only to diagram the reasons behind the success of a small, relatively unknown club in Oxfordshire, but also to broaden his brief to criticise England's tactics under Dick Best. Interestingly, that did not prevent Dick Best from supporting Woodward's campaign to become the RFU's performance director many years later, in 2011.

Woodward's potential as a head coach had first been noticed by Don Rutherford, the union's technical director. While searching for the right candidate for the under-21s coaching role, Rutherford had observed that Woodward 'struck me as a man who could make a difference, a man who could change things.' At the end of his three years with the under-21s,

Clive Woodward's appointment as full England coach was then driven forward by the two men at the top of the RFU, chairman Cliff Brittle and vice-chairman Fran Cotton. Both Brittle and Cotton supported a vision of the English game with

- Reduced influence of the clubs within the RFU
- Revived divisional competition
- Central contracts for top players.

Brittle had for example signed Lawrence Dallaglio to a central contract with the union at a secret meeting at St Albans, only to have the contract blocked by a legal challenge from Dallaglio's club Wasps. He had also declared quite unequivocally that 'the total financial success of the RFU depends on one thing – the success of England' – in other words the success of the England national team.

At the other end of the scale were the club owners. Having bought into professional rugby so heavily at its inception in the UK, they now wanted at the very least to manufacture a workable financial situation for the clubs they owned. After the initial excesses [a £13m deficit in the first year of professionalism], they had to cut their wage bills drastically in advance of the 1998/99 season. Those that either didn't or couldn't, went to the wall. The benefactor of Richmond RFC in south-west London, Ashley Levett, announced an annual loss of £1.8m and total losses of £8m, and Richmond simply ceased to exist as a professional entity. When the club finally went under, its wage bill was discovered to be a colossal £230,000 per month, set against income based on an average home gate of only 3,600. Another of the power-brokers in rugby union's brave new world, Sir John Hall at Newcastle Falcons, admitted to losses greater than Ashley Levett's. Even Newcastle, the champion team from the 1997/98 season, were only attracting average gates of just above 5,000 at less than 50% of ground capacity. Two thirds of the clubs in the league averaged attendances of less than 6,000 spectators per match and even those who regularly 'maxed out', like Bath at their Recreation Ground, were severely limited by the poor overall capacity at their outdated stadia – and in Bath's case by the fact that the local council owned the 8,200-capacity Recreation Ground and therefore controlled the possibility of redevelopment. Clubs with great kudos in the amateur era [Bristol, Blackheath, Coventry and Moseley] followed Richmond out of the professional door, although Bristol were revived by the intervention of a new benefactor in the shape of Malcolm Pearce.

The solution apparent to all the leading club owners was *ring-fencing*. Ring-fencing meant abandoning the notion of promotion and relegation. A reduced number of elite clubs would sit securely at the top table of English rugby with their considerable investments protected against the threat of loss of income represented by relegation to the second division of English rugby. The owners of those that were not already sitting at that table, like Bristol and Worcester in the 1998/99 season, looked at buying out franchises that were [London Scottish for Malcolm Pearce at Bristol and Sale Sharks for Cecil Duckworth at Worcester], if they could not achieve the desired status by promotion.

So there were two radically different views on how the professional game in England should be run – on the one hand, a game led by the needs of the national side, with central contracting of the top players by the union and the potential for divisional revival; on the other, a game dominated by the needs of the clubs and their owners, with the assets [the players] firmly under their contractual control, an elite ring-fenced club league with no relegation and no possibility of the divisions being resuscitated.

Clive Woodward formed part of the Brittle–Cotton axis in this civil war when he was first appointed in 1997, at a time when the clubs were beginning to get a solid foothold in the legal debate. The Mayfair Agreement of May 1998 firmly rejected the idea of central contracts and an increase in the number of international fixtures, which Clive Woodward had supported. He had gone on record with his admiration of the southern hemisphere administrative systems, where 'the top players are contracted to the union [and] everything is totally under control. They play less games but play together more'.

Worse was to follow. Cliff Brittle was voted out of office in July 1998 at the union's Annual General Meeting, and Fran Cotton felt compelled to follow him by falling on his own sword shortly afterwards. This left Clive Woodward without the support of his two most prominent political buttresses as he sought to build the identity of 'Team England' into something stronger, with more 'buy-in' attraction than any of the clubs in the land. A new England coach intent on development by revolution rather than evolution, dropped into a political situation that was already so deeply polarised? It was a volatile mix.

Clive Woodward's focus on creating an elite situation with 'Team England' started with a management consultant named Humphrey Walters. Walters had just finished an eleven-month round-the-world yacht race going 'the wrong way' around the globe, mostly into a force

10 gale. As he said, 'The oceans do not wait or accept excuses – nor do most successful teams.' Walters always began his presentation with a slide that challenged the audience to count [under time pressure] how many letter 'Fs' were contained in a single sample sentence. Most would pick out the accented letters at the beginning of words but overlook the little connecting words like 'of'. The lesson was in the importance of the little connective details that are often glossed over or missed out entirely at the start of a project.

We were introduced to Humphrey Walters who ran a training company called MaST International. I have to admit that I was slow to see how a businessman, even if he had successfully completed the eleven-month BT Global Yacht Challenge around the world, could help us make England a more successful team. But gradually Humphrey won me over with his ideas on teamwork and loyalty. Clive was quick to pick up on his statement too that all that was needed to produce a world-class team was to do one hundred things one per cent better.

One of Clive's best mission statements was '*to create an environment that the players would never want to leave.*' Planning and creating this environment became our first task. Some immediate improvements were the 'branding' of the old unmarked team coach and the All Blacks lesson – to fill the away changing-room with our memorabilia and motivational tools when playing away from Twickenham.

John Mitchell suggested that we could improve the way we welcomed players to the team hotel, particularly the newcomers. In the All Blacks, this was such an important occasion that it had become like an initiation. Mitch had been met by the team manager, who escorted him to his hotel bedroom where he found his training kit and 'number ones' complete with the Kiwi emblem neatly folded on his bed. When he tried on his blazer and took a look at himself in the mirror he thought 'I've made it'.

However this was only one part of the initiation rite. 'I met with one of the senior players and the meeting lasted for about half an hour,' Mitch continued. 'He explained to me what it meant to be an All Black and the standards I would have consistently to achieve in order to remain in the team.' He walked out of the room but then the footsteps stopped and his head suddenly re-appeared around the frame of the door. After a short pause he said, "You know John, every boy born in New Zealand wants to be an All Black and every girl wants to marry one – but no-one wants to know a player who only played for the All Blacks once." It was a humbling moment for those of us who thought we had arrived.'

With the benefit of his NFL experience, Dave Alred suggested that we needed two team rooms rather than one. It was a good idea for the squad to have a large room in which to relax, but it was also psychologically important to have another dedicated solely for the business of winning games. To divide war from play and work from relaxation was essential, and so the 'war-room' was born.

All the while, Humphrey listened. We were determined to create an elite environment for our team and used Great Britain Rugby League, Manchester United from soccer, the New Zealand All Blacks and Minnesota Vikings as our benchmarks. Deep down we were determined to fulfil Clive's mission statement and create a better environment than the players were used to at their clubs.

Clive Woodward had also come upon the business self-help guide of a Brisbane dentist, Dr Paddi Lund, when he was still coach of the England under-21s back in 1996. The book was entitled *Building the Happiness-Centred Business*. Dr Lund had begun his career as a dentist with all the usual trappings of a new practice – the big plaque outside the front door, the whitewashed anxiety of the waiting room, the oversubscribed client list. It drove him to the point of contemplating suicide. When he came back from the near-dead, Lund decided to rescue his vocation by creating an 'elite' environment. He wrote to all his many customers, separating out the profitable 20% from the unprofitable 80% and only retaining the kernel of his clientele. He took down his plaque and removed his name from the phone book, and new clients were only added by invitation or the referral of existing customers. Those pre-selected clients were sent luxurious welcome books indicating the standards of behaviour expected of them, and the courtesies they would receive in return. The customers were served tea [30 different varieties] from silver service or coffee from Lund's gleaming new Italian espresso machine, along with 'dental buns', as they were welcomed into their own individual waiting lounges – and so the 'theory of critical non-essentials' was born.

Lund understood very well how psychological associations worked – that if you can make someone feel better in one area, their emotions will begin steadily to transfer that positive 'note' to all of your dealings with them. The opulence and emotional ease of the environment Lund created made his customers more willing to take on trust his expertise as a doctor, and over time eased out the usual fears connected with 'a visit to the dentist'. Clive Woodward took this theory on in his creation of the 'Team England' environment. Given the political circumstances which surrounded him, he wanted every player to build up a network of positive associations with 'Team England' that surpassed or supplanted the same associations with their clubs.

Neil Back noticed the difference between Woodward's environment and those he had experienced under Jack Rowell and Geoff Cooke immediately:

> The first thing that changed under Clive Woodward was communication. Where there had been no channels of communication open between player and coach, or newcomer and senior player – at least in my experience of the Cooke and Rowell eras – now information flowed freely, aided by the developments in email, text and mobile phone.
>
> One of Clive's first aims was to make the experience of playing for England completely the opposite to his own – something so special and unforgettable that it would represent the pinnacle of a player's career. I have to say that I never hesitated to call him on the phone or even drop in on him at home to seek clarification. Clive and his wife Jayne operated an 'open house' policy and you always felt relaxed about discussing issues with him. Jayne was particularly good with the wives, girlfriends and families and helped create a much wider sense of the 'England family'. After all, if you are happy off the pitch you are much more likely to play well when you are on it. My daughter Olivia was born on the day before the squad met up for the 1999 World Cup, and Clive was very generous and understanding. Jayne would always be on the phone to Ali, checking that everything was all right, and she invited them to our pool game against New Zealand at Twickenham. They were given the full VIP treatment, and Jayne even announced their arrival off the wives' and partners' coach ahead of the two royal princes William and Harry! We really appreciated those little touches.
>
> The culture where players did not really speak to each other also changed under Clive. A special effort was made to welcome

newcomers, and the 1997 Lions policy of an unselected player making a proactive effort to congratulate the guy chosen ahead of him was introduced. There were standards – a dress code, and a 'no swearing' code in public. We were all expected to turn up on 'Lombardi time', ten minutes before the start of a meeting or a session, and we were all expected to contribute something positive to it rather than just sit back passively and let it all happen to us.

The most important single contribution to the network of positive associations with 'Team England' was the move to a new training base in Pennyhill Park, a luxurious five-star hotel and spa resort boasting its very own two-Michelin-starred restaurant.

The most important improvement did not occur until December 1999 but it was to be highly significant in our future progress. We moved from the relatively small but picturesque Petersham Hotel on the banks of the Thames in Richmond to Pennyhill Park, a luxury hotel set on a 120-acre estate in a secluded part of Surrey near Bagshot. Pennyhill Park had its own nine-hole golf course in the grounds but more importantly, the owners agreed to upgrade a big lawned area into a full-size rugby pitch and they improved the indoor training area into a full professional standard gym over the course of time. Having quality training facilities and accommodation only a short distance from Twickenham eradicated those frustrating journeys through the heavy traffic in Richmond town centre between the Petersham and the Bank of England practice pitches, and it enabled players to do extra individual or group training on their own time. With the hotel's gym, spa, swimming pool and ice baths all easily at hand, the recovery programme after training was likewise facilitated.

The rule of 'two to a bedroom' was changed, so that every player had a bedroom to themselves marked by their own name plaque above the doorframe, and returned to the same bedroom on each visit, creating a cosy sense of privacy and familiarity. An 'open door' policy was also adopted to ensure that the players mixed easily and cliques were not formed.

All those involved with the squad – players, coaches and backroom staff – were made to feel that little bit more special, while at the same time the opponents who witnessed the extent of England's support system could be forgiven for going away feeling like the poor relation. Instead of going cap in hand to his RFU budget-makers and asking for permission for the frequently expensive new changes, Clive Woodward tended to act first and then require the RFU to adapt to what had already been accomplished, so that he had the initiative in the next 'round of negotiations'.

We started to train at Twickenham when it was still unauthorised. But Clive went ahead and did it anyway, and although there was some gnashing of teeth and tearing of hair at HQ it was quickly accepted and became the norm. Likewise, the home changing room was immediately and completely transformed. The players had individual cubicles each with oak plaques bearing their names. It was brightly coloured and festooned with motivational statements. After initially failing to persuade the RFU to fund it, Clive then approached the television crew from *Real Rooms* who were only too happy to take on the project! As the players entered the changing room, they looked up at a board which proclaimed: 'THROUGH THIS DOOR WALK THE NATION'S TOUGHEST COMPETITORS'.

Our kit man Dave Tennison, a motivational character in his own right, took on the responsibility for decorating our changing room when playing away from home. He would plant cross of St George flags everywhere and attach our mission statements to the walls. When the players walked through the doors to change in readiness for the game they immediately felt at home and that in turn created a positive on-field vibe.

A custom-made luxury coach replaced the old team charabanc, with a large rose and 'England rugby' tattooed on the side tastefully banishing the memory of that anonymous journey down Stretford Way before the first Test against New Zealand. Our 'number ones' were designed by Hackett and our shoes by Oliver Sweeney. Nike provided quality personalised training kit and matchday jerseys individualised with the player's name and cap number, the date of the match and our opponent. It was indeed an elite environment designed for an elite team.

Clive's cultural architecture was completed by a magnificent leather-bound tome with 'This is England' stamped on the front, defining our code of conduct, policies and objectives. All of the players had debated the content [as well as the coaches], so to sign up to it became a very real example of player ownership.

Perhaps the greatest compliment I can pay Clive is to say that, of all the teams with which I have been associated either as a player or as a coach, my time with England in the Woodward era was by far the most *enjoyable*. We spent a lot of time away from home, cooped up together in hotels under intense pressure – but every day it was not only a privilege but also a pleasure to be involved. Out on the training field in all kinds of weather, Clive would often whisper to me, 'Phil, isn't this is the best job in the world?' and I would nod my head in agreement.

There were however some dark clouds on the horizon as spring passed into summer and the end of the 1998 season exposed the deep-seated rift between club and country. In the middle of a Five Nations tournament where England were ultimately to finish in second place behind France, the outspoken owner of the Northampton Saints, Keith Barwell, announced that he was withdrawing his Saints players from the forthcoming seven-match tour of Australasia and South Africa. According to Barwell, Clive Woodward responded by threatening to de-select any players who weren't available for the summer tour for the remaining two games of the Five Nations against Scotland and Ireland: 'The players went to a training session [at Bisham Abbey] but they didn't do any training. Woodward told them that if they aren't committed and available between now and the World Cup they wouldn't be considered and he'd rather play a Pisspot United against Scotland.' At a later meeting the 12 EFDR clubs fell into line behind Barwell and the players were consulted about vetoing the tour entirely, which was described as a 'punishing schedule' following a 'gruelling season'.

The crux of the matter was the length of a playing season, which for a top player [with commitments to both club and country] could easily top 40 games, compared to the 25-game maximum that had already been established as the gold standard in New Zealand.

During the Five Nations tournament, the names of Lawrence Dallaglio, Richard Hill and Neil Back in the back row, Martin Johnson in the second row, Jason Leonard and Darren Garforth in the front row; Will Greenwood, Jerry Guscott, Mike Catt, David Rees, Kyran Bracken and Paul Grayson in the backs had become automatic on the selection sheet.

These 12 players had been the backbone of England during my short time coaching the team and they all made themselves unavailable for the tour. Several fringe players joined them. As the implications of the tour became clear we were devastated, but on the other hand I had tremendous sympathy for the situation the players were in and also fully understood the problems that had confronted the directors of rugby.

The game at the elite level was now professional and the players were full-time. They could now devote all their time and energies into improving their performances. Rugby union is a collision sport, not just a contact sport, and those collisions became more severe as the players became significantly bigger, stronger, faster and more powerful with the time and the equipment available to train regularly in the gym lifting weights, and on the track increasing speed. More rest, better diets and intelligent recovery systems only intensified the process.

The medical associations of 'collision sports' such as American football and rugby league had suggested a 25-game season as a maximum, and the championship-winning Denver Broncos team of 1998 had just played through a 19-game season, including the play-offs. This represented the maximum number of games it was possible to play in an NFL season. Rugby league complied by reducing the number of teams in Super League to 12, therefore restricting the amount of regular season games to 22. The maximum number of games that could be possibly played in a season, even if a team reached both the Challenge Cup Final and the Grand Final, was 30. The majority of top English rugby union players were being asked to appear in over 40 matches, which was nearly twice as many as they should have been required to play.

So we were in a 'no win' situation. The tour itself was arguably one of the most demanding series ever devised for an England touring team. It was certainly tougher than any Lions tour, containing four Tests against our strongest opponents and another unofficial 'Test' against an extremely powerful Maori team who had only lost one home game in the last 20 years [against the 1977 British & Irish Lions]. We were going to do it without three quarters of our starting side, including both of our two outstanding captains. It was like attending a gunfight with a knife, and every time I looked up to see the motto of our kit sponsors Nike: Just Do It right in front of me, a rueful grin would pass across my face.

Of the men who were called in to replace the top 12 missing stars, Spencer Brown, Steve Ravenscroft, Tom Beim, Scott Benton, Ben Sturnham, Richard Pool-Jones, Dominic Chapman, Dave Sims, Stuart Potter, Jos Baxendell and Rob Fidler all became 'one-cap wonders' of the kind John Mitchell so dreaded, while uncapped others like Matt Moore and Tony Windo would also never be seen in England colours again.

> Our first game was against Australia at Lang Park, Wally Lewis's old stamping ground – now modernised and renamed Suncorp Stadium after its sponsors. Australia thrashed us by 76 points to nil and the gymnasts who performed press-ups under the posts every time Australia scored ran out of energy just after half-time. It didn't say much for the athleticism of the Australian gymnasts but it said even less about us as an international rugby team. Our performances in New Zealand were not much better; we lost 64 points to 22 at Dunedin after Danny Grewcock had been rightly sent off, and then by 40 points to 10 at Eden Park, Auckland. South Africa beat us 18-0 to round off the nightmare, and all three southern hemisphere giants had shown they would give no quarter when we were down and out, either on or off the field. It was a very salutary lesson.

In the political context of the 'Tour of Hell' as a whole, what was happening off the field turned out to be much more meaningful than what happened on it. It was an emotionally unstable time for Clive Woodward, who had to fly home before the second of the two Tests against New Zealand to attend his father's funeral. This led to some confusion about responsibilities among those remaining, with the RFU technical director Don Rutherford taking over the central management role on tour instead of the designated team manager Roger Uttley, and John Mitchell temporarily abandoning Clive's principle of delegating training time to the senior coaches:

> The death of his father meant that Clive had to fly home and he left Mitch in charge of the coaching. Mitch reacted to the extra pressure by taking more responsibility on his shoulders and while

I understood that he had a reputation to protect coaching on his own doorstep, I found that my training time with the team virtually disappeared and that was very frustrating.

Roger Uttley's role in particular came under increasing scrutiny during the summer tour because of the new coaching structure. Clive Woodward's own ability as a manager overlapped with Uttley's role significantly, and as a full-time master at Harrow School, where he taught PE, Uttley was never going to be more than a part-timer with England. He had a full and rewarding life outside rugby. Clive Woodward had already put down his marker regarding part-time employees, and as he was quite capable of managing the media relationship and liaising with the RFU himself, all he really needed was an administrator to get the squad from place to place on time and make sure that the hotels were suitable. This role hardly accorded with an international ex-player and ex-England head coach of Roger Uttley's calibre and the two clashed frequently. As Roger Uttley recalls sadly, 'He [Woodward] and I used to have stand-up rows about everything – all to do with control… He said to me, "I think I should have complete control", and [ultimately] I didn't feel I had any choice but to let him have it.'

A similar overlap of roles had already occurred with Don Rutherford. The story of how Clive Woodward arrived on his first day of work at Twickenham to find no office, no secretary and no laptop waiting for him has already passed into the stuff of myth and legend. Don Rutherford's view of this event is rather different:

'I know much has been made of this "no office" thing… [but] the plan all along, as Clive knew, was for him to go out to the clubs, meet everyone and work with them for England rugby. We never envisaged it as an office job.

'We had this vision of clubs being integrated and working together on training and talent identification. Clive didn't want that though, and that's why he had so many problems with the clubs farther down the line.

'Before Clive joined, I had employed Dave Alred and Dave Reddin with the aim of building a coaching team who would tour the country working with clubs and representative sides and raising the whole level of English rugby. No-one ever envisaged Clive being locked away in an office and using every talented coach entirely for the England team. That wasn't what we agreed.' [quoted by Alison Kervin in her excellent biography, *Clive Woodward: the biography* Orion, 2005]

Don Rutherford wanted England coaches such as Dave Reddin and Dave Alred to tour the country and behave in exactly the way John Muggleton did in Australia – irrigating the lower levels of the game with the 'water' of cutting-edge knowledge in their own specialist areas. As the CEO of Premier Rugby Howard Thomas pointed out, 'The long form agreement between the RFU and the clubs does stipulate that centrally-funded coaches should work inclusively rather than exclusively. We are trying to operate a fair, even-handed league and there are things here that need to be resolved.' For Clive Woodward however, 'Team England' was exclusive, full-time work and there was no time or need for his coaches to function as coach educators in this larger setting. They would work with him and all would be based in either south-west London itself or the nearest suitable training base outside it.

Phil Larder could appreciate both views. He had connected with Dean Richards at Leicester and progressed both his defensive systems and the techniques and understanding of the Tigers' England players – but he had done it as 'the invisible man'. His presence and impact was largely unknown, even to those regulars in the club shop!

I had visited the clubs in an attempt to gain more time with the players and most of the directors of rugby were supportive. I felt that if I could inspire the clubs to introduce defensive training into their weekly training programmes there was little doubt that England would benefit in the long term. Nigel Melville at Wasps was the coach who picked my brains the most, while Matt Dawson at Northampton and Jerry Guscott at Bath were two players who persuaded their directors of rugby to invite me in to run a day's training and then developed their own defensive pattern based on what I'd shown them. However, nothing happened on a consistent basis outside my involvement at Leicester.

My background was in coach education as a former national director of coaching in rugby league, and therefore my first instinct was to facilitate the trickle of knowledge from the top end of the game all the way down to its roots. In 1982 Australian Rugby League had thrown open its doors to me with the words 'Show him the lot'. Peter Corcoran, Frank Johnson, Frank Stanton, Jack Gibson and Ron Massey had not held anything back in the process of widening my knowledge base and rugby education, and at the AIS I had experienced an environment in which intellectual property was transferred freely between sports. The Australians always gave freely because I think it spurred them to on to make new discoveries 'under pressure'.

Therefore I believed that what we were doing as England coaches should be drip-fed down into every level of rugby in England. With his business background Clive was of the opposite opinion. He regarded intellectual property as a precious commodity, the contest for it as a battleground and he ring-fenced the senior England team. He was very sensitive to the loss of intellectual property and he wanted to make 'Team England' as watertight as possible – the sealed war-room with no-one outside 'the circle of trust' allowed in was as good an image of that as any.

On the one hand I feel that Clive was probably right. For example, I only became aware of just how much other coaches had learned from observing my defensive sessions with the 2001 Lions after that tour had ended. Graham Henry appointed Clive Griffiths, another rugby leaguer like myself as his defensive coach with Wales immediately after the Lions tour finished. The tour manager, Donal Lenihan, then contacted me with a shortlist of professional rugby league coaches [all with Irish connections] and asked for my recommendation. I pointed him in the direction of Mike Ford, a former pupil of mine at Saddleworth, who had impressed me when qualifying through the Rugby League National Coaching Scheme – so much so that I had taken an interest in his subsequent coaching career. Donal took my advice and appointed Mike, who did an excellent job as defence coach with Ireland before going on to work with the 2005 Lions and England at the 2007 World Cup in the same capacity. Once the importance of specialist defensive coaching was recognised and the techniques and patterns were out in the open, all the other European nations found people to teach it, like Dave Ellis with France and Alan Tait with Scotland. My presence on the Lions tour enabled those countries to catch up to the advances we'd made more quickly.

On the other hand, the ring-fencing of rugby knowledge did not help when it came to re-negotiating a new EPS [elite performance squad] agreement in 2004. After a core of senior players retired after the 2003 World Cup – especially Martin

Johnson and Neil Back, plus the long-term injury to Jonny Wilkinson – England performances began to tail off dramatically. When that happened, it put the relationships between 'Team England' and both the RFU and the clubs under considerable strain. Those relationships weren't good enough to attract the same allowances as before, and I believe that increasing the flow of coaching information down to grass-roots level could have played an important role in helping to sustain the goodwill between the national squad set-up, the clubs and the RFU.

When Graham Henry returned to New Zealand in 2002, first becoming a defensive advisor at the Auckland NPC and the Blues franchise, then being elected the new All Black coach after the unsuccessful World Cup campaign mounted by John Mitchell in 2003, he did it as a defensive coach. I had spent many enjoyable hours in his company in Australia [writing his book of the tour] and the subject to which he returned again and again, was the beauty and simplicity of Phil Larder's defensive system. For someone like Graham to be so interested meant that it was a very important development in the game as a whole, because Graham was always at the forefront of new trends in rugby union, either creating them himself or appreciating the importance of those that had been developed by others – sometimes before they even realised it themselves! He had diagrams of how Phil's defence responded in every situation, sheets and sheets of them, and he would show them to me over lunch in Brisbane or Manly or Melbourne.

Graham's confidence in his own ability as a coach had temporarily crumbled after the Lions series and he was burned out. When he had recharged his batteries after leaving Wales and returning to New Zealand, at first he re-invented himself as a defensive specialist with Auckland in the NPC and the Blues' Super Rugby franchise. With Graham's understanding of the game there was never any possibility that he would not be able to translate Phil's system for Super Rugby use. After finishing sixth and 11th in the two previous years, in 2003 with Graham Henry back in the saddle, the Blues won the [then] Super 12 title conceding more than 60 fewer points than the next best defensive side in the competition.

Defence was Graham's primary coaching responsibility in the three-man group that included Wayne Smith [backs] and Steve Hansen [forwards] when he became head coach with the All Blacks. The shift in defensive pattern that Graham Henry introduced was a seismic event for the All Blacks, because New Zealand teams usually defended 'the other way around' compared to the Phil Larder system. As Andy Robinson says,

> New Zealand always used to mark from out-to-in defensively. Their edge defenders would mark up first and there would always be a space around the 10 channel, which the back-row would be expected to fill. Phil's system was in-to-out, with defenders marking from the ruck perimeter outwards, pushing up first and then out towards touch – and that was the pattern Graham brought back from the 2001 Lions with him.
>
> It was probably a key event for New Zealand rugby, because ever since Phil's defensive pattern was introduced they have been trotting along at an 88% win ratio over nearly 150 Test matches, which [bar the Fred Allen period back in the mid 1960s] eclipses anything in even their illustrious history.

Previously Graham had tended to specialise in attack, and some of the most enjoyable moments of the Lions tour in 2001 for Phil Larder were the contests between Graham's attacking ideas and his own defensive pattern:

> One of the most stimulating aspects of the 2001 Lions tour for me was the coaching interaction with Graham Henry. Graham is the best rugby union coach with whom it's been my privilege to work. We would go on to the training field and Graham would come up with a move, then it was my job to find a way to defend it. If I couldn't see the solution on that training day, I'd be lying in bed at night trying to come up with an answer the following day… If I did provide a solution Graham would then go to the next level trying to find another attacking refinement. It was a tremendously stimulating to-and-fro exchange between two rugby minds on opposite sides of the fence, conducted through six- or seven-a-side games.
>
> Graham took my defensive system back to New Zealand and eventually introduced it in the All Blacks when he took over the national coaching reins, and they still use more or less the same system. I was watching the All Blacks on TV the other day, and after a bit of rewinding I could see all the characteristic features of the pattern I developed. At the same time, a lot of Graham's attacking ideas, such as the two lines of attack, have been taken

back to the UK and were developed with England when we came back from Australia.

At the same time, Phil had been unsure whether he was really going on the Lions trip with Clive Woodward's blessing:

> After I had been invited to coach the 2001 Lions I had approached Clive for permission to accept the invitation. He said that he had no problems with my selection but added that chief executive Francis Baron was opposed to the idea. This did not concern me too much at the time, because in my eyes Clive was my line manager and I reported to him. Later after problems had arisen, I found out that it was Clive and not Francis who was opposed to my going on the Lions tour.
>
> Whilst the Lions were in Australia, England were busy touring North America playing two internationals against Canada and the United States, both of which England won comfortably. I was delighted that Clive appointed my old buddy Ellery Hanley as defensive coach. Ellery – or 'the Black Pearl' as he was fondly known in league – had had a full season under his belt with Bath and I knew that he would go well and earn the respect of the players. As Pat Sanderson [with whom I would later link up at Worcester Warriors] said after the tour, 'He's awesome, you just listen and learn. He was just the greatest as a player and he understands exactly what England are trying to do.'
>
> During the tour review Clive surprised me by offering me the position of performance director [on an increased salary], and suggested that Ellery would take over from me as defence coach with the England senior squad.
>
> I replied, 'Clive, sorry but I am not interested. I have been there and done that in rugby league and I am only interested in coaching and player education.' I reminded him that England had the best defence in world rugby for the last two years before adding:
>
> 'Ever since the Lions tour finished, I have been inundated with calls asking me for advice on defensive coaching appointments. Every conversation begins with "Phil, are you happy working with England?"'
>
> Clive then suggested that Ellery might begin working with the Saxons and the other England teams, which I thought was

an excellent idea. I had great respect for Ellery and understood that the future for England would be much stronger if he was in place, perfecting the tackling skills and defensive understanding of these up-and-coming international players.

As luck would have it, I bumped into Ellery a couple of weeks later when Leicester Tigers entertained Bath at Welford Road, and he told me that he had finished with England because the deal he had received from the RFU bore no resemblance to the one promised by Clive. 'I could never work for anyone that I could not trust,' he added. With that Ellery walked away sadly into the distance, and he was back with his family in Sydney before Christmas.

Clive's desire to ring-fence the intellectual property contained in the England coaching group was very, very real. None of us were indispensable in that respect. It was a warning that 'Team England' had to come first, even if you had been offered the chance of a coaching lifetime with the Lions.

Clive was not given a budget for his needs at the beginning of his job and had to apply for every individual financial requirement through Don Rutherford. With his business background, he didn't accept the situation and he was not a man to take 'No' for an answer.

With Humphrey Walters in his corner, he pushed forward on his proactive course, acting and then forcing the RFU to react to a *fait accompli* rather than begging for money with cap in hand. It was a little like the situation at Keighley Cougars, where Mike Smith and Mick O'Neill would embark on a course of action first, then find the finance for it afterwards. Clive Woodward was unafraid to make unilateral decisions and the first climax came at the end of the 1998 'Tour of Hell' in South Africa:

> Clive had now rejoined the squad and I was secretly wondering how he was going to recover from his own very personal difficulty and our sporting distress on tour. He was in the public eye and he was the key to our future.
>
> We were staying in Cape Town, and I was both intrigued by the country's problematic racial history and in awe of what Nelson Mandela had achieved, using the Springboks to unite a nation at the 1995 World Cup. I liked the people, both blacks and whites, and the passion they had for rugby football.

The three-star Holiday Inn Motel, set in a suburb of Newlands, didn't match any of our professional needs. It was hot and busy, the food was mediocre and there was little in the way of security – so the 'war-room' was a non-starter. We felt we had been treated very well by our Australian and Kiwi hosts, but the accommodation in Cape Town left a lot to be desired. Insult was also added to injury when the Springbok under-21 squad arrived in midweek, as if to reinforce the regard in which we were held by our South African hosts.

Clive knew that the full Springbok squad was staying at a luxury five-star hotel across town in a safer part of the city, and that on their last tour to England the RFU had financed their stay at the five-star Berkeley Hotel in central London. The knowledge that we had been viewed as the poor relations by the host union was one thing, but the deeper concern was that our own administrators had not seen fit to correct the error in perception.

Clive and Jayne went out on a reconnaissance mission to the nearby Mount Nelson hotel, known locally as 'the Pink Palace', another five-star establishment set in lush gardens at the foot of Table Mountain. They met the Germany soccer team just on their way out of a training camp. After that we knew there was trouble around the corner, and the first indication that something was afoot was when we all arrived back at our rooms on Thursday evening before the game. We all had a note from Clive under our doors telling us that there was to be a major meeting at 8am the following morning. This was an hour before usual.

The players who descended in the lift with me for the meeting could sense that something big was about to happen, particularly when I told them that I was just as confused as they were and had no inside information to relay. The team manager Roger Uttley, who had done everything he could possibly do to make me welcome when I had first arrived from league, sat down alongside me and whispered 'What is this all about, Phil?' I shrugged my shoulders. Clive was certainly keeping his cards close to his chest.

Clive walked into the room and was brief and to the point. First of all he congratulated the squad on the way they had handled a difficult tour. Then he took a breath before exclaiming:

'You don't deserve the way you're being treated and this hotel sums it up... Pack your bags, we are moving out of here right now!'

The players had been taking bets on what was going to happen and Clive's resignation was odds-on. The loud cheers that greeted his announcement confirmed that they were firmly behind him.

We moved into the Mount Nelson, popularly described by the local guides who passed in front of it in their little red tourist buses as 'the best and most famous hotel in the whole of South Africa.' It was both spectacular and spectacularly expensive too, and both the Woodwards took the hit on their credit cards.

The South African Rugby Football Union was furious and threatened to cancel the forthcoming return fixture in the autumn. The RFU were also up in arms – 'you just do not do that sort of thing' – and there was no guarantee that Clive and Jayne were going to get their money back.

I understood that the move was primarily political. Clive had taken this brave and decisive step to make a point to the RFU about where 'Team England' stood, or should stand in the order of priority.

It not only cheered up the group in South Africa but was respected by the senior players back home. Clive had proved to us once and for all that he was not full of hot air, but he meant what he said and he was prepared to put his own career on the line to move us all forward.

Clive Woodward has been described as a 'transformational leader' and there is little doubt that this description fits him well. Transformational leaders have gained currency in the modern era, and they are becoming increasingly popular on television.

Sir John Harvey-Jones set the trend with his *Troubleshooter* programme in 1990 and more recently Gordon Ramsay [*Ramsay's Kitchen Nightmares*] and Alex Polizzi [*The Fixer*] have followed in his footsteps. All three visit ailing, failing businesses and effect quick turn-around solutions. Then they leave, perhaps returning a few months later to check whether the changes they instigated have been followed up by the owner of the business. The features of transformational leadership have concrete points of relationship in Woodward's approach to 'Team England':

- **Idealised influence.** *The leader is charismatic and is prepared to engage with followers as 'whole' people rather than just employees.* Clive Woodward invited Lawrence Dallaglio and his family to stay in his own home while *The News of the World* scandal was in full swing, and Neil Back's view of how he felt free to call or drop in on Woodward at any time is already documented. Clive Woodward actively built up the level of trust and loyalty in his group, which in turn allowed him to make changes more easily. That sense of loyalty was absolute.

- **Motivation and commitment to a vision.** *The leader is able to broaden the interests of his followers [beyond self-interest] and inspire them with his vision.* Woodward had an inspiring vision of the way 'Team England' could play and achieved a collective buy-in to that vision from coaches and players. The result was the most enjoyable coaching environment Phil Larder had ever experienced, in either code.

- **Intellectual stimulation.** *The leader encourages creative and innovative solutions.* Woodward wanted coaching solutions that were at the cutting edge of rugby union, and employed coaches who could deliver them in the areas of defence [Phil Larder], conditioning [Dave Reddin] and kicking/psychology [Dave Alred] especially.

- **Raising the level of achievement and 'morality'.** *The leader raises the level of achievement and 'morality' within the group by a conscious change of values.* The code of conduct and 'This is England' bible set new standards and was perceived to raise the moral level of the group above that of the world outside it. Every little detail of the behaviour of those in the group mattered, whether it was in time-keeping, dress code or proactive contributions to training sessions and meetings.

Development by upheaval always means a much rougher ride than evolution within the system, and the impact of transformational leadership can be undermined when it clashes with the traditional culture within which it is embedded. The RFU itself represented a very powerful amateur tradition within rugby union in the UK – and one which was highly unlikely to be swept out wholesale by Clive Woodward's new professional requirements for the national team. At the same time an entirely new club culture, driven forward by businessmen-benefactors just as successful and driven as Clive Woodward, was also marking out its territory in rugby union's 'new age'. In 2005, the amateur institution of the British & Irish Lions would also prove itself to be largely immune to Clive Woodward's transformational style of leadership, and has only succeeded since then by recovering much of its traditional format and meaning – under a Lions archetype in Ian McGeechan, and [ironically] a Kiwi coach in Warren Gatland.

The second potential issue is that the possibility of transformation becomes entwined too inextricably with the leader's own personality, to the point where he is seen as the only conduit of change, whether for good or for ill. One of the chief proponents of transformational leadership, Bernard M. Bass, suggests that an organisation with a transformational leader can suffer from over-dependence on his persona and that in turn retards the development of fully participative decision-making. In England's case, Clive Woodward's sudden resignation in September 2004 exposed a lack of succession planning, and produced a dramatic collapse of morale and results thereafter. England's win percentages in the three seasons leading up to the 2003 World Cup were 91% [2001], 89% [2002] and 94% [2003]. In the three seasons afterwards, they dropped to 45% [2004], 50% [2005] and 38% [2006]. The fact that a transformational leader's energy is invested primarily in the turn-around does not always allow him to participate in the consolidation phase that follows.

Compared to the All Black 'legacy' in New Zealand, Clive Woodward's situation was not an enviable one. Where the All Blacks culture was fully supported by the NZRFU, who have always had firm control of elite player contracts and therefore player welfare, the RFU could not provide Woodward with the same level of backing. They were fighting on two fronts, trying to satisfy both the club owners and the national coach. It is likewise impossible to compare the England rugby culture with that of the All Blacks. Where Woodward had to either rediscover or reinvent that culture virtually from scratch, All Black coaches have always been more comfortable in the knowledge that they are 'passing through the jersey' and their own positions of responsibility, with the aim of 'leaving it in a better place'.

With Graham Henry as their head coach from 2004 to 2011, the mini culture-crisis of his first year in charge was repaired by the shift to what is now called *Participative Leadership*, whereby 'leaders create leaders, and arm their subordinates with intent. And then step out of the way.' The end result is that continued New Zealand success has not depended on the personality of Graham Henry, it has been seamlessly reinforced by his successor Steve Hansen. Even though he was replacing a coach with a outstanding 86% win percentage, he has actually improved it to over 90%. Succession planning, the sharing of information and empowerment of coaches and players have not been issues because of the coherence of New Zealand rugby union culture as a whole.

Except for a brief period after the Tri-Nations tournament of 2004, it was not wholesale transformation that was required in New Zealand. A return to traditional All Black values, with far greater participation by the players and other coaches in the leadership process, was required. As Graham Henry has said on many occasions, 'I just got out of the way and allowed it to happen.'

Clive Woodward's position was vastly different, and for him it was necessary to occupy more leadership space rather than less for the changes he wanted to occur. His need for more control of the direction of 'Team England' was facilitated by the removal of the two men whose areas of responsibility overlapped with his own. Early in January 1999 both Roger Uttley and Don Rutherford received their termination notices from the new CEO Francis Baron in a large round of cost-cutting exercises. Clive Woodward drove to Harrow School himself to hand over the letter to Roger Uttley, while Don Rutherford found himself required to clean out his office on the same day. It was a sudden and ignominious ending to Rutherford's productive 30 years at rugby's HQ, and it came three years before he would have been able to draw his full working pension. When Andy Robinson joined the England coaching group as a replacement for John Mitchell in mid-2000, the delegation of responsibilities within the coaching group was streamlined further, and the working structure for 'Team England' was finally in place. It would carry the group forward all the way to the 2003 World Cup.

* * * * *

The first real litmus test of how far England had travelled on Woodward's pathway to success came at the 1999 World Cup, after he had been in charge for 23 matches and 23 months in the job.

> The 1999 World Cup did not excite me as much as it should have done. Everything was in our favour with the competition being held in the northern hemisphere and with all our pool games

being played at Twickenham, but at the time I did not think that we were quite ready to win the most treasured trophy in the game. We had only one victory to our credit over the southern hemisphere 'big three' in 11 attempts up to that point so as yet we didn't have a great deal of background to the self-belief Clive was trying to instil.

One of Clive's favourite tactics when announcing the team to the squad was to put up the names of the players in both teams, side by side and position by position on his ever-present flip chart. Then he would turn around to face his audience with the question: 'Which team would you rather be playing for?'

On several occasions in those early days I would think to myself, 'Bloody hell Clive, I would prefer to be playing for the opposition' but as we gradually improved I found myself opting more and more for England. It was a pleasant surprise and an increasingly pleasant feeling. As the World Cup approached however, I was still not fully convinced of our ability to handle our three major rivals from the southern hemisphere. New Zealand was the bookies' favourite but it was Australia who had impressed me the most. They had a competent set piece, an expansive attacking game with some experienced and exciting outside backs, and a dependable goal-kicker in the shape of full-back Matt Burke. Above all, they had a superb defence drilled by John Muggleton. To me they looked like a complete outfit.

Defending tends to use up far more energy than attacking, so it is essential that teams who rely on their well-organised defence to win tournaments have a supreme fitness base, and enjoy the psychological edge that comes from that. This was simply not the case for England in 1999. The squad's inconsistent standards in that area had been quite evident during our stay in Couran Cove. Too many of the players were nowhere near fit enough to be playing international rugby let alone to aspire to become world champions.

Dave Reddin had only just been appointed full-time, and the 1999 World Cup was too early in the cycle for him to have made the huge strides forward in conditioning that we required. Mitch had blended our forwards into a strong unit at the set piece and contact area, but I believed that as defences improved more, much more had to be expected of them. Sport has a tendency to first adapt, then to take another evolutionary step – it is like a staircase of progress. My phone was already 'hot' with other top nations asking me for help and advice on defensive formations and I was well aware that international coaches were analysing the rugby league alignments that both John Muggleton and myself were using. It would not be long before they had devised methods of breaking us down.

As defensive coaches, we had created a numerical advantage by first improving the tackling ability of the tight five forwards and then spreading a defensive line across the pitch. As long as this remained the status quo, defences would continue to dominate. The only pathway forward for attacking coaches therefore, was to encourage their own tight forwards to become more involved in the attacking structure of the game.

As I analysed the opposition attacking formations, it quickly become evident that the Australian and New Zealand forwards were far more skilful and made many more meaningful contributions to attacking plays than England's. I repeatedly suggested in our coaching meetings that our forwards should develop footwork, power running and handling skills and that we should also include game-awareness drills to encourage the forwards to move away from the set piece and contact areas and offer support to the first and second receivers. We already insisted that the backs should readily secure the ball in the rucks, so it appeared obvious to me that the forwards should compensate by being more involved in our attacking structure.

The merging of the traditional responsibilities of backs and forwards was already producing a generation of backs in Australia and New Zealand who were as physically imposing as previous generations of forwards. Men like Joe Roff and Chris Latham for Australia, Va'aiga Tuigamala [for both New Zealand and Samoa] and Tabai Matson for Fiji, were all either 6ft 4in or 100+ kgs, and frequently they were both. Back-line size had taken on a whole new meaning at the 1995 World Cup, when the New Zealand giant Jonah Lomu, all 6ft 5in and 120kgs of him, first burst into the Test rugby arena. Lomu was still around, and playing in England's group in 1999.

The player agent David McKnight had first 'tipped' me about Jonah in 1992 during my first year at Widnes RL. The conversation was quite bizarre.

'Phil', he said, 'there is a giant of a 17-year-old playing youth rugby in NZ who is tearing the game apart. His performances are so outstanding that he is attracting coaches from the NFL, as well as Australian RL and New Zealand RU to sign him. They are like bees around a honeypot. You need to get on a plane today and go and get his signature.'

'Good idea, David… but Widnes is so short of cash at the moment that they have halved the contracts of their existing playing staff and can't even raise the money to attract local youngsters. I tried to sign a 16-year-old called Kieran Cunningham last night but we hadn't enough cash to lure him. Thanks for the tip David – but wrong place, wrong time… Please keep me posted.'

Jonah eventually signed for the NZRFU and gained his first cap in 1994. He exploded on to the Test scene one year later scoring seven tries in five games in the 1995 World Cup, including four to put England away in the semi-final. In that game he had dismissed competent defenders like Mike Catt, Tony Underwood and Rob Andrew like speed-bumps. In 1996 Jonah had been diagnosed with a rare kidney disorder and had to take some time off from the sport, but since his return he had proven he was as dangerous as ever. He had huge strength and size, he had speed and he could swerve around defenders in addition to running over the top of them. What more do you need?

It was best to try and stop the ball getting to him, but the All Blacks were well-coached and streetwise and made sure that he was around the ball as often as possible. They would pass the ball to his wing to create a one-on-one down the touchline, or use him in midfield as a runner or decoy. The key for the tackler was to get really close to him, inside his huge fend, drive the shoulder in hard and low and above all keep the legs driving forward. If you couldn't get close or you stopped driving the legs, you were history. An assist-tackler was also a great help and South Africa used this ploy effectively in the 1995 final with their aggressive scrum-half Joost van der Westhuizen tracking the ball to the wing every time it moved in Lomu's direction.

There were six players from the 1995 semi-final still in our squad and I did my best to provide reassurance by reminding them of all the tackling drills and improvements that had been made in the last couple of years. I also made scrum-half Matt

Dawson aware of the cover defence that South Africa used in the 1995 final, showing him two clips of Joost van der Westhuizen tackling Lomu from the side. However Matt was an integral part of our pendulum defence, covering in behind the line to defuse any short kicks and organising the defence in front of him. Our tight forwards leaned heavily on his direction at the back of the breakdown, and he enabled our full-back Matt Perry to concentrate fully on his deep positional play. That was important as New Zealand were expert at controlling territory via the kicking game of Andrew Mehrtens at fly-half. I felt I had no choice but to accept Newton's law that strength in one area would mean weakness in another – so we kept the same pattern, and I simply told Matt to defend as usual but to be aware of Lomu's threat. Matt was an intelligent player who could read the game as it unfolded in front of him and usually made the correct decisions. I therefore backed his judgement and was fully confident of his ability.

After studying New Zealand's previous games I had become convinced that their cover defence was poor and that they were vulnerable to an intelligent and varied kicking strategy, and in fact France chose this approach in their semi-final victory over the All Blacks. However Clive decided that we should keep the ball in hand and take the game to them. This was probably the correct decision because after 60 minutes we were level at 16-16 and the momentum was in our favour. However we lost the ball in a heavy tackle out on our left and before we had time to readjust New Zealand had spun the ball across the width of the pitch to Lomu in acres of space on the far touchline. Jerry Guscott had the side angle but was victimised by Lomu's great fend. Austin Healey went low but couldn't get close enough, and both Matt Dawson and Dan Luger were always struggling to stop Lomu in full flight near the goal-line. Suddenly it was a re-run of the semi-final in 1995 and the psychological stalemate was broken. New Zealand put us to the sword in the final quarter and finished with a comprehensive 30-16 victory after scoring a third try when we were vainly trying to play out from our own 22.

The loss meant that we had an extra game to play which created an unenviable schedule – 15 October versus Tonga in the final group game, four days' rest before a play-off against Fiji on the 20th, then only three days before a quarter-final against

South Africa in Paris on the 24th. Although the scoreboard recorded two comfortable wins against both the Pacific island teams [Tonga by 101-10 and Fiji by 45-24], the England medical team would tell you a very different and much tougher story. Both Tonga and Fiji played to type and tested us physically to the limit – leaving us victorious, but battered and bruised in the changing room afterwards.

To play three matches of tournament intensity in the space of nine days was totally unacceptable and suggests that the people who put the schedule together either had no idea of the physical demands of rugby in the professional era or no consideration for the health of those that played it. Add to that another day wasted travelling to Paris and the result was one solitary day's preparation before the biggest game in the youthful history of 'Team England'. It was a ridiculous situation.

Unlike ourselves, South Africa had been under no pressure at all in the group stages, beating Scotland, Spain and Uruguay easily and walking straight into a quarter-final spot. I assumed they would know that our energy levels were depleted after the midweek fixture with Fiji and our late arrival in Paris, and would therefore keep the ball on the pitch as long as possible in an attempt to run our tanks dry. In our 'war-room' meeting I suggested that we play territory and do everything we could to spend most of the game in their 22, and Clive was on the verge of selecting both Jonny Wilkinson and Paul Grayson together to give us the coverage of the field we needed in the kicking game. However he finally came down on the side of our usual game-plan – trying to create a faster tempo than the opposition by playing with ball in hand. In my opinion, this was one occasion where Clive should have gone against his admirable desire to 'get bums off seats' with an attractive style of play, and played simply to win.

In the match itself we defended well but our precision was off in our decision-making and the kick/run balance. We turned the ball over 18 times and they finally converted one of their turnovers on the stroke of half-time. Despite televised replays suggesting that van der Westhuizen had been forced into the corner flag as he grounded the ball over the goal-line, South Africa were awarded the score and they did not look back. In a 31-minute period during the second half their fly-half Jannie de

Beer, who was covering for the injured Henry Honiball, kicked five consecutive drop goals, two from over 45 metres, and then finished us off with a cross-kick for Pieter Rossouw, the try helping South Africa to 44-21 win.

It was a horrible way to lose a game, like a kind of Chinese water-torture. At the same time I was proud of the players, who had given everything they had but come up short. I felt that 1999 was too early for us but I saw something that afternoon that gave me hope for the future. The nucleus was there, it just needed further development and addition.

In the end, the tournament was won by the team that defended the best throughout it – Australia. The former England number 7 Peter Winterbottom had told me that he was convinced that Australia had been doing defensive training for the 1991 World Cup, and that preparation came to fruition eight years later. John Muggleton's D conceded only one try in their six games and none at all in the crucial knockout stages of the competition. If your opponents can't score tries against you then you are highly unlikely to be beaten, and so it proved. Australia beat France easily in the final 35-12 after France had memorably upset the All Blacks in the semi. 'Muggo's' defence gave the French no encouragement whatsoever and snuffed out everything they attempted. By proxy it was a victory for Jack Gibson because John had been one of his players and disciples at Paramatta, and that too gave me an optimistic feeling about England's future under Clive Woodward.

In contrast to the opinions of most of the coaching staff, the newly-appointed England captain Martin Johnson felt that England were good enough to win the competition. 'It's easy to see things differently with the benefit of hindsight', he says, 'but I've watched that pool game with New Zealand and we were definitely in the driving seat after we got back to 16-all. We had all the momentum and if we had scored next, I think we would have gone on to win the game. The quarter-final at Stade de France was a one-off, a freak performance by a guy [the Springbok number 10 Jannie de Beer] who just had one of those days when everything he touched – or more accurately kicked – turned to gold. You can't legislate for that. I just felt we lacked a bit of conviction in our own abilities. We lacked the self-belief to back up our ability, rather than the ability itself to win those games and the tournament as a whole.'

The appointment of Martin Johnson as captain turned out to be a pivotal moment. Up until the middle of 1998 the captain of choice had been Lawrence Dallaglio, but there is little doubt that the combination of Clive Woodward at the coaching helm and Martin Johnson as the on-field translator of his wishes represented the most potent danger for England's opponents. 'Clive and I are as different as chalk and cheese as people. He'd come up with a load of ideas ranging across the whole spectrum from great to barmy, whereas I probably had my feet on the ground a bit more. The whole Yehuda Shinar thing for example, the Mossad computer game, I couldn't get my head around it… At one point Clive told us that selection would be based on how well we did in the game – all the younger guys who had been brought up on the PlayStation were of course great at it…!'

With his background at Welford Road, his experience as a winning captain away from home at the highest of levels [as Lions' tour captain on the 1997 tour of South Africa] and his excess of common sense and dry humour, Martin Johnson was the perfect foil to Clive Woodward, the pragmatist balancing Woodward's idealist. He took nothing on trust and calling a spade a bloody shovel was second nature to him. With Johnno as captain, England won 88% in the Woodward era; without him, that winning percentage dropped to 57%.

Clive Woodward probably needed this counterpoint of personalities somewhere within the leadership structure. As a player, he had thrived in a centre combination at Welford Road with Paul Dodge, a player who represented the solid, grounded qualities he lacked. Dodge was dependable, had a good range of skills and seldom had a poor game. As Les Cusworth, the Tigers' fly-half of the time remembers, 'Clive joined us in the late 70s and he had bags of flair – though Paul Dodge was the cement that kept a talented back-line together and made Clive look a better player.'

The Leicester coach Chalkie White himself felt that 'to some extent Woody relied on other people, and if Dodge had not been there, he would have been a more ordinary player. Dodge was outstanding. Didn't drink, didn't smoke, didn't sit in the back of the coach along with the rogues.'

Despite the apparent disaster of a loss at a home World Cup, beneath the surface matters were coming together nicely for 'Team England'.

Jack Gibson had emphasised to me the importance of the administration to a coach's success.

'First look at the front office,' he had said. 'If that is not functioning on all six cylinders then forget it, because there is no chance the team will be successful, however good a coach you are.'

This advice came back to haunt me during the build-up to the World Cup when I realised that administrative problems were compromising our efforts. Clive had had to fight his political battles in 1998 and 1999 and upon his re-appointment after the World Cup took direct responsibility for all issues in this sphere.

Clive Woodward now had the complete control of team affairs he needed as a 'transformational leader'. He could liaise directly with the new CEO Francis Baron over budgets and he had the elbow-room to challenge the distribution of RFU funds. He had created the cultural architecture he wanted with the help of Humphrey Walters and Paddi Lund, and engineered a positive, enjoyable squad atmosphere in which players felt they could communicate informally with each other, the coaches and Woodward himself. He had taken steps to ring-fence Team England's intellectual property and prevent avoidable leaks. All his primary coaches were now full-time and he had the captain he really needed in Martin Johnson. When he gave a rousing speech at the disappointing conclusion of England's 1999 World Cup campaign, he was able to make it against a background in which it had real meaning. Clive Woodward had said previously 'Judge me on the World Cup' and there had been a lot of calls for his head in the media now that England's tournament was over. If he went, others would inevitably go too. But instead of falling into the self-pity trap and dwelling on the team's misfortunes, he thanked everyone for their effort and said that this was a new beginning rather than the end. He had an evident sense of pride in what England had achieved and he wasn't afraid to let it show. At the darkest moment of his tenure as England coach, he was able to find the silver lining, provide inspiration and turn around the mood in the room. He said that England would go on to win the 2003 World Cup. It was a moment of transformational leadership right out of the textbook.

Chapter eight

Becoming number one

One hundred and five days, from 24 October 1999 until 5 February 2000… That was the time we had to spend kicking our heels and brooding on our losses before our next fixture. It was a long wait but I was excited. For the first time since switching codes I was fully confident in my ability to solve problems by using my knowledge and experience in rugby union, rather than having to think what would I have done in league and then try to translate it to the other code.

With the images of Jonah Lomu and other massive southern hemisphere backs fresh in our minds from the World Cup, we added two youngsters in centre Mike Tindall and wing Ben Cohen who would bring considerable size and power to our back-line. Both were well over 6ft tall and 100+kgs and both were there to stay.

Changes to the back room staff were equally significant. Our new physiotherapist Phil Pask turned out to be one of the best in his area of expertise and Dave Tennison had joined the group as kit man. The unsung relationship between the kit man and the players is often a litmus test of team morale, and Dave was an ex-Marine who we had first encountered in our training camp at RM Lympstone before the World Cup. He was very positive, a 'cup half-full' man, he loved his job and would do anything for the players.

The changing room should give the team security and comfort as they prepare to play one of the hardest sports in the world and Dave always created the right atmosphere. He did a priceless job and the players loved him for it.

The most significant additions to the coaching group were Brian Ashton and Andy Robinson, who would replace John Mitchell as the forwards coach in June 2000 and in time for the summer tour of South Africa. Although Brian Ashton had been a part of the group since 1998, the full benefit of his coaching did not make itself felt until 'Robbo', a fellow Bath club man, came in to reinforce his attacking philosophies with the forwards. Brian was a self-effacing ex-teacher who had enjoyed considerable success with the Bath club. *The Daily Telegraph* columnist [of the time] and ex-England international Paul Ackford recalls meeting Ashton after Bath had won another Heineken Cup game and asking whether he was celebrating. 'No, I'm off walking', came the reply. As Ackford goes on to relate, hill-walking was his passion, 'Which tells you something about the man. That he is contemplative. Not afraid of his own company. His is not a forceful personality. And he is not exactly impressive to look at. In fact, he usually looks shabby and dishevelled, as if he might have spent the night sleeping on a park bench.'

Brian Ashton shunned the limelight and instinctively distanced himself from the world of media relations in which Clive Woodward revelled. But his influence on the attacking play of teams with which he was involved was druidic in its force. He may have wanted to merge into the very powerful intellectual background of the England coaching group more quietly than most, but the lantern of his attacking genius was shining as brightly as any – at least up until 2001, when the advent of rugby league-style defences changed the landscape of the game for good.

Brian had joined England in 1998 after coaching Ireland for only the first year of his six-year contract. I remember him as a fragile but tough and competitive scrum-half with Fylde, a delightful club on the north-west coast near Blackpool. He made his name as a coach of Bath. I had run into him at the Loughborough Summer School in 1991 when we were both heading up rugby coaching courses. The RFU had made it clear to me after I had returned from the Rothman's Foundation in Sydney that they wanted nothing to do with rugby league coaching courses, so I was both surprised and delighted when Brian suggested that our two groups join forces one afternoon. I took both groups for a tackling session before Brian ran an excellent session on support play which the rugby league coaches enjoyed tremendously. Both groups mingled in the bar that evening and several new friendships were formed.

I next bumped into Brian in 1996 when, as the incumbent head coach of Great Britain I attended the early season cross-code match between Wigan and Bath at Twickenham. It was the second game in the so-called 'Clash of Codes', in which the top union and league sides took each other on in two matches under both sets of rules. Wigan had won the league match 82-6, and Phil Lowe, the GB manager, booked me into the Runnymede Hotel, set in idyllic surroundings on the banks of the Thames for the return match. The Bath squad also happened to be staying at the hotel and that evening I had a couple of beers with Brian chatting about the prospects for the following afternoon. It became clear that Brian wasn't interested in his team exerting their undoubted advantages at scrumming and mauling to win the game: 'I can't see the point of that… The spectators will want to see some fast-flowing action so we will run the ball at them at every opportunity. We understand that will play into Wigan's hands but it will make more of a game of it.'

There was the clue to Brian's psyche in a nutshell. He challenged his players to embrace risk and find their own solutions, even if the risks were not strictly necessary. Bath promptly mauled the ball upfield from the kick-off all the way to the Wigan 22 as if to say 'that is what we could do', but then with the goal-line at their mercy, passed it wide as if to say '…but we won't because we are going to make a game of it!'

Bath eventually won 41-19, but it was Wigan's all-international back-line who stole the show. At one stage they created a superb try from a scrum near their own goal-line, inter-passing all the way down the pitch before scoring under the posts. Don Rutherford's wife Sue, who was sitting just ahead of me, turned round in uncontainable excitement, shook her fists in the air and shouted: 'Phil, this is the best rugby we have ever seen at Twickenham!'

Brian often referred to that try when he was coaching the England backs, not only drawing the players' attention to the accuracy of the passing and lines of support, but also emphasising the rugby league mindset – that tries can be scored from anywhere and at any time during the game. 'Open your eyes,' he would say, 'be brave and back yourself.'

Brian was an innovative coach who engineered his sessions to be both interesting and challenging. He spent a lot of time developing real-time decision-making and would have my defence running against his attack. His favourite drill would be to have the attack facing the wrong way with their backs to the defence, which would be 10 metres away. He would then ask me to create a deliberate weakness in our structure by leaving a hole in the middle of the defence, or having the defence in a tight line on one touchline leaving a large space on the far side. When he put the ball down and blew his whistle the attacking players would turn around and quickly identify our area of weakness before attacking it. The practice was well-devised but it was his coaching that made the difference. He improved the players' vision, helped to make their communication shorter but more decisive, and sharpened the lines of running in support of the ball. He had a gentle way with him, but like all successful coaches he was incredibly demanding, and insisted on total commitment to the process he wanted to develop.

I had been pointing out in our coaches, meetings for some time that Australia and New Zealand were developing a 15-man game and that there was a real danger that we would be left behind if we did not develop and nurture the attacking skills of our forwards. Brian agreed wholeheartedly and when Andy Robinson became forwards coach in June 2000, he allotted Brian time in our weekly training programme to work with the forwards. That was a crucial adjustment.

I can still remember the first session when Martin Johnson walked up to Brian [who's about a foot shorter than Johnno] with furrowed brow and said, 'Brian, do you really want me to run and pass the ball?' 'Of course I do Johnno, can you handle it?' came the reply. 'Course I can,' said Johnno and his face lit up like a small boy's, '…but no-one has allowed me to pass the ball before.'

Largely as a result of Brian's influence, we scored 20 tries and amassed 183 points in the five games of the 2000 Six Nations tournament, entertaining the crowd and repeatedly achieving Clive's overall aim of playing at a higher tempo than the opposition and 'getting bums off seats'.

Andy Robinson also believes that:

> Brian was a supporter of the 15-man game when he was head coach at Bath and I think his confidence flowed into Clive's veins in that respect. It also encouraged him to select the footballers who could achieve that vision like Will Greenwood and Mike Catt. With myself and Brian and Phil in place, all espousing similar attacking values, the message began to be transmitted to the players because it was consistent in coming from all the main coaches.

Even though England were creating more positive selection choices in the backs and steadily increasing their overall attacking effectiveness, the question of mental toughness at key moments remained unresolved. Mental toughness was Vince Lombardi's main qualification in order to become a consistent winner, and in two successive Five/Six Nations tournaments England had blown opportunities to complete a grand slam with victories in the final match of the competition.

> At the beginning of April 2000, we knew we were already champions after four rounds of the new Six Nations format, and we travelled to Scotland chasing our first grand slam against a side who had not registered a victory in the competition. The scene was set for complacency and complacent is exactly what we were in our preparations. We trained at Heriot-Watt University and stayed at a superb hotel outside Edinburgh, complete with its own golf course. The problem was that we were there for the whole week and that was far too long. We got bored, our focus drifted marginally and training lacked the necessary bite. That is complacency for you – things look the same on the surface, you seem in good spirits but the edge is missing. There is a huge difference between wanting to do something and feeling that you have to do it, that there is no other option.
>
> The Scots clearly felt they had to rescue something from their season and came at us as though they had been on the set of *Braveheart* all week, fuelled by a grave feeling of injustice and utterly determined to send King Edward's army back over the border 'tae think again'. They hit us with everything they had in their arsenal, causing several of our players to lose their self-control, whether by fair means or foul. That was not in our script.

Although we led 10-9 at the half, the light drizzle which had begun to fall was a warning of the Scottish deluge to come.

The team changed their shirts at half-time, the new kit designed to create a new focus in the opening 10 minutes of the second period, but the horrid weather and our lack of ability to adapt to it swamped all our best intentions. The rain became torrential, the drains could not cope and the pitch became waterlogged in several areas. Duncan Hodge kicked his fourth penalty goal to put them in front, and then continuously forced us back into our own 22 with long accurate punts into the flooded areas. We tried to run out of our end and Scotland fed off our errors, and when Hodge slid over to score Scotland's only try from close range it was the final straw. We had lost the grand slam for the second year in succession – and to make things worse, we failed to turn up for the presentation of the Calcutta Cup afterwards.

Much the same thing had occurred one year earlier at Wembley, when Wales stood between us and a grand slam in the [then] Five Nations. Only the weather was different. It was a day flooded by spring sunshine on perfectly-manicured grass which I regard as the home of rugby league finals. It is every Englishman's dream to play at Wembley. I had been there before, leading out both Widnes to play Wigan in the 1992 Challenge Cup Final, and England in the opening game and the final of the 1995 Rugby League World Cup. It does not matter how many times you have been there before. As soon you walk out on that hallowed turf you get goose bumps and the hairs on the back of the neck stand up in nervous anticipation of the grand occasion to follow.

As against Scotland we'd started well, scoring three tries on our way to a 25-18 lead at half-time, with only the superb goal-kicking of Neil Jenkins keeping Wales in the hunt. We were still leading 31-25 with 80 minutes showing on the clock, we were camped deep in their half and the game looked to be over. The white streamers had already been attached to the Five Nations trophy, for heaven's sake! The South African referee André Watson then penalised Tim Rodber for a hard [but in my view perfectly legal] tackle on Colin Charvis, Jenkins found touch on our 22 and Scott Gibbs scored a marvellous try straight from first phase, changing his angle of run to take a short pass off Scott Quinnell from the ensuing lineout and slaloming between five defenders to touch down. It was a match-winning try scored by the red jerseys of Wales, but manufactured by the red jerseys of Wigan RL! Neil was never going to miss and duly converted to win the game for Wales by one point. We were completely devastated. This was not in our script and it was not meant to happen.

Tim Rodber was distraught afterwards, not only for conceding the penalty that gave Wales position, but also for missing the first-up tackle on Gibbs on the scoring play itself. He stood up and apologised to everyone in the changing room, and told me quietly as we were sitting together that he was still thinking about the penalty and was not concentrating fully when Gibbsy came at him from the next lineout.

The only sure thing in any competitive match is that you will make mistakes when you're out in the middle, particularly when you're under pressure. You can be sure of it. So it is vitally important that you pass through errors immediately, and get your mind back on the job. That is what mental toughness, and 'making the second effort' means. You stop negative mental associations immediately. To be successful at this level you must always remain grounded, live in the moment and not dwell on the past. Tim's miss certainly underlined the importance of 'thinking correctly under pressure' – or T-CUP as Clive had abbreviated it – and I began to emphasise the point more fully in our future preparation.

We decided to approach the underlying problem of 'thinking clearly under pressure' through the issue of discipline. We had conceded 18 penalties against Wales, and lost to Scotland one calendar year later because they were able to kick four penalty goals from inside our own half to win the match.

In rugby union, the consequences of giving penalties away are far more severe that in any other sport. Give up a penalty in American football or a free kick in soccer and you give up yardage but you cannot give up three points. In union you can concede two penalties for a couple of technical infringements and find that their value exceeds that of a try you may have struggled so very hard to create! Moreover, conceding too many penalties makes it almost impossible to achieve the advantages in territory and possession for which most teams strive, and see as the signposts of success in a game.

We discussed the possibilities at a number of meetings after the two grand slam debacles. I suggested that the presence of a qualified referee during 'live' defensive training sessions might be of great benefit. Clive nodded his head in agreement, but we were all taken aback when he announced the very next day that he had approached international referee Steve Lander to join our coaching team.

The work that Steve did was extremely valuable. He refereed all contact situations during our preparation, advising defenders on the fine line between legal and illegal involvements and on how to 'manage the referee' in the heat of battle. To give one example, our line-speed was quicker than that of most other teams and some referees had penalised us for offside when we were clearly onside. Steve suggested defenders should continue to shout 'Back foot!' at ruck-time to indicate to the referee that we were onside, with those close to him asking, 'Are we okay here, sir?' to draw his attention to our discipline. Steve would meet with the official in charge the day before the game to get a clear idea of his main criteria and the areas of the game he tended to referee most severely. Steve's input reduced our penalty count significantly, which in turn improved our ability to win games. It was a classic example of one of Clive's CNEs [critical non-essentials] working out in practice.

After the Scotland loss we also began to pay far more attention to the meteorological report for the day of the game and weather predictions were pinned up every day at the front of the war-room to keep us abreast of developments. But for me, by far the most important task was to challenge the players to become 'the best defensive team in the world' before the end of the next World Cup cycle. I had been waiting for the moment to turn the screw and the timing was vital. A meeting at the end of the 2000 Six Nations seemed like the perfect moment.

The atmosphere was very relaxed and banter was still flying around the room as I pressed 'play'. The clip-reel displayed some of the soft tries we had conceded before the 1999 World Cup on a large screen. There was an immediate hush as the laughter died away and I could almost hear the sound of some jaws dropping open. Finally Matt Dawson shook his head and said ruefully, 'I didn't think we were as bad as that.'

And in truth they weren't, but I was prepared to let them mull it all over a little more before striking my next blow. Lawrence Dallaglio put his hand up and said plaintively: 'Phil, please tell us we have made some improvement?'

I didn't respond, instead I played a short three-minute sequence highlighting our excellent defence in the recent win against France, set to the background music of 'Something inside so strong' by Labi Siffre. 'When they insist we're just not good enough… when we know better, just look 'em in the eyes and say, we're gonna do it anyway… Something inside so strong, you thought that my pride was gone – oh no!–…something inside so strong.' In the complete silence as I ran the two sequences, the difference between winning and losing could not have been more stark.

'That', I said, 'illustrates our journey – where we came from, to where we are now.' I knew now I had their whole attention.

'Improvement like that does not occur easily. It reflects the effort and determination you have put into both your preparation and into your game. I am proud of you, every one of you. I have waited a long time for this moment because I wanted it to happen earlier, but I am confident that you are now ready.

'It is time for us to draw a line in the sand and move on. We have the ability to be the best defence in the world, to be the best defence that rugby union has ever seen. But you will have to step up once again.'

With that I unveiled a statistical table including the three Tri-Nations teams of South Africa, Australia and New Zealand, the Six Nations teams of Wales, Ireland, Scotland, France, Italy and ourselves, plus Argentina. Ten countries, and every time one of these countries played one another I intended to record every try conceded. The challenge for the England team was to concede the fewest tries and finish at the top of the table by the end of the World Cup cycle in 2003.

'It is the hardest challenge that I have ever set a team of players but I am confident that you have the courage, ability and sheer bloody-mindedness to achieve it. You cannot do it on your own, it can only be achieved if every single one of you buys into it with your heart and soul. Not 99% of you but 100%.

'Defence is the only part of rugby that is all "team". It is only as strong as its weakest link, and at this level and with all our games on TV, the opposition will soon scent any weakness and send all the traffic that way. I want you to look at every one of your team-mates one at a time. I want you to ask yourself as you look at them, "Can I trust him, in the heat of battle, when we are breathing through our backsides and under intense pressure… can I trust him to do his job and not let me down?" Ask the question of everyone around you but also ask it of yourself, because everyone else in the room will be looking back at you and asking it too. No shirkers, and no more discussion now. I am finished here. It is one hell of a challenge and if you are all up for it, you can tell me tomorrow.'

Afterwards I found out that Neil Back and Martin Johnson had led the response among the players.

'We will have to work hard,' Backy had said. 'If we decide to do it there is no turning back. We all either give it everything we have and put every bit of our body and soul into it, or we tell Phil "No thanks mate".'

'It's a no-brainer,' said Johnno. 'If we want to win the World Cup we have to be the best defensive team in the world. Let's get on with it.' As with all debates that included Martin Johnson, his word was the final word. He and Backy were the living embodiments of mental toughness, and we shared a similar outlook on the winning of games. Vince Lombardi and Jack Gibson would have been proud to have them.

The weekly build-up to a Test match now became a detailed, intense but well-oiled process. After a match on the Saturday, Sunday was a recovery day for the players, but a hectic one for all the coaches. Like Ron Massey, Phil would study the tape of the game. He would assess both the collective defensive performance and complete an individual report on each player. This would include work rate, total tackles and missed tackles, tackle effectiveness, turnovers, discipline, errors of judgement and decision-making – all depicted numerically as a percentage. The team analysis included a detailed report on England's defence at the ruck, set piece, in line, pendulum, kick chase, and in reaction to turnovers. Phil's work was not finished at this point, because then he would have to turn his attention towards analysing England's next opponents. He would examine their attacking structure, the strengths and weaknesses of individual attackers, looking at whole games run in real-time to get an idea of opposition momentum, their current mindset and tendencies.

'I could not relax until I had a complete picture of both "them" and "us" and related one to the other in my head, and I couldn't plan the week's sessions without a sense of that relationship', Phil says. Once he was satisfied, the session planning could go ahead.

- **Monday** – performance review presented to the entire squad. Collective and individual performances came under the microscope. Criticisms always occurred in public and never behind closed doors. 'We were a band of brothers and I was no different to them,' Phil says. 'We all looked in the mirror and asked, "Could I have done more?" If I had given them faulty or incomplete information or over-trained them, either I would own up to it – or they were free to criticise my performance as I would criticise theirs.' That equality fostered healthy relationships based on mutual trust. After the review there would be a light session based on minimal contact situations run at half-pace. Kick-chase was a favourite, with the emphasis falling on communication and line integrity.

- **Tuesday** – mostly devoted to attack but with a small 20-minute morning slot for defence. Concentrating on communication or 'small talk' with the full squad of players divided into two groups, one attacking and the other defending, with the groups swapping roles halfway through the session. Emphasis on alignment, spacings and defence against different types of attacking play. The group in possession had some temporary advantages, either extra players or 'quick ball'. 'I did not tell them at the time – quite deliberately I might add – that the quality of their decision-making and "small talk" had now overtaken that of the league teams that I had coached.'

- **Wednesday** – defence day, often called 'murder-ball' by the players. A brief three- or four-minute video on the opponent's key set-piece starters, to be followed by a session of about 45 minutes on first-phase defence by the backs, mostly chat and discussion, with the replacements and squad players impersonating the opponent's offence and enacting their key starter plays. The back-row would always be included in the practice and the major transition zone between the first back #10 Johnny Wilkinson and last forward #7 Neil Back would be scrutinised and checked for strength. In fact, the relationship between these two players, the two best tacklers on the team, was an area of huge advantage to 'Team England':

Most teams have to hide their fly-half in the defensive line or fill his channel with support, but Jonny Wilkinson was the exception to this rule. Jonny attacked every ball-carrier that came his way as if it was a personal challenge – a challenge he was not going to lose. I am sure that he enjoyed flattening an opponent with a big hit more than he enjoyed scoring a try. To have a number 10 who could deliver hits of such coruscating power, like the one with which Wilko levelled the big French wing Emile N'tamack in the Stade de France, lifted the whole team.

Even in training, Clive was often concerned that Jonny would injure himself. He would run out with a yellow bib that indicated the injured players who weren't ready for contact. He would say, 'Phil, give this to Wilko – we can't risk him being injured for the weekend.' I would go up to Jonny and relay the message: 'Mate… Clive wants you to put this on,' and hand the bib to him. 'No way!' he would shout, throwing the bib on the floor before accelerating away into another hit.

After lunch, there would be a 12-minute video preview compiled by Tony Biscombe, based on the opposition's last three matches. Phil would explain their attacking philosophy and shape, flag up key individuals and how he expected them to attack England's defence. The afternoon session would begin with small-sided games designed to test individual decision-making, with the attack having either extra numbers or varied angles around the ball-carrier – no more than ten minutes. This would then be followed by a tackling drill, but with the attacker and defender close enough together to avoid unnecessary impacts or injuries. Any faults in individual technique would be picked up either 'live' or on video replay afterwards.

The final segment of the session would see either England Students or London Irish [coached by Brian Smith] imitating England's upcoming opponents for 20 minutes, with the session starting as a 'grab' and finishing full-on. 'I handed the defence over to Backy, who would control both the intensity and length of the session. As soon as he was satisfied with the structure and level of commitment he would give me the nod and I would end it.'

- Although **Thursday** was a rest day, Backy would often visit individuals to iron out any issues by speaking to them one-on-one, and these informal chats were invaluable, especially coming from a fellow player rather than a coach sitting somewhere in the stand come Saturday. The captain's run, which took place on Friday, was a relatively short but vital session because the players were in charge and made all the decisions. It always finished with a run-through of our drop-goal routine which was to prove so important to our ultimate success.

The appointment of Andy Robinson as a direct replacement for John Mitchell in June 2000 was another large step forward. Andy Robinson had previously worked with Clive Woodward in the England under-21s set-up and the two of them had enjoyed mischievously posing on-field dilemmas for the senior side run by Jack Rowell, to the point where Rowell would walk across and tell them to cut it out. This was a little like saying to the rabbit 'you must not eat the lettuce'.

> Andy bought into Clive's vision of specialist coaches whole-heartedly and gave Phil Keith-Roach (scrum), Simon Hardy (lineout), Dave Reddin (fitness), Dave Alred (kicking), Brian Ashton (attack) and myself (defence) total support. He encouraged us to take full responsibility for our own areas, where Mitch had wanted to do it all himself and was loath to delegate.

Andy Robinson immediately made some important technical adjustments to the forward pattern employed by John Mitchell:

> In terms of set-piece technique and accuracy there was no question of the value that John Mitchell had added. But I felt I could add something different again. Instead of John's two pods of four wrapping around each other continually, I opted for three pods, with a 3-3-2 split of the forwards. This helped us cover the width of the field better, developed the handling skills of the forwards and tended to keep more of them on their feet for longer.
>
> The philosophy was the one I'd learned from Brian Ashton at Bath, having more people in the game and on their feet as decision-makers – rather than being 'pre-programmed' where to go. That's why I enjoyed working so much with our locks at

the time – Martin Johnson, Danny Grewcock, Simon Shaw and Ben Kay. They all had an appetite to expand the range of their games, to carry the ball more and pass it in contact, to make more tackles – and for me, that expectation was built with England rather than at the clubs.

There was an increased emphasis on passing the ball and offloading in contact and I started comparing the number of passes our forwards made with the world leaders in that area, New Zealand. We wanted two lines of attack and people on the edges, and it was a challenge for us because it was not what we were used to. Ideally I wanted a set-up with backs ahead of the forwards, but with those forwards able to step up past the backs and become the first line where necessary.

With the Bath club 'old firm' of Brian Ashton and Andy Robinson in harness, the advances made by England's attacking game increased exponentially, and Phil Larder could see the changes happening:

Brian and Andy began by insisting that at least one attacker be on each touchline, which was a clever way of spreading out the defensive line and forcing our opponents to increase the spacing between individual defenders. With our facility at the cross-kick, the threat on the touchline was too definite to ignore. Secondly, they started to evolve the 'two lines of attack' principle, which featured a second line of attackers who would support our first and second receivers [usually Jonny Wilkinson and Will Greenwood], give them passing options and change their angles of running depending on what they saw in front of them. These extra passing options would often cause defences to either fly up and guess at the receiver, or hold too passively awaiting developments – both of which created opportunities for our attack to make line-breaks or keep the initiative. The key was the selection of a mobile pack of forwards who were comfortable with ball in hand, and able to read the game and adjust as it developed, and this is what Brian and Andy sought to develop.

The results of their work came to fruition in the 2001 Six Nations tournament, where the brilliant running and inter-passing of England's attacking play accrued six tries apiece against Wales, Scotland and France and ten tries against Italy. We produced a festival of attacking rugby which thrilled and enthralled the

England public and generated an average of 49 points per game. Jonny Wilkinson became England's all-time highest points scorer at the tender age of 22, and Jason Robinson was introduced off the bench. He immediately showed the changes of direction at speed which had terrorised defences in rugby league and hinted at the excitement to come. Graham Henry told me afterwards that England's performance in the 44-15 win at the Millennium Stadium in Cardiff was the best he had ever seen from a northern hemisphere team, while Scotland captain Andy Nicol shook his head remembering that, 'We were out on our feet with 20 minutes to go… then there was a huge cheer echoing around the ground as England brought on Jason Robinson.'

Andy Robinson's background as a number 7 also helped Phil to improve England's work at the defensive breakdown, an area of comparative weakness up to that point:

> Robbo increased our defensive effectiveness by taking control of the contact area. It was a 'no brainer' for an ex-number 7 and specialist ball-stealer to coach the intricacies of the tackle area, rather than an ex-rugby league player who had been allowed to tamely regain his feet and play the ball after every tackle!
>
> There had been times when I'd relied too much on my fail-safe maxim *If in doubt, stay out* at the breakdown, but with Robbo's help the players improved both their body angles and their ability to get over the ball and stay there after the tackle. Above all, Robbo improved their recognition of the situation so that they made better decisions – when to stay in the tackle area, and when to pull out into the defensive line.

The first test of how far England had come after their shattering loss to Scotland at the end of the 2000 Six Nations occurred just over ten weeks later, when they faced their nemesis from the 1999 World Cup, South Africa, in a two-Test series. In contrast to the threadbare 'Tour of Hell', England were able to take a full squad of 42 for the five tour games with none of their 'names' missing, and they were based at the five-star Westcliffe Hotel in Johannesburg, built on a hill overlooking beautiful zoological gardens.

It was a huge turn-around in planning and scheduling compared to 1998. England trained at the local university and had the use of a nearby gym which was frequented by some of the strongest and best-known body-builders in South Africa. It became the battleground for some serious lifting competitions, and even the body-builders put down the tools of their trade and stopped work to watch young Andrew Sheridan squat-lifting with as much as 275kgs on the bar. As Phil recalls, 'I am not sure exactly how much weight he had on the bar but it began to sag around his shoulders and the entire gym applauded when he had finished lifting!'

> We had a setback before the first Test. Jonny Wilkinson felt ill during the night before the game. He thought he would recover during the morning, but his condition only deteriorated. The decision to give Austin Healey the number 10 shirt was made only an hour before kick-off, and 'Oz' responded positively and had an outstanding game, aided by the presence of a second kicker in Mike Catt playing at inside centre. The set piece [with tight-head Julian White winning his first cap] was solid, giving us quality possession, and the work that Robbo and Brian Ashton had been doing with the forwards was clearly evident as we played a 15-man game and created the lion's share of the chances.
>
> Towards the end of the game Oz took a quick tap from inside our own 22 after we had been defending for over three minutes. I think the Springboks expected us to kick to touch to buy some time whilst we recovered, but instead we launched a length-of-the-field attack which took them by surprise. The move culminated in a chip and desperate chase to the Springbok line, and Tim Stimpson was tackled in the act of reaching for the ball to touch it down. The entire stadium, apart from the South African video referee, thought that he had been taken out early and that it was a penalty try, but it was the TMO's opinion that mattered. The try was disallowed and South Africa won 18-13, via six Braam van Straaten penalties.

Clive had recently brought back some fresh ideas from Israel, and one of them was the rather Old Testament concept of 'when attacked, retaliate immediately' which was then translated as 'fight pressure with pressure' for the benefit of the players. They liked it and bought into the new motto, and Austin Healey's tap-and-go from his own line was the first example of the policy in action – Woodward even congratulated him in the post-match review afterwards!

Everywhere the England squad went, there was evidence that the cussed creed of 'an eye for an eye, a tooth for a tooth' was just what was needed to beat South Africa on their own patch. As Neil Back says, 'The impulse of the Afrikaner is to circle his wagons. He has fought against ferocious indigenous tribes like the Zulu and he has fought with his back to the Zulu against the English colonial empire, so his hardness is inbuilt. It is reinforced by a sense of spiritual entitlement from his Calvinist beliefs, which arguably created the situation known as apartheid in the first place. As a race, South Africans are hard, they are bonded and they are confident to the point of arrogance.' The *laager* was like a mobile fighting village, complete with women and children. The Afrikaner was used to carrying his whole existence, everything that made life worth living, on his own back – and defending it with his life. A Boer commander would secure his wagon-circle even if there was no enemy within 50 miles. Not for him a battle of manoeuvre or attacking élan; the *laager* was based on proven low-risk principles, giving nothing away and an impregnable defence was at the core of it. As one 19th-century British witness put it, rightly or wrongly, about his Boer neighbour, 'You feel somewhere deep in his heart there is a tyrant – and he wants to rub you out.'

> We took the midweek team to the University ground to train on Sunday morning, but there was a dog training programme already taking place and we were refused entry. I walked around the corner with some curiosity and when I reached the practice ground I was amazed to find well over two hundred owners training their guard dogs. Both the barks of the dogs and the commands of the owners were made of the same stuff – guttural, low and rasping. South Africa is a strange mixture – an outstandingly beautiful country with a dark, unbending iron in its soul. The two police bikes which usually accompanied the team coach as an escort to the stadium on matchday were in South Africa replaced by two armoured cars, with a police helicopter overhead.
>
> Frustrated by their inability to score a try in the first Test, we knew that the Springboks would throw the kitchen sink at us in the second match at Bloemfontein. They had all the possession in the first quarter and most of it was in our half. Our back-row of Richard Hill, Neil Back and Lawrence Dallaglio were magnificent as we kept our goal-line intact. Gradually we began

to exert pressure of our own in retaliation and, in a reverse of the first match, we were the ones to win the game by penalties. Jonny Wilkinson, now fully recovered from illness, scored all our points from eight penalties and a drop goal. Twice we had a player sin-binned and on the second occasion we defended resolutely for 20 phases with South Africa failing to make a line-break. With less than ten minutes left to play, and South Africa trailing by 12 points, Joost van der Westhuizen was awarded a dubious try by the video referee André Watson. We certainly deserved our 27-22 victory but this was not the first occasion, nor would it be the last, when André Watson would make controversial decisions that rendered the finale of important matches more nerve-wracking than they needed to be!

We were delighted with the win. It was only the third occasion that England had won a Test match on South African soil and we were duly proud of what we had achieved. The midweek team won all of their three games too and we left South Africa with a proud record of four wins out of five.

By now Phil Larder felt he had worked out the South African mentality. Understanding the opponent's psyche goes hand in glove with understanding how their strengths can be turned into weaknesses. The Springboks were physically the biggest, hardest group of players that Phil had ever coached against, and from that point of view they presented the most imposing challenge he had faced in either rugby code.

They knew it, they were proud of it and they played to their strengths. They took to the field determined to win the physical battle and dominate us physically, so when we met them again in the autumn of 2000, the entire theme in our build-up was to be smarter and cleverer than them.

My first step was to modify our structure, shortening the defensive line and deliberately closing the gaps between players. I knew that it was a matter of pride for them to run over the top of us rather than around us, and that by narrowing the gaps between defenders we would be able to hit their runners in twos and threes, in gang-tackles. However big, strong and determined their ball carriers were, we would win the collisions as long as our technique was good and the tacklers worked together.

In the three-man tackles I envisaged, it was critical that one tackler rolled away quickly and reloaded into line, otherwise we would be short of defenders on the next phase. Matt Dawson at scrum-half, although officially part of the pendulum, would now be more involved than usual in marshalling the defensive line and ready to quickly fill in when gaps occurred around the breakdown.

We worked on our alignment all week and the England Students became the Springboks against us on Wednesday afternoon. The game itself was exceptionally tough, as we knew it would be, but our gang-tackling was explosive and allowed us to achieve our aim to dominate the majority of collisions. We were always in control and won the game far more easily than the 25-17 score suggested. Will Greenwood scored our only try, with all the other points coming from Wilko's boot.

Phil Larder knew that, with the Boks' own traditional defensive strengths, England would be unlikely to score many tries against them, but he felt that his defence would concede even less. Two tries conceded in three games against South Africa in 2000, became two in four after our 29-9 victory in the autumn of 2001, and two in five after the 53-3 rout at Twickenham one year later. England had won the psychological war in the build-up to the 2003 World Cup, where the Springboks would once again provide England's main opposition at the group stage, and the Springboks knew it.

South Africa had not varied their game plan or tactical approach when they arrived at Twickenham for our last game of the year on 24 November 2001. In my opinion, South Africa went way over the top in this game. Rugby league can be a tough uncompromising sport but nothing had prepared me for the brutality that the English players had to endure that afternoon.

The two coaching boxes at Twickenham are next to one another, and I always sat on the left-hand side adjoining the opposition box. I could clearly see and hear their reactions, and when in the very first minute Jason Robinson was felled by a tackle that was both high and late, two of the Springboks' back room staff smiled and nodded to one another as if they'd scored a try! Worse was to follow as Jonny Wilkinson was singled out for special attention. They were even stooped over him, cussing him out while he lay on the floor recovering from a hit, and so it went on… Phil Pask ran on to the pitch just before half-time to drag Neil Back off – Neil was bleeding heavily from a head wound. Lewis Moody replaced him. At the next ruck a head butt felled Richard Hill and Ben Kay replaced him.

I ran down into the changing room were Backy was being stitched. 'Get Backy ready,' I shouted, 'we need him.' Backy had already been stitched and the medics were covering the wound with a bandage.

'How are you, mate?' I asked him. 'Can you give us five minutes before half-time?'

'Try stopping me' was his reply.

The changing room was like a military hospital at the front line at half-time and our doctor, Simon Kemp, did a superb job to patch everyone up for the start of the second half. I have never seen a team so determined as they jogged on to the field to begin the second half. They were quieter than usual, but the steely resolve in their eyes was unmistakeable. We put the Boks away 29-9. We didn't hide from the challenge that afternoon, nor did we retaliate and lose our self-control as we had against Scotland. Every last one of the England players took the hits, maintained maximum concentration and gave it everything they had. Each one played with every fibre of his body and soul, from the top of his head down to the soles of his feet. This was mental toughness, from 1 to 15.

The game represented an important milestone for me. I felt that we had come of age and nothing could stop us. The trust was there for all to see, it was there in bucketloads, and there was no 'weakest link'. Even now, on occasion I delve into one of my desk drawers at home, and bring out a photograph of Neil Back, his head covered in bandages, blood seeping through even after the repair work, putting his head in where it hurt – two inches from Braam van Straaten's boot as he attempted a drop goal. The oceans do not wait or accept excuses, and neither did Neil Back.

By the time England got to the World Cup in 2003 – with the Springboks the main opposition in our group – I am convinced they were psychologically 'gone' against us. We had absorbed all the physical batterings they could dish out and they had completely forgotten how to score tries against us. We had taken their psyche to pieces and when they again left the field try-less after their 25-6 loss at Subiaco Oval, they had gone fully 286 minutes of game-time and three calendar years without crossing the whitewash against England. That was mental domination.

Defence against Australia was a completely different kettle of fish. The Wallabies didn't have the power and size of South Africa, but they had better balance in their side. Their lineout was of high quality, they had a great open-side flanker in George Smith and they had a number of big multi-skilled backs who could both run and pass, and had the size and power to make an impact at the cleanouts in multi-phase attacks. England had experienced two narrow losses against the Wallabies [11-12 in November 1998 at home, and 15-22 the following June away] and one narrow win [22-19 at Twickenham in November 2000] so they knew they were closely matched.

Clive had introduced another new concept – '20 seconds to score' – before the game against Australia in our 2000 autumn international. Tony Biscombe had shown us clips of how little time was really needed to score a try, and that in turn helped reduce our anxiety in 'catch-up' situations near the end of the match.

The game itself was not a great spectacle, and as the game went into 'added time' the Wallabies were leading 19-15. With less than a minute to go they missed touch and we had one last throw of the dice, and we managed to force the pressure back on to them by carrying strongly into their 22. With Matt Burke up in the line, Iain Balshaw was able to kick down the short-side for Dan Luger to win the desperate race to touch down in the corner at the very last gasp. Wilko duly converted from the touchline, the whistle went and we had won 22-19. The players had embraced both the 'fight pressure with pressure' and '20 seconds to score' concepts and we had won the game by executing them quite clinically.

Australia were also our first opponents in the autumn of 2001, by which time they had changed their coach. Eddie Jones had taken over from World Cup winner Rod Macqueen. In the shape of captain George Gregan and his half-back partner Steve Larkham, they had the most dangerous attacking pair of half-backs in world rugby. Outside of them Matt Burke, Chris Latham, Daniel Herbert, Nathan Grey and Joe Roff were all world-class backs. All of them had experienced rugby league coaching in the junior ranks and instinctively cut intricate angles, supported well and made decisive choices in situations where there were more attackers than defenders.

I had enjoyed some interesting discussions with first Pat Howard and then Rod Kafer – both former Wallabies who enjoyed distinguished spells at Leicester Tigers. They had told me that Eddie Jones's major attacking principle was the 'three minute offence'. His aim was to keep possession and play through structured phases for three minutes, typically with an attacking call between each phase or group of related phases. Eddie knew that any defensive pattern would start to lose its shape if the Wallaby attack was able to keep hold of the ball for longer than three minutes and/or 20 plus phases.

Therefore I invented the 'four minute drill', asking my England players to defend for up to four minutes in one sequence. During the drill there would be no competition for the ball at the breakdown allowed, and the attack would get the ball back immediately whenever they dropped it. We found it demanding for the defence to keep its shape for that period of time, particularly if the opposition generated quick ball.

Initially our defence experienced some problems, particularly when a defender was required to move from one side of the pitch to another across the back of a ruck, so I reduced cross-breakdown running to a bare minimum. From a scrum, our blind-side wing forward would take control of the short-side defence, our open-side wing forward would have a roving role after first phase and endeavour to create as much mayhem as possible in the contact area. Meanwhile our no.8 would defend in midfield. I would try to keep the same structure from lineout but sometimes with the roles of number 6 and number 8 reversed.

Our hooker would defend in the five-metre channel on opposition throws and would shift to the short side from all scrums to defending inside our number 6. After first phase one of the midfield backs [either 10, 12 or 13] would move back across to the short side and extend the line outside 6. This was the only cross-breakdown running that would take place.

Drawing on my experience from rugby league I had created a zonal pattern, which had quicker more agile defenders on each side of the field after second or third phase and prevented mismatches occurring down the sidelines. This was an innovation in union at the time, based on the comparison with league, where there will always be one centre defending on each side of the pitch at all times. Sometimes our two props would defend side by side, but by now our decision-making and communication was sufficiently advanced so that all the props could control the spacings around them intelligently.

Obviously having a back-row of Hill, Back and Dallaglio was a huge asset. All three were world-class players in their own right, but the sum of their parts outweighed even their own individual strengths. As a defensive unit they were by far the best in the world, and I appreciated how lucky I was to work with them. Hilly in particular was never out of the top three tacklers in the side, and in the final and semi-final of the 2003 World Cup he was our top tackler.

We also concentrated on ways of disrupting Australia's attack so that they would not have possession for such long periods. Johnno usually played a big part in our lineout defence. He was our front jumper but if the ball was thrown over his head, as it usually was in our half, he was able to get to the far side of the first ruck – that was a big advantage from a big man starting at the front of the lineout. This created extra defensive numbers if they attacked with the flow [or 'same-way'] so that we would have fast line-speed on second phase with a chance to force them backwards or even to turn them over. Johnno was blessed with good genes thankfully – his mum was a distance runner so he inherited her big engine, and his dad was born in Wigan so he inherited a shrewd football brain!

In the event Australia could not handle our raw power. We were invariably on the front foot and controlled territory and our defence repeatedly turned the Wallabies over or forced penalties at the breakdown. Jonny Wilkinson kicked two splendid drop goals, one off each foot and three penalties to give us a 15-0 lead at half-time. Although the Wallabies came back into it with a couple of second half tries, we kept the scoreboard ticking over and our 21-15 victory was our fourth consecutive win against the southern hemisphere big three.

The side England had beaten was almost identical to the one which had recently squeezed home by the narrowest of margins against the British & Irish Lions, on the last play of the last game in a titanic three-match series – one which has subsequently been acknowledged as one of the highest quality Test series of all time. The only notable absence for Australia from the Lions series was lock John Eales, who had since retired. It was probably no accident that England succeeded where the Lions failed. The strength of the 'Team England' identity had been reluctant to dissolve back into a form [and era] of preparation which most of the England coaches felt languished behind the high standards they had set since the 1999 World Cup.

By the end of 2001, Phil Larder was able to turn over the pages on his flip chart to reveal the following table. The challenge set down, and the long journey begun at the end of the 2000 Six Nations was not complete, but the players had reached their aim ahead of time. They had overtaken the Wallabies as the best defensive team in the world. At the same time, Phil Larder was at last able to shrug off the spectre of sporting inferiority to Australia which had followed him in both codes. He had used the models freely given by the likes of Jack Gibson, and eventually he had surpassed them: 'I never thought that we would achieve the goal so quickly but by the end of 2001 we had the best defence in the world, measured by the fewest tries conceded and average tries given up per game. It was an extraordinary testament to the efforts the players had put in.'

Team	Games played	Tries conceded
England	17	16
Australia	16	19
South Africa	20	27
France	18	33
New Zealand	18	35
Wales	13	31
Ireland	13	35
Scotland	15	48
Argentina	10	38
Italy	14	69

While England had become increasingly confident that they could handle both the Wallabies and the Springboks on defence, there was still something missing: the X-factor, the moments of genius against which no defence in the world could legislate. Against Australia and South Africa in 2000/01, despite the improvements made by Andy Robinson and Brian Ashton, England had only registered four tries in six matches, an average of less than one try per game. It was only in 2002 that England confirmed their attacking potential, with 12 tries in the three autumn internationals against the triumvirate of southern hemisphere superpowers. The missing ingredient, the vital X-factor, was a rugby league full-back-cum-winger named Jason Robinson.

I had felt for some time that we lacked a game-breaker, someone with the 'X factor', a player who would cause defensive coaches like Australian John Muggleton some sleepless nights, just as Jonah Lomu and Brian O'Driscoll had tormented me! Although some pundits in the media [like Stuart Barnes in *The Sunday Times*] had assumed, quite wrongly, that I preferred defensively-minded players as a selector, in fact the reverse was true. As a defensive coach I always looked for players who worried me for their attacking threat, and I transferred that way of thinking into the England selection meetings of which I was part.

Jason Robinson was the answer to the X-factor question. When Clive first informed me of Jason's move from Wigan RL to Sale Sharks, I immediately thought, '*He* could be the final piece of the jigsaw.' Jason was a player who had something really special, the skills to shred the best defensive game-plan to pieces.

I first saw Jason playing scrum-half for Wigan's second team at Central Park against Sheffield Eagles. Anne and I had gone to the game to watch our 17-year-old son Matt make his debut for the Eagles at stand-off. The first time Jason received the ball the crowd roared in expectation as he danced and jinked through the Eagles defence to score. Matt was a great tackler but he could not get a shot on Jason. He shook his head afterwards as he said to me: 'I don't know who that scrum-half is, but he has the fastest feet I have ever seen.' 'Billy Whiz' was just too fast, too smart and too elusive. I went with one expectation and left with another – good as it was to see my son play, I could not get Jason's performance out of my head.

The following day the Wigan coach, John Monie, phoned me to ask my opinion on Jason's best position.

'Bloody hell, John,' I replied, 'you have someone special there. I honestly don't know where I would play him. He is not really a scrum-half but whatever number you put on his back you need to modify your tactics and give him the ball as often as you can.'

'You can bet on that, mate,' was the reply. John finally played him on the wing but encouraged him to come infield as often as possible.

Wigan had a scouting system and a youth policy which was the envy of the league. With no salary cap and Wigan attracting both the highest attendances and the most lucrative sponsorship deals in the league, they had the finances to sign the best players in the world and they proved to be excellent role models for the youngsters pouring out of their academy. Wigan were in the process of becoming the most successful club in the history of rugby league under the stewardship of John Monie, who had been Jack Gibson's second grade coach at Parramatta Eels. There was no doubt about it, Jason had signed for the best of the best.

When I coached Jason in the England and Great Britain teams I quickly realised that he was blessed both with unique evasive skills and the magic ingredient of mental toughness. He was a game-breaker who rose to the occasion and would score tries against the meanest of defences – often when his team needed the points most of all.

Jim Mallinder and Steve Diamond approached the responsibility of coaching Jason at Sale Sharks sensibly, particularly in the first season when he was learning the intricacies of rugby union. I remember watching some of his early games, confidently expecting him to carve up the defence as he had done so expertly in league and being mystified because he appeared to be attracted more to contact than space. I would turn and nudge Jim or Steve in the ribs and say, 'Where is Jason?', and they would reply quietly, 'At the bottom of another ruck.'

When I asked him about it in the clubhouse afterwards, he explained that he wanted to be tackled as many times as possible until he had mastered both the laws and techniques involved in the tackle area. The breakdown was alien to rugby league players and Jason was determined to be its master. There was no way that he would take the easy option. Jason wasn't built that way and he took every step necessary to be a success – falling the right way in contact, movement on the ground to throw off the ball-poachers, accurate placement of the ball.

Whereas at Sale the contact area had been the challenge, at England level it was Jason's kicking game. No-one in league could remember Jason kicking a ball. Not even a chip-and-chase, which is a trademark skill in most wingers. I remember him coming to Welford Road when I was involved with Leicester Tigers. We deliberately kicked behind him and sent a fast four-man chase after the ball knowing that he would retrieve, turn and accept the challenge of beating the chase with ball in hand. We were well-organised and able to stop him in his tracks and Jason would be penalised for not releasing the ball.

Jason understood that he needed to develop his kicking skills in a kick-based game like union and he worked tirelessly with Dave Alred on improving his punting technique. This impressed everyone in the squad, particularly Jonny Wilkinson. I think Wilko recognised a kindred spirit in Jason Robinson. 'DA' did such an outstanding job that Jason was soon kicking competently off both feet. Meanwhile Jonny was so impressed that he asked both Dave Reddin and Steve Black [his trainer and mentor at Newcastle Falcons] to devise obstacle courses to help him to become a more evasive runner. 'Blackie' dutifully came up with a run which had Wilko tiptoeing and dancing for his life between heavy, medieval swinging bags that would have knocked Jonny into the middle of next week, had they made contact. Jason and Jonny inspired each other to reach new heights of excellence and practised for many hours outside the official training periods – the hallmark of all great sportsmen. They were two English backs who would have been accepted without question by the southern hemisphere nations in a composite World XV of the era.

With England progressing well on both sides of the ball, possessors of the best defence in world rugby and reeling off five successive wins against Australia and South Africa up until the end of 2001, there remained only one final obstacle – to prove to everyone else that they were now the best by winning a tournament in which all the premier rugby nations were competing. Welcome to the World Cup, Australia 2003.

Chapter nine

Seeing is believing

IT is 30 March 2003, and only the prospect of a grand slam divides England and Ireland, who have both won their opening four games of the Six Nations tournament this year. The trophy stands figuratively at the halfway point between them as Martin Johnson leads the England team out of the tunnel towards the South Terrace end of the pitch. Behind him, his Leicester club-mate Graham Rowntree glances briefly towards the Havelock Square end before following his captain in the opposite direction. With that glance, the battle lines for the day have already been drawn. There will be no quarter, and as Johnno will later say, 'it was do or die'. The Irish players, who are used to lining up for the national anthems at their lucky South Terrace end, are taken aback that England are already standing in 'their' space. Brian O'Driscoll looks sheepish and there are a few raised voices of complaint as the Irish players shuffle past, so that both teams are now standing to the right of halfway. Out to the left the red carpet stretches away into the distance like forgotten royalty.

The England team has some form for this kind of thing. In 1999, they had occupied Wales' space at Wembley, invading the 'home' changing room and festooning it with their mottos, banners and memorabilia before Wales arrived to find themselves, quite unexpectedly, as the 'away' team. Graham Henry had dismissed it with a wave of the hand and it had concentrated rather than diminished Welsh resolve on the day. Wales won by 32-31.

That was premeditated. In Dublin it is different, it is an unexpected contest of wills and it is the Ireland squad who are starting to look like spare parts. Their team services manager, Ger Carmody, tears up out of nowhere to remonstrate with Martin Johnson, and there is a priceless moment when Carmody gestures 'West' as Johnno points 'East'. A couple of barks from the big man and Carmody is despatched. Johnno turns around to Graham Rowntree and Wiggy grins back at him: 'You're right mate, we can't move now.'

When President Mary McAleese arrives in her smart camel-hair coat to greet the players from both sides, she unexpectedly has to walk through the soft, sticky grass to get to the Ireland team. Martin Johnson and England have won their battle already. As Johnno recalls,

> We had already been warming up at the South Terrace end so we went to stand there for the anthems. You normally stand on the side where you've done your warm-up. But the atmosphere for the game that year was incredible, like no other I'd experienced in Ireland. Normally the Irish lull you into a false sense of security. They spoil you with their hospitality and flatter you in the build-up, sometimes they will even applaud you out of the hotel. 'Sure… you're England, you'll be far too good for us', then they try to take your head off during the game and the crowd [probably including some of those guys who have spoiled you during the week] are in a frenzy, baying for blood. In 2003, there was a hardness to the atmosphere right from the moment we set foot in Ireland, so we hadn't been softened up and were in no mood to accept second best.
>
> If the Ireland boys had stayed where they were [at the Havelock Square end], then President McAleese's shoes would have been on the red carpet all the way. Having said that, if you look at the tape she was quite happy greeting both sets of players and her feet are on the grass all the time, so it was no big deal.
>
> The guy coming out of nowhere to move us on triggered everything, he appeared so suddenly. I told him where to go and BANG! – it was all going off around us, a major diplomatic incident. I looked back at Wig and he just smiled and nodded. At that moment it was a case of 'None of us are going to move, and if anyone does move, I'll kill them.' That's what I told the players out on the field and I'd given them the same message in the changing room – no-one was going to push us around that afternoon.

England entered the game with an attitude far different from the last time they came to Dublin in 2001 with the prospect of a grand slam in front of their noses – or for that matter Murrayfield in 2000 or Wembley 1999. It is Martin Johnson's presence which makes all the difference: 'We had a mindset going into that game that if we win with a deflected drop goal in the ninth minute of injury time, we could be the happiest people in the world, because we just needed to win.' Without Johnno in 2000 and 2001, England did not have the same focus:

> My strongest impression was the influence that Martin Johnson had on the team. Before leading them out on to the field he had said, 'Listen, this is our day. Don't let anyone mess you about. Stay focused, don't let anyone knock you off your game or cause you to lose concentration.'
>
> I think he had been given instructions on where England were supposed to line up before the game. Whether he had turned the wrong way out of the tunnel deliberately, been given the wrong information or misunderstood it, it is all irrelevant. We had arrived at the last match of the Six Nations with a grand slam in our sights on three previous occasions and blown it each time – on the last occasion at Lansdowne Road. Clive Woodward had raised the stakes in the build-up by emphasising that we could not win the World Cup if we did not win the grand slam in the Six Nations tournament in 2003. When Johnno refused to move for the national anthems, he was 100% focused on leading England to a grand slam. He would never have disrespected Ireland or their president intentionally.
>
> Ironically, we had disrespected Ireland two years before, in 2001, when Johnno was injured. The game had been rescheduled to October because of the outbreak of foot-and-mouth disease throughout the UK and Ireland earlier in the year, which also caused the cancellation of the Cheltenham horse-racing festival and the British Rally Championship. Moreover, it was only a couple of months after a Lions tour where many of our players were either injured or in a recovery cycle and looking for form. We had been unable to negotiate any more training days from the clubs and we were undercooked, and we compounded the problem by trying to blow Ireland away right from the start by throwing the ball about all over the park. So our arrogance was right there, reflected in the fact that we had completely forgotten

our foundation belief – that preparation was the key to success, and we adopted the wrong tactics as a result. Ireland gave us exactly what we deserved, there were no two ways about it. They had already played two games against Scotland and Wales and they had firm foundations. They kept the ball tight, kicked for territory and did everything in their power to unsettle us. We forgot our basics, Ireland remembered theirs and we were humbled. It was ever thus in rugby of either code.

If anything can be pleasing in defeat, I was happy that Keith Wood, for whom I'd acquired a great deal of respect on the Lions tour, was the instrument of our downfall. Keith was a warrior, the sort of player you always want on your side when the going gets tough, and he'd peeled around the back of the lineout like a runaway train to score Ireland's try from a close-range lineout in their 20-14 win. It was a big day for Keith. He became the most-capped Irish hooker and eclipsed Tom Kiernan's record for most games as Irish captain. Brian O'Driscoll summed the game up perfectly afterwards: 'Our entire build-up was that it was our turn from among the Celtic nations to stop England from winning the grand slam, as Scotland had done the year before and Wales had done the year before that.'

In 2003 Johnno was determined to make sure that performance was not repeated, and that we built a foundation for victory and played to our strengths. Our forwards gradually got on top, we dominated possession, we played in Ireland's half increasingly, defended strongly and used our superior fitness. We opened the game up and went for the jugular in a final quarter which we won by 29 points to nil.

At the same time, England successfully controlled Brian O'Driscoll, who had become the most potent midfield attacking force in world rugby. England only conceded six points to two penalties in the first period, and nothing at all in the second.

Although on one occasion Mike Tindall lost patience and shot up out of the line and O'Driscoll escaped around the outside, for the most part our plan for handling him was implemented well. I looked at the 'O'Driscoll problem' in connection with the 'O'Gara problem'. Their outside-half Ronan O'Gara was such an accurate kicker of the ball and so astute at controlling territory that I had decided to keep our open-side winger much further back than usual to give him fewer targets. This obviously gave Ireland a numerical advantage when they ran the ball, so the idea was for the defence to hold, content to drift across, link up with our winger and tackle the player who attacked the line. Although this policy did concede some yardage, we were able to implement it because we knew Paul O'Connell would always take the ball off their number 9 on second phase, without any intention of passing. As a result we moved up at speed and gang-tackled him, which then redressed the initial losses, put us on the front foot and back in control. Everything we gave up at first we took back with interest thereafter.

Where Ireland had one Brian O'Driscoll, New Zealand had a number of quality attacking backs in the same sphere of operations as the young Irishman. They had Tana Umaga in the centre, a 10.7 seconds 100 metres sprinter in Dougie Howlett on the right wing, and the monster that was Jonah Lomu on the left. Orchestrating all the pyrotechnics was one of most talented, if flaky ball-playing number 10s of his generation, Auckland's Carlos Spencer, at first five-eighth. By the end of 2002, although England knew they had the measure of the Wallabies and Springboks having beaten them on seven consecutive occasions, the All Blacks remained the great unknown.

England hadn't played New Zealand since the 1999 World Cup group game and they had yet to beat them in five attempts in the Clive Woodward era. They had lost those matches by an average score of 37-16 and they had conceded an average of 4.6 tries per game while doing so. As always with international rugby in the professional era, New Zealand was to prove the ultimate test of England's World Cup winning aspirations.

The first game of the 2002 autumn series was against New Zealand. We had not played the All Blacks since putting together a string of 15 consecutive victories at Twickenham after our 1999 World Cup defeat at their hands. During the last two years New Zealand had scored 75 tries in the 18 Test matches they had played against the ten best teams in the world at an average of over four tries per game. That was 21 more tries than we had scored in the same period. However, since they had also conceded 35 tries [more than twice as many as us], there was a counter-weight to the argument and we went into the game with bags of confidence.

As was Clive's way, he wanted to run the ball at every opportunity and fight fire with fire. I wasn't sure this was the best policy given that New Zealand had a pack of forwards who could all handle the ball in addition to some outstanding backs. Carlos Spencer usually pushed the game and at times he had magic in his hands, they had accurate, clinical passers and – in the shape of wingers Jonah Lomu and Doug Howlett – they had try-scorers with both the power and speed to finish moves. The All Blacks were dynamic in the contact area and they reacted decisively off turnover ball, penetrating quickly before the opposition defence had time to reorganise.

Although we began the game strongly, taking a 6-0 lead off two Jonny Wilkinson penalties, New Zealand gave notice of the threat they would pose by scoring the first try. Jonah Lomu had already barged up the middle from a scrum close to our goal-line before he scored in the corner off a lineout from much the same position. The All Blacks moved the ball wide with two decoy runners in midfield and we couldn't stop Jonah tumbling over near the corner flag. Although there was a suggestion that Mike Tindall had prevented the great man from grounding the ball properly, the try was awarded by referee Jonathan Kaplan nonetheless.

We showed some ambition of our own and had the crowd on their feet when we launched an attack from our own 22 with forwards Trevor Woodman, Steve Thompson and Richard Hill inter-passing in a breakout that went for over half the length of the field. We were determined to demonstrate that we could play some 15-man rugby as well!

Although Wilko dropped a goal to regain the lead in the 28th minute [see https://www.youtube.com/watch?v=kFctRUpALko], New Zealand quickly responded with their second try of the game. Tana Umaga finally intercepted a Richard Hill pass after both sides had their chances and Dougie Howlett simply ran away from our cover defence, Jason Robinson and all, to score. The try had come from a situation where we tried to 'fight fire with fire' and run turnover ball out of our 22, but as the game wore on it became clear that neither our ball retention nor our handling were quite up to New Zealand's clinical standard.

On the other hand, the pressure we were exerting was forcing the Kiwis to concede penalties. The penalty count late in the first half was 6-1 in our favour and two further goals from the boot of Jonny brought the score back to 12-14. Lewis Moody then scored our first try on the stroke of half-time after James Simpson-Daniel and Jonny Wilkinson had probed a short side defended only by forwards. Five minutes after the break, the change of shirts at half-time again did the trick after we had broken out from a turnover near our own 22. Simpson-Daniel made another break and with their full-back Ben Blair caught at the bottom of the next ruck, Jonny was able to chip the ball delicately over the line and collect it unchallenged for a try under the posts. When a strong tackle by substitute Ben Johnston a few minutes later dislodged the ball and Ben Cohen raced away to score, our lead had moved out to 31-14 and it looked very much like 'game over'.

New Zealand had other ideas. A strong All Black lineout drive from outside our 22 took play all the way up to the goal-line, and Lomu scored his second try after the combination of a loop in midfield by Andrew Mehrtens and a decoy run outside him had given the big man a one-on-one with Mike Tindall. As strong a tackler as Mike was, he was never going to win that contest! New Zealand had used a similar move in the 11th minute of the first half to break us on second phase from lineout, with their scrum-half Steve Devine running around a pivot and a blocker outside the loop providing interference on the cover defence.

Another rampaging run by Lomu down the left sideline set up New Zealand for a wide attack off an Andrew Mehrtens cut-out pass and only desperate defence near our own line saved us. Then their number 8 Sam Broomhall went through a gap after another 'loop with decoy' off Mehrtens from a lineout in the 71st minute. The dam had to break and it did on the very next phase, with their scrum-half Danny Lee scuttling through the middle of the defence to score to the right of our posts. The gap had closed to only three points at 31-28, and we had to acknowledge that New Zealand had all the momentum in their favour. It was time to dig in.

With less than five minutes to play Clive threw on Austin Healey as a replacement. I knew Ozzie's game really well from my days at Welford Road and felt that he was unlucky not to have been given more game time with England. I bounded down the steps three at a time to offer some support when I realised that Clive was putting Oz on the right wing for 'Sinbad' [James Simpson-Daniel].

'Ozzie, be quick mate you're on,' I shouted in his ear. 'About bloody time!' he replied, 'I'm freezing my nuts off here.'

As he took his tracksuit off he looked at me: 'Where Phil?... scrum-half?' 'No Ozzie, wing... right wing.' I gave him a long look as I let the information drip down.

'Bloody hell! Up against Lomu?'

'You will be fine,' I said. 'Back yourself, get in close, hit him hard and low and keep your legs pumping.'

New Zealand were awarded a lineout on the opposite side of the pitch on their 40-metre line as Austin trotted on to the pitch. I expected them to fire the ball across the field to give Lomu a one-on-one with a substitute who had not yet acclimatised to the pace of the game. Oz was obviously thinking the same thing but unfortunately, the All Blacks were not. On this occasion they used Lomu as a decoy angled into midfield, and for one split second Oz was caught looking in at him, with his shoulders turned slightly to the inside. Oz had 'planted' his feet and that was all New Zealand needed to spring Dougie Howlett free on an arc outside him, with their full-back Blair flying up in support.

The spectators watching the overlap materialise must have thought the game was lost – and I have to say that opinion was shared by everyone in the England coaching box, as headsets were thrown down and hands covered faces... But I was still Mister Cool, because I knew that defending this kind of situation was an integral part of our preparation, it was something we had trained for. Howlett did his part, drawing our full-back Jason Robinson and timing his pass perfectly to give Blair a run to the corner – but Jason stepped into Howlett and put him on the ground to take him out of the support play. This was critical, because as Blair surged for the corner our one remaining cover defender, left wing Ben Cohen, came into his view on a perfect angle to prevent any inside swerve or step inside. With Howlett out of play, the two players closest to the man with the ball both wore the white of England. Blair's only option was to pin his ears back and go for the flag, but Ben Cohen bundled him into touch and then bear-hugged him as if to say, 'No way mate – you're mine.'

The fire had been put out only one metre from our goal-line with less than two minutes left to play…

Even then, New Zealand manufactured one last throw of the dice from a lineout only five metres from our line. You could hear the proverbial pin drop as Ben Kay followed Ali Williams's backpedal every step of the way to get in front and steal the throw majestically.

Oz came up to me after the game and apologised for being drawn out of position, but I told him not to worry because I would have made the same error in those circumstances. 'Yeah Phil, but I am a better player than you were,' he replied with a cheeky grin. Some people must always have the last word!

I felt that Andy Robinson's DNA was also all over the England performance. He had blended the forward pack into a dominant force and improved the team's ability at the contact area, but more than that he had encouraged the specialist coaches to take full control of their own areas of responsibility. The coaching team was a far happier unit because of his presence in it and was now giving maximum return.

At the same time, I was also aware that John Mitchell, the coach whom Andy had replaced, was in charge of a very special squad of players. I now understood that New Zealand would present the biggest threat to England at the World Cup. They had cut our defence to pieces at times, with the ease and precision of a surgeon's knife, and that was something I would have to address.

But when all was said and done, I felt that those who claimed we had struggled to defeat a weakened New Zealand team were missing the point. This was a full international, New Zealand had put out their strongest available team and we could only beat what was in front of us. England won, New Zealand lost, and our winning sequence of wins against the southern hemisphere had continued. That was the whole of the story, and it didn't need any qualifications or 'What ifs?'

The reaction to England's win in the media was muted. New Zealand were missing 12 of the players who had started their final game of the 2002 Tri-Nations tournament, including their captain Reuben Thorne, their entire first-choice forward pack and other game-changers like full-back Christian Cullen, scrum-half Justin Marshall and open-side flanker Richie McCaw. As Robert Kitson put it in his newspaper article in *The Guardian*, 'Even Clive Woodward, England's head coach, wore the look of a general whose troops had just launched an all-out assault yet gained only a few muddy yards of no-man's land.' Although the reaction in the press was understandable, it underestimated England's new-found resolve and mental toughness under fire, which was precisely the quality they had been accused of lacking in the key moments when losing three grand slam deciders. Now they had it, and it was here to stay.

As Robert Kitson also observed, the game had come down to two plays by the 'big Bens', Cohen and Kay, which perfectly exemplified both that mental toughness and the depth of our preparation. Ben Kay's lineout steal in the last seconds of the game was a result of detailed analysis by Simon Hardy, with input from Ben Kay himself and under the overall gaze of Andy Robinson. Simon would begin to study the opposition lineout nine days before the game itself, adding in any new developments or information as he went. Without an outstanding aerial athlete in the England back-row, and with Neil Back's principal responsibility to defend the area underneath Jonny Wilkinson, the defensive lineout formation evolved as a '3-3-1' – two pods of three with Neil Back playing 'loose' at the tail:

{1-Johnno-3}…{6-Ben Kay-8}…7.

Occasionally Ben Kay would slide back in between Lawrence Dallaglio and Neil Back, but only on the understanding that Backy would leave him in the care of the front lifter in mid-air in order to honour his defensive commitments.

As Simon Hardy recalls,

> If the opposition wanted ball off the top we would compete, but in our own 22 the contest would be restricted to one jumper. This would usually be Ben Kay because he was the best at reading where the ball was going. So in the 2002 autumn international against New Zealand, Ben competed right at the death because the ball went to the middle/back of the line, but if they had thrown to the front we would have stayed on terra firma and defended the drive instead. It was a small but critical detail on which the result of the whole game may have hinged.
>
> Johnno and Ben were automatic choices by the time the World Cup spun around in 2003. Of course Johnno was the best in the world in his position, but Ben was an excellent complement to him. They played at Welford Road together and were used

to each other, and Ben had a very calm and reassuring presence about him [especially at the pressure lineouts] to which the other forwards responded positively. I would have Tony Biscombe's camera plugged into my laptop so that I could analyse calls and patterns of calling as the game went along, and then relay the right messages on to the field to Ben.

There is no doubt we benefited immeasurably from having Phil Vickery standing at number 3 in the line. This was an important position [especially on our throw] because the lifter would have to go 'two ways' – as back lift for the man in front of him, and as front lift for the receiver behind. Phil was what the Americans call a 'quick study' and he was an exceptional reader of lineout situations, while at 6ft 3in he could jack the jumper a long way up in the air and hold him there. There was a lot of banter about who was really winning the ball: I would review one of Ben's steals on tape and Phil would point at the screen and say, 'But who's holding him up there?' with a big grin on his face.

We were always looking for little ways to improve, and the addition of Sherylle Calder as the 'spatial awareness' coach before the 2003 World Cup had an unexpected fringe benefit. I always spent time in preparation trying to work out the opponent's calling system via the 'ref mike'. We had the Springboks in our group and their lineout caller Victor Matfield would call in Afrikaans, a language which was beyond me but in which Sherylle, as a native South African, was fluent. So Sherylle taught Ben the Afrikaans numbers from 1 to 10 and when he passed through the language barrier he found that Victor's lineout calls were very simple. That enabled us to win two or three balls in our group game against the Boks by knowing the target space where the ball was going to be thrown.

If it was another example of small details making an impact on the overall outcome of the game, it was also a very useful way of getting under South African skins and instilling self-doubt in their psyche, because the lineout is the area of the game on which South Africa prides itself. With Martin Johnson moving to jump against the throw at the tail of short lineouts on the previous summer tour and relatively late on in his career, it gave us a priceless advantage in the 'critical non-essentials' of the lineout in the lead-up to the World Cup. Johnno's ability to counter-jump against the Wallabies' 'walk-in' five-man lineout in the 2003 final was vital to our ability to stop Australia attacking with tempo from an uncontested set piece.

I think the introduction of Andy Robinson to the coaching group was important from my point of view. Although I had a decent working relationship with John Mitchell, Mitch always had a very clear idea of what he wanted and there was not much elbow-room for discussion.

He was not a great delegator and Robbo was far more inclusive – he would always be prepared to debate the options with you. We'd worked together before for Bath and it was Andy who had first asked me to coach the throwers with the England 'A' team that he coached. Andy, Ben and myself would liaise before the game to discuss our lineout options, then Robbo and I would have a private meeting before selection to make sure we were on the same page and gave very clear advice in the selection meeting itself.

Clive Woodward brought us all together, and I think his realisation that he could be the best manager in the world was a brave and essential step forward. Clive was highly innovative and had the ability to combine everyone's skill sets and dovetail them into the big picture – the 'crossword effect' if you like. He also understood that, in order to be potential World Cup winners, we had to have at least six players in our team who were the best in the world in their positions. Clive was also very sympathetic in terms of bringing our families into the environment. In 2003 I slept away from home for more than 200 nights, so that was vital to my sanity!

My favourite player was our hooker Steve Thompson. 'Thommo' was an ex-back-row forward so he added something special to both our attack and defence. His throwing was effective but needed management, and playing on the ovals often seen in Australia created extra problems for him because of the disorientating effect. So he required lots of practice to create more 'feel' and maintain his rhythm. He probably made more throwing repetitions in a week's training than Wilko did kicks at goal – and that is saying something… When he came up to me before the presentation of the World Cup and shook my hand and said 'Simon, I don't think I would have made it without you', it meant everything in the world to me.

New Zealand still loomed as the big challenge to be met before the World Cup began in earnest in October 2003, and the challenge materialised as early as England's tour of Australasia in June. The challenge was further brought into focus by the absence of Brian Ashton, who had left the England coaching group for the calmer, more educational waters of the National Academy after the 20-15 loss to France in the 2002 Six Nations. England had been struggling to score tries against the countries who'd adopted rugby league-type defences. Although they scored two tries in defeat, Yorkshireman Dave Ellis had been brought in from rugby league by Bernard Laporte and he had fashioned the France defence on similar league principles to Phil Larder's own.

Brian Ashton had some domestic issues at the time which probably intensified the fragility, rather than the toughness inherent in his temperament. A couple of the senior players who had been coached by Brian at Bath, Mike Catt and Mike Tindall, were convinced that England's chances of winning the World Cup were following Brian Ashton out of the door. In Phil Larder's view, fine coach and educator that he was, Brian Ashton was struggling to move with the times as more and more international sides adopted defences with rugby league principles underpinning them.

> Brian definitely developed the players' ability to play 'heads-up' rugby, of that there is no doubt. He could teach them how to spot weaknesses in a defence and attack them. The players themselves enjoyed his coaching sessions and he was an energising force as a result.
>
> However, in my opinion Brian did not understand how rugby league-type defences were constructed and therefore had little idea of how to break them down. It was one thing 'seeing the space' and picking off relatively static northern hemisphere tight forwards trying to defend huge line spacings up until 2001. But when Wales employed Clive Griffiths, Ireland Mike Ford and France Dave Ellis after the Lions tour, those spaces and the easy mismatches began to disappear and the defensive lines became far more disciplined.
>
> Graham Henry would spend many hours on the 2001 Lions trip with me, learning how a league-style defence was built and the essential foundations which the attack had to destabilise in order to be successful. He saw that a whole new set of attacking

solutions were needed, but I didn't feel Brian had made the same recognition and as a result his attacking ideas didn't 'grow with the modern game', as for instance both Graham's and Wayne Smith's did when they returned to New Zealand. The result was that I felt our attack, in international terms, was treading water.

The absence of an attacking coach in the short term reinforced the pressure on Phil Larder's defence to pick up the slack. New Zealand's wrap-around plays had caused problems at Twickenham and Phil was aware that he had to tighten up this area of defence before the Test match in Wellington.

Carlos Spencer had created uncertainty in our defensive line by passing to the second receiver [usually the Kiwi number 12] and then running round him. Once he received the return pass he either passed to a runner or attacked the defensive line himself. New Zealand wanted the opposition defence to wedge in, thereby creating numbers for their fast and elusive backs on the outside. The safest way to defend dangerous plays like this was for the defence to 'hold' whilst the move was being executed and then simply tackle whoever received the ball. This was too passive for my liking. Spencer was probably the most dangerous and creative attacker in world rugby if given space, so I wanted to see how he handled the pressure that a fast line-speed would bring.

Therefore my improvement – and the next counter-play in the intellectual warfare that international coaches wage against their key opponents – was for the defender marking Spencer to accelerate across field and destroy the pivot as soon as Spencer passed to him. The idea was that the defender marking the pivot would then be released to author a 'king hit' on Spencer as he came round the corner to complete the loop. We christened the play 'Shift'.

There was however a problem. Throughout my coaching career I had always asked myself 'What if?' in order to visualise all the eventualities. What if Spencer realised what we were doing, dropped off a couple of metres and executed the move from a deeper position? Our two aggressive defenders would be unable to make their tackles before the loop was completed. This would leave Spencer with ample support and running at a fractured line, which was certainly asking for trouble.

So we had a choice to make between the two calls – 'Shift' and 'Hold' – but we still needed a defender in the right position, and with the vision to make it. The obvious answer was Kyran Bracken as the sweeper behind the line, but we found that he was too far back to read the play quickly enough.

The only sensible solution was for the player marking Spencer to make the call. As this could be a number of different players depending on the situation, Clive extended the main Wednesday training session to give me an extra ten minutes, but the feeling we were entering the unknown persisted.

As usual, the local weather prediction was for very strong winds with squally rain, and both were scheduled to appear during the game. The round, flat shape of the 'Cake Tin' stadium was both susceptible to the gales blowing in off the Cook Strait, and whipped up the winds inside it into an unpredictable, cyclonic swirl that made life very difficult for kickers. It was no surprise that the Super Rugby franchise based on the Wellington provincial side had been christened 'The Hurricanes' as a result.

The other significant 'uncontrollable' factor was the refereeing appointment of Stuart Dickinson, a late replacement for his fellow Australian Peter Marshall. Dickinson had issued the most yellow cards of any referee in the current Super Rugby season and he was especially hawkish at the breakdown. The scene was therefore set for a stop-start game with a heavy emphasis on the quality of the kicking game, both off the ground and out of hand.

Right from the start we pressurised Carlos Spencer, whom we felt did not possess the same mental toughness as our own Jonny Wilkinson, and Ben Kay charged down his clearing punt from the opening kick-off. We were awarded a penalty which Jonny Wilkinson goaled to give us the lead. Spencer went on to miss a kickable penalty in the eighth minute and four others in the course of the game, so that part of the plan worked well.

The referee was a different matter. He started by awarding eight penalties within the first 15 minutes of the game and by the end of the half he had awarded 19, with England definitely on the wrong end of his decisions. We conceded 14 penalties to New Zealand's five and most of those occurred at the breakdown. By the start of the second half both teams were on a yellow card warning for repeated infringements in the same area.

With Jonny kicking into a hurricane and our hooker Steve Thompson having problems mastering both the swirling wind and the disorienting effect of the oval-shaped pitch on his lineout throwing [we were losing the lineouts by 11 to 2 at half-time], we found it impossible to either win or maintain ball and were committed to defending in our own end for long periods in that first 40 minutes.

The wind got so bad that both Wilko and Spencer required a team-mate to hold the ball securely in place when kicking for goal. Even then, you could see the ball wavering on the tee as the kicker approached it! I was surprised that New Zealand only used their signature loop/decoy play once in the first half, given all the problems it had caused us at Twickenham. As soon as they did call it in the 22nd minute [https://www.youtube.com/watch?v=ZGDivBtzfMM] off a lineout deep in our own 22, we were in trouble.

Spencer wrapped around his second five-eighth Tana Umaga and got the ball back just as the decoy [13 Ma'a Nonu] crashed down taking out both our centres. Spencer moved the ball on to Joe Rokocoko in the hole that been created but 'Smokin' Joe's' pass wasn't accurate enough and it checked their left wing Caleb Ralph. This meant that our cover defence of Jason Robinson and Josh Lewsey was still in play and able to stop Ralph near the corner flag.

It was one of three clean breaks New Zealand made, but failed to convert in the first period. First Spencer broke free from a midfield scrum on our own 22 after Kyran Bracken had followed round to the base and took himself out of the defensive line. I immediately sent on a message to Kyran to make an adjustment in our scrum defence, after Will Greenwood had put out the fire with an interception near our own goal-line. Only a minute-and-a-half later, we rashly tried to run the ball out of our 22 to relieve the growing pressure and lost the ball. Fortunately for us, Ralph received the ball and failed to make it to the corner for the second time.

I didn't understand why New Zealand didn't take us on again with their wrap-around/decoy play, which had achieved such a high success rate previously. For some reason they preferred to direct their attack down the inside of Spencer with a series of drop-off plays and inside passes. This played directly into our hands because our defence in that area was one of our great strengths. As I scratched my head in bewilderment, I thought to myself: 'Whichever coach has devised their attacking strategy has given Carlos and his team the wrong information.'

I felt we had done extremely well to reach half-time at 6-6, given the All Blacks' total domination of the lineout, penalty count, territory and possession. Deep down, I wondered whether we would be able to hang on in there in the last quarter of the game. Defending uses up far more energy than attacking, and the massive pressure of having to defend for so long on our own line would have been mentally draining. The impact would be compounded by the fatigue of a long season which tended to leave even supremely fit international players 'playing from memory' on a summer tour. So it both surprised and delighted me to hear all the talk from the players in the shed. It was all so positive, all about their pride and determination in keeping the winning sequence alive and maintaining momentum. There was no mention of holding on, it was all about going out and giving it to the All Blacks. 'We are fitter and better than them... so let's go out and do it!' was Johnno's parting shot as they charged back out and on to the pitch. Their conviction was complete.

The second half started exactly on that note, with surging hit-ups by both Lol [who had an outstanding game and completely overshadowed his opposite number] and Johnno taking play into the New Zealand half and forcing a penalty out of the All Blacks. Wilko again converted superbly from 40 metres out and we were back in the lead at 9 points to 6. However, in the 46th minute the inevitable finally happened and we were the first to slip off the refereeing 'ledge'. Stuart Dickinson's general warning materialised as not one, but two yellow cards for us. Backy, who had defended superbly and set a wonderful example throughout, was sent to the bin for one breakdown infringement too many – to be swiftly followed by Lawrence only a couple of minutes later! Not only were we down to 13 men, we were missing two key defenders and two specialists in slowing down ball at the contact point.

New Zealand reacted immediately to Neil's absence, and we were turned over as we tried to pass the ball across field. New Zealand countered decisively and with our three-quarters in or around the contact area Spencer was able to round Johnno on the far side and carry the ball deep into the 22. New Zealand always reacted quickly to turnover ball and this was no exception. A black tide flooded deep into our 22, and it looked like our sea-wall had to crumble when they were awarded a penalty and put down a series of scrums only five metres from our goal-line. Once, twice, three times the eight-man Kiwi pack attempted to drive our six men – Graham Rowntree, Steve Thompson, Phil Vickery, Martin Johnson, Ben Kay and Richard Hill – over the line. Three times they were repulsed by fair means or foul, and the grip was finally broken when Rodney Soio'alo was penalised for a double movement after taking a tapped penalty rather than resetting another scrum. Back to seven men, our pack immediately forced a penalty on the All Black feed and Wilko, whose kicking for goal had been magnificent throughout, made another goal from the touchline to boost our lead to 12-6. It was fast becoming a heroic performance.

With numbers now even, we extended our lead out beyond one score, to 15-6 after Lol had won a turnover near the New Zealand 22 and we went through seven phases, including one tremendous charge by Phil Vickery before Jonny dropped a goal from in front of the posts. As it turned out we really needed that nine-point cushion because the All Blacks scored the only try of the game almost immediately. We won a ball against the Kiwi lineout throw, which was an event in itself, and Jonny hoisted a bomb into midfield without pre-calling it. All of our three-quarters chased the ball, including Ben Cohen who had appeared outside Wilkinson expecting to hit the ball up in midfield. As soon as Josh Lewsey and Jason Robinson made the first two tackles on the kick return we were in dire straits, because the player who would have been covering at the back [Ben Cohen] was already out of play. There was nobody home and Carlos Spencer knew it. He pumped a long kick downfield and there was no way that Lawrence Dallaglio, who was covering valiantly, could match Dougie Howlett and Ralph stride for stride. Howlett duly scored and suddenly it was 15-13 with the conversion. Although television replays showed that both Howlett and Ralph were marginally in front of Spencer before he kicked the ball, I felt New Zealand deserved the points because they had read the situation so well. We were quite simply out-thought on the play and the seven-pointer was fully deserved.

Although New Zealand fought to the very end of the match, just as they had done at Twickenham, Howlett's try proved to be the last score of the game. In the changing room afterwards, thoughts raced through my head quicker than I could track them – a deep sense of gratitude towards the two Daves, Alred and Reddin, who prepared a side that could defend for 85–90 minutes and a kicker who could bisect the posts in the most adverse of conditions, whatever the pressure... an even deeper sense of admiration for a set of players who could pull off a defensive performance like that while enduring the mental fatigue of defending for such sustained periods near our own posts, and at the end of an over-long season. I congratulated each and every one of them and I meant it.

The game had been played in conditions similar to the grand slam match of 2000 against Scotland, and on this occasion we had adapted to them far better than our opponents. Our leaders had made more correct decisions in the heat of battle than New Zealand, and as a result England had played and beaten the All Blacks on their own soil for only the second time in our history. The previous occasion was 30 years previously, back in 1973. I believe our leadership was superior to New Zealand's at that time, and I also believe that both sides knew it at the end of that game in the 'Cake Tin'.

Yes, we could play a lot better and we knew we would need to, in order to stand a real chance of winning the World Cup a few months later. But we had won, and we had shown we had the mental toughness to win in adversity, against our most dangerous opponents. That was after all, the sole object of the exercise – wasn't it?

After the excitement of the match had died down and the immediate reactions had washed away, the more observant critics realised what had been accomplished. John Mitchell acknowledged that England's victory had given them a definite psychological advantage in the tournament to come.

The vice-captain of the New Zealand team, Tana Umaga, summed it up best when he said: 'The people in New Zealand should respect them for what they have done. What else do they have to do? It's what teams do that counts, not what they say, and these guys are doing it all. They have something that travels the world with them wherever they play. They are what we are striving to be… They know their game-plan, they all believe in it, and their defence on Saturday was one of the best I've seen. They've beaten us twice in a row and they operate like a club side playing week in, week out.'

At the same time, Phil Larder realised that the New Zealand puzzle was not one that England had yet solved, despite their two consecutive wins. Compared to Australia, New Zealand had the more dangerous playing personnel but the Wallabies were a better-coached and selected team.

Fortunately, the All Blacks had some issues of their own with selection for the 2003 World Cup, with experienced Test players like Jonah Lomu, Andrew Mehrtens, Christian Cullen, Anton Oliver and Taine Randell seen as surplus to requirements – leaving the average age of the squad at 25 years old, and under the relatively inexperienced captaincy of flanker Reuben Thorne.

Certainly Graham Henry felt, upon taking over as All Black coach after the World Cup, that the most immediate issue to be addressed was that of the brittle leadership layer, in which New Zealand were depending far too heavily on a couple of individuals in the shape of scrum-half Justin Marshall and centre Tana Umaga. Marshall and Umaga were the only All Blacks with more than 50 caps to their name at the start of the 2003 World Cup, and one of them was absent for the crucial semi-final against the Wallabies. When Graham Henry finally led New Zealand to World Cup glory in 2011 there would be nine players with over 50 caps, and two players in Richie McCaw and full-back Mils Muliaina with almost one hundred [97]. But it took eight long years to get there.

In the event England put all their technical issues – the lineout, the kicking game and above all their discipline after conceding 18 penalties at Wellington – to rights on the very next weekend, in a win which ranks as the pinnacle, in terms of performance quality, that England achieved during the Woodward years.

> It was a relief to play under a closed roof at the Telstra Dome in Melbourne after the extreme weather conditions at Wellington. Neil Back – probably our most down-to-earth squad member – could feel a special performance in the air and he was right. We proved all the critics wrong – or at least those only capable of seeing the same characteristics in *this* England side that they saw in *every* England team.

We announced our intentions after only five minutes of play, with a 14-phase, 15-man attack from lineout producing a try for Will Greenwood and that set the tone for the rest of a half where we threw the critics' jibes back in their faces. We played a brand of adventurous rugby that even the best defence in the southern hemisphere was powerless to oppose.

Our second try on the half-hour mark was built off a slick peel by the forwards, with Johnno rolling around the tail off a catch by Richard Hill, and Lol's inside pass springing Trevor Woodman through a half-gap. With the Wallaby back-row out of play and their defence contracted in midfield, it was 'quick hands' – or should I say 'dream hands' – right on the gain line, by first Jonny Wilkinson, then Steve Thompson and finally Will Greenwood setting Mike Tindall free on a scoring run to the corner. When he touched down 'Tinds' still had Josh Lewsey, Jason Robinson and Ben Cohen all unmarked outside him, so clinical had been our build-up play. It was a special moment.

We were leading at half-time by 12 points to 3 and were controlling both territory and possession in a way we had failed to do at Wellington. Our lineout problems were a thing of the past with Thommo addressing his issues on an oval, and that gave us a platform for the drive. At one point we rolled them back all of 40 metres, all the way back to their own goal-line before just failing to convert via a Wilkinson cross-kick into the Aussie in-goal area.

Although Australia came back strongly in the second half, Ben Cohen scored our third try after 65 minutes after another lineout drive, from one of our banker starter plays. Will Greenwood pulled away to the outside and Ben came through like a steam engine on to a short ball from Wilko, split the Wallaby centres and rounded full-back Chris Latham to score. Although the Aussies played to the final whistle, as they always do, the final score was 14-25 and I felt we had made our point.

As Bob Dwyer, the Australian World Cup-winning coach of 1991, said after the game, Martin Johnson had been a 'colossus'. He made 15 hit-ups during the game as a whole, and at one stage carried four times in the first 10 minutes, getting up off the ground after one surge to carry again on the following phase. He was third in the tackle count, top of the ruck cleanouts and at the epicentre of the driving maul. It was the work rate expected of an elite rugby league forward. Dwyer also observed the depth of leadership within the side with all of Johnno, Neil Back, Lawrence Dallaglio, Jonny Wilkinson, Kyran Bracken and Phil Vickery having captained the side on previous occasions – it was the exact opposite of the situation within the All Blacks at the time.

He went on to note the exceptional skill, speed and footwork of England's front-row forwards Woodman, Thompson and Vickery, considering them 'four times more effective than their opposite numbers' – and of course Thommo was able to relax and enjoy his work in the open field knowing that his lineout throwing basics were now solid. Bob Dwyer praised the number of involvements of wings Jason Robinson and Ben Cohen in midfield. Above all, what impressed him was England's awareness in contact situations: 'Each player has a whole checklist of options. If he is taken low, he pops the ball up. If he is taken high, he gets the drive on until he feels the support. If he goes to ground, he lays the ball back on a plate. The result is constant pressure on the defence.'

According to Dwyer, England were probably 'the first team in rugby history that can attack through all 15 players'. In the process the last ghost, the failure of northern hemisphere sides to win down under, had been exorcised, and it had been exorcised in style.

> We had achieved something that most people thought was impossible. We were the first England team to beat Australia on home soil. We had defeated Australia and New Zealand home and away in the space of six months, and had defeated the three Tri-Nations teams on ten consecutive occasions. We had finally won the grand slam in the Six Nations tournament and recorded 21 consecutive home victories. We were ranked as the number one team in the world and the bookmakers had us as favourites to win the World Cup. It was the players I was most pleased for. They were the gladiators in the arena, the ones who had to endure and enjoy the greatest pressure, and now the winning habit was in their DNA.

Chapter ten

The last thousand feet

TRUE climbers never 'conquer' the mountain they have successfully ascended. There is too much respect for the process through which the ascent has been accomplished – and too much awareness of potential disasters at every turn, given a slight tweak of circumstances. As if to underline this reality, the final few hundred feet of the world's most imposing climbs are often the most difficult.

During the golden age of mountain climbing in the 1950s, a British party led by Charles Evans made the first successful ascent of the Himalayan peak of Kangchenjunga, at 28,169 feet the third-highest mountain in the world. Kangchenjunga has five separate summits, but none are approachable directly. The final thousand feet is a vertical pyramid of rock and ice, defended by the constant threat of mudslides, avalanches and seasonal monsoons. During one morning before the 1955 expedition set out from their base camp, summit climber George Band looked up at the top of the mountain and counted 48 avalanches in the space of one three-hour period. Charles Evans himself knew the truth of the last thousand feet only too well. He had gotten to within 300 feet of the summit of Mount Everest in 1953 before being forced to turn back. It was only three days later that Edmund Hillary and Tenzing Norgay sealed the 'conquest' and walked into history, although Hillary significantly refused to be photographed by Tenzing at the summit.

A 24-year-old Lancastrian plumber by the name of Joe Brown was one of the potential summit climbers in Evans's party in 1955. After a couple of failed initial attempts to climb the final few hundred feet, Brown led the way up a sheer, overhanging face to find himself near the top of the mountain. He stopped five feet short of the actual summit, in accordance with Charles Evans's agreement with local Sikkim leaders that the party would only go as high as they needed to verify their claim that they had climbed Kangchenjunga, and no further. The highest point of the mountain itself was still sacred to the mountain gods, and therefore remained inviolate.

The feeling of humility did not just happen by prior agreement, it was Joe Brown's real emotion upon reaching the top: 'I didn't feel like I'd conquered the mountain. I don't know why people use the word conquered – it's such a stupid word. You never conquer a mountain. You either reach the top if you're lucky, or if the weather's bad you've had it. When I reached the summit my overwhelming feeling was relief that I didn't have to keep going up.' The tradition of stopping short of the actual summit has been emulated by every climbing party since Brown and Band.

For the England rugby union team of 2003, all the goals they had set themselves had been achieved. They were ranked the number one side in the world according to the new IRB rankings, and as Clive Woodward had said to the squad, 'We have achieved our objectives. We are ranked the number one team in the world, and we fear no-one. The World Cup is in our hands. If we perform at our best, no-one can beat us.'

Phil Larder's defence moreover, had fulfilled its pledge to become the best in the world for three consecutive seasons:

Nation	Games Played	Tries Conceded
England	31	33
Australia	33	51
New Zealand	35	58
France	36	64
South Africa	37	79
Ireland	28	73
Scotland	28	81
Argentina	19	55
Wales	28	86
Italy	22	106

Only the final ascent up to the top of the mountain remained – and the humility needed to achieve it was fully realised. Phil Larder had it in mind to repeat the same exercise, and therefore complete the cycle that he had started back in 1997, with individual defenders trying to tackle attackers in a narrow corridor, one-on-one. This was the point at which England had started, psychologically speaking, at ground-zero seven years previously:

> It was the final training session before we were due to fly out to Australia for the World Cup. I had decided to complete our preparation with the identical drill that I had used the first time that I had coached the team, before the South Africa match at Twickenham in 1997.
>
> The players had improved considerably since then so I increased the pressure on each defender by widening the corridor, and the space in which the ball-carrier had to work by one full metre. Between 1997 and 2003 the ball-carriers had also improved their footwork and were far more powerful, so the exercise was now much more difficult than it had been.
>
> I was delighted with the results. Back in 1997 none of the defenders had successfully made all their tackles, and the average success rate was below 50% overall. Seven years later, 28 of the 30-man squad completed all their tackles successfully, with two players missing one and two tackles respectively. Every member of the squad would be urging the defender on as the ball-carrier approached the channel, so that the attacker had to navigate both the defender and a hostile tunnel of noise. The tackler was encouraged not only to complete the tackle but to make it a quality effort. There was simply no comparison between either the attitude or technique of the players now and seven years earlier and that was reflected in the results. The players were like the men in a 'before and after' advertisement. As usual, it was Johnno who summarised the mood in the huddle, turning around slowly and looking at each player individually before announcing in his own incontrovertible way: 'We are ready.'
>
> This was not the end of the story however. My normal routine would involve helping Dave Tennison to pick up the cones and clear up after the session, but on this occasion there were only 40 minutes before we were due to be collected by coach for our farewell dinner. As I hurried off the pitch I heard some breathless

footsteps behind me. I could almost sense the anxiety in that patter of feet even before I looked around to see Jonny Wilkinson standing there, desperate to repeat the exercise after being the only player to miss two tackles in the session.

I explained that we had nine days in Perth before we played Georgia [in the first group game] in which to run the drill again, and added some positive reinforcement:

'Look Wilko, I am not at all concerned about your tackling ability… Relax, and enjoy the reception.' But I could see that my words were evaporating into thin air. Jonny was not listening.

'I can't travel like this,' he mumbled.

I didn't fully understand Jonny and I didn't realise the extent of the problem until I was at the reception kindly organised by our sponsors O2. Backy was sitting at my table, and he was commenting on the excellence of training ironically, when the wife of O2's CEO leaned in over out of nowhere and announced:

'Are you Mr Larder?… If you are, I must tell you that Mr Wilkinson is still brooding about training this afternoon. He is not eating his food.' Backy just looked at me, shook his head and shoved his face into his hands.

I went over and engaged in a long one-to-one with Jonny. I listened as he emphasised how important the process of mental rehearsal was for him, and how his self-confidence and technique was reinforced by successful rehearsals and visualisations. He would finish final practice before matchdays with six goal-kicking attempts from in between the two 15-metre lines. If he missed a kick he would start the whole process again until he finished with a 100% success rate:

'I can only leave the practice after strengthening this feeling to the point where my confidence is absolute, by replaying all those successful kicks in my head.'

I quickly began to understand that it was the same with his tackling:

'I tackled poorly today Phil, and if I don't sort it out it will play on my mind throughout the journey. I will have picked my self-confidence apart by the time we set foot in Australia. I can't travel like that.'

Our excellent manager Louise Ramsay had informed us that pick-up at Pennyhill Park would be 9am sharp in order to meet the tight deadlines later in the day, so there was only one answer.

The following morning we were placing the cones again, as the sun came up over the horizon just before 6am. Backy organised players as guinea pigs for Jonny to tackle, Otis warmed them up, Phil Pask and Simon Kemp stood on the sideline in case of injuries. I ran the drill again while Clive just closed his eyes and crossed his fingers, hoping that everyone came through the exercise unscathed. Inevitably Jonny Wilkinson was successful with all of his tackles and boarded the plane later that day with a look of sunny contentment on his face.

Although Jonny often suffered from 'performance anxiety' in this respect, ultimately I believe it was a sign of the humility which underpinned his character. He never believed anything was a 'given' and as a result he, more than any other player I knew, was willing to go back to basics, forget all his past successes and behave in training as if he had achieved nothing at all…

The natural educators within the coaching group would reinforce this kind of attitude by insisting that only 'perfect practice makes perfect' – not just practising the skill, but performing it with exactly the right mechanics so that the results became consistent.

It was just this kind of attitude we needed in order to ascend the last few hundred feet of our own personal mountain-top at the World Cup in Australia.

England had flown into New Zealand for the beginning of their summer tour on 2 June. They had beaten the Maoris in New Plymouth on Monday 9 June, New Zealand in Wellington on Saturday 14 June, and Australia in Melbourne on Saturday 21 June. The return journey was routed via Perth in Western Australia so that the squad could take stock of their home venue at the World Cup, with the players flying back to the UK on 25 June and the management following them the very next day. Training camp would start with fitness tests at Pennyhill Park on Monday 21 July, so the players had the best part of a month to rest and recuperate. It was during that period of designated 'R & R' that Phil Larder discovered a renewed sense of his own humility, by brutal *force majeure*:

My wife Anne and I flew to Portugal, hoping to get away from it all. But as luck would have it, we bumped into Lawrence Dallaglio and a couple of his friends at a local restaurant in Vale do Lobo.

Lol explained that he had to go easy on the alcohol because he was committed to completing one of Dave Reddin's conditioning runs the following day and he wasn't looking forward to it. We all agreed to help Lol out and arranged to meet at Barrington's Sports Centre the next day at noon.

We had all enjoyed the evening, so to speak, but we must have been short in the head to agree to the run because the sun was high in the sky and beating down at well over 30°C the following day. We had forgotten the reality of that 'testing tomorrow' completely, so it really was a case of *Mad Dogs and Englishmen…* for all of us! After a series of demanding sprints ranging from between 50 and 300 metres with short rest periods in between, we were well and truly cooked. Anne rightly played hell with me and my Peter Pan complex, because I was diagnosed with atrial fibrillation shortly afterwards.

Atrial fibrillation is a condition whereby the normal heart rate is disturbed by random electrical impulses which override the heart's natural timer. Instead of pumping blood in and out of the atria slowly and rhythmically, the heart rate becomes much faster and more irregular. During the process, I started to feel a fluttering sensation in my chest because my heart was beating so fast, and the breathlessness rarely left me. It was always worse in the morning and even the climb to the top of the stairs was an ordeal – it felt like I was carrying a sack of coal on my back. The doctor told me that there was also a danger of blood clots forming in the heart chamber and I was prescribed warfarin to prevent the clots from forming. I have been on it ever since.

For a person like myself, who had always prided themselves on their active lifestyle and athletic prowess, the sense of my own fragility came as a shock – a warning of how brittle the sense of being alive could become. Like the breathlessness and the warfarin, that feeling is still my constant companion.

When I laid back and tried to relax in my business-class seat on the flight out to Australia, it was with a renewed feeling of gratitude for virtually everything that I could call 'mine' in my life. The RFU and the Zurich Premiership clubs could certainly not have done any more for us and gave the elite squad their total support. From 31 May onwards, after the 2003 Zurich Premiership Final in which Tigers had squeezed past Saracens in extra time, the selected squad would be completely under our control for 177 days – until we returned home from the World Cup on 24 November after winning another nail-biter in extra time against Australia.

The summer training camp had been divided into three periods.

- 'Period 1' began on 21 July and lasted for three weeks. It was designed to increase fitness levels and improve individual skills without contact.

- 'Period 2' began on 18 August with three Test matches on consecutive Saturdays: against Wales at the Millennium Stadium on 23 August, France in Marseilles the week after, and France again at Twickenham on 6 September.

- 'Period 3' commenced on 15 September, with the final World Cup squad of 30 players undergoing an intense conditioning and coaching programme designed to bring them to peak readiness.

The process of settling on a 30-man squad for the World Cup had not however been without its own difficulties. It had proved hard to condense the squad down to the 30-player maximum, and a number of very good players, like the Wasps and Lions lock Simon Shaw, had to be left out. For Phil Larder, the two most painful omissions were those of his Leicester charges, Graham Rowntree and Austin Healey:

> In my opinion the most unfortunate player was Graham Rowntree, who had been a regular in the England squad since 1999 and been a Lions tourist to South Africa in 1997. I had gotten to know 'Wig' really well while coaching him at Welford Road and I held him in the highest regard. He was an immensely likeable character, thoroughly dedicated, tough, reliable and without a malicious bone in his body. He was one of Clive's 'energisers' rather than a 'sapper' and an excellent squad man.
>
> He was also an outstanding scrummager and, along with Darren Garforth and Richard Cockerill, made up the famous 'ABC club' at the Tigers that had won the respect of the entire Zurich Premiership in the professional era. He had been quick to develop both his tackling skills and defensive understanding after I'd started teaching my system at Tigers, and he was regarded

as a source of inspiration and education by the young academy players. They would flock to him for advice, and even then it was obvious to me that Wig had the gift of being able to pass on knowledge to others, so his future as first England's scrummaging coach, and then forwards coach came as no surprise when it began to gather momentum a few years later.

Wig had been told that he had made the World Cup squad for sure after his outstanding performance in the win over New Zealand in Wellington. He was the cornerstone of the six-man scrum which had held New Zealand on our own goal-line after both Dallaglio and Back had been yellow-carded. At the final selection meeting there was a change of course and it was decided that Wig had to be sacrificed in order to accommodate six back-rowers, three hookers and three scrum-halves in the squad, rather than five props which had been the original intention. Trevor Woodman was the number one loose-head and Jason Leonard had the ability to cover both sides of the scrum, so it was Graham who had to miss out in the most unfortunate of circumstances.

There was a powerful lesson in his omission about the importance of not making critical decisions in the heat of the moment. Emotions had been running high in the changing room after the win in Wellington and it was then that Wig was told 'You're in.' He had already booked places on the plane for his young family to fly out for the quarter-final in Brisbane on that understanding and therefore had to cancel his arrangements when there was a change of mind. It was all very disappointing and although it will be no compensation on missing out on potentially the finest moment of his playing career, I am delighted with the coaching success that he has enjoyed since hanging his boots up. Wig is a very special guy and he deserves every success that comes his way.

The second Leicester player to miss out was Austin Healey. Ozzie had played a key role in my Tigers defensive pattern at scrum-half. He was a superb communicator with a shrewd footballing brain and well-respected by the other members of the squad. He was able to organise the defence around the breakdown, guide players quickly into position and generally act as our defensive quarterback. The forwards, in particular, trusted him and followed his directions implicitly. He was also a player with a big-match temperament and enjoyed his two best performances for Leicester in their two Heineken Cup final victories against Stade Francais at the Parc des Princes in 2001, and against Munster at the Millennium Stadium one year later.

Oz's problem was his versatility. He was multi-skilled and could play in several positions – wing, scrum-half and outside-half. Until Jason Robinson arrived on the scene he was probably the most elusive player in the Premiership. He'd played in all England's games in the 1999 World Cup on the right wing until he was moved to scrum-half against Fiji. Then in 2000 he had an outstanding game against South Africa in the first Test at number 10, as a late replacement for Jonny Wilkinson. I sensed the danger of the perception of Austin as a 'jack of all trades' and we had several talks based around my efforts to persuade him to specialise at scrum-half. I didn't feel he was a world-class winger but I did think that his speed and skills would be a huge plus around the base of the scrum or ruck.

Increasingly however, the England selectors began to consider him as a replacement able to cover several positions and therefore best suited to the bench, and I feared for his future in the team. If you're not starting, you cannot cement your position and you are not in the 'shop window' regularly enough.

Ozzie was placed on standby and stayed at home, but with Kyran Bracken's injury history I felt there was a good chance of him making the tournament at some point during the six weeks. As it transpired, Kyran's back flared up again and Austin was summoned in the week before the semi-final against France on 16 November. The World Cup rules were however unequivocal. Each team could only maintain a squad of 30 players in the same hotel. When Ozzie arrived in Manly only to learn that Kyran was now fit and raring to go, he couldn't even stay in the Manly Pacific with the rest of the players and coaches he had gotten to know so well over the years. He only had time to have a brief coffee with his Leicester team-mates in a bar close to the hotel before returning to Sydney airport for the long and lonely flight home. Loaded down with superfluous luggage, he cut a forlorn figure. Perhaps it is better to know you are on the outer right from the beginning, than to have your hopes raised and then dashed as both Wig's and Ozzie's had been.

Phil's statistical table meanwhile would prove more prophetic than even he realised. All four of the top-rated defensive teams – England, Australia, New Zealand and France – would reach the semi-finals of the competition, with the top two going through to meet in the showpiece event itself. But Phil was still not satisfied with the number one ranking, and the humility of small margins dictated that more improvements would be necessary. During the period of extended preparation in the UK, he had decided to experiment with the idea of using the 'up and in' defensive method popularised by Shaun Edwards at Wasps in order to stay ahead of the game.

I had been interested in the 'up and in' defence coached at Wasps by Shaun Edwards for some time and decided to introduce it to the England squad. I had a meeting with the Wasps contingent and then threw it into training on 22 July. In all we had six training sessions, beginning with small groups of six players, then increasing it to 12 before finally playing a full-sided game. This was followed by a meeting with the team leaders – Neil Back, Martin Johnson, Richard Hill, Lawrence Dallaglio, Phil Vickery, Jonny Wilkinson, Mike Tindall and Jason Robinson – to discuss our impressions.

There was a difference of opinion on the value of such a major change so close to the World Cup. At the start, Lol and Johnno were supporters of the new idea, Jason thought that it might be useful as an option when we were defending in our own 22, but Backy was dead against it: 'If you are the best in the world at something, why change it?' he said.

Although we tried to introduce Shaun's pattern in our 13 July training session, it created more problems than solutions. One of Wasps' premier defenders, Joe Worsley, would often be caught in no man's land, and even Neil Back, our defensive captain, conceded a try at Guard when he flew in and mistimed a hit. To say it was a shambles would be an exaggeration, but it was certainly not a success.

Looking over the footage of the session afterwards, it became obvious that the decision-making processes which I had developed so patiently over the past six years could be fatally compromised by an entirely new mode of defensive thinking and behaviour. Could every single player in the squad be expected to switch from one system to the other and back again under the white-hot pressure of the knockout stages of the World Cup? Would the 'up and in' take up too much of my allocated coaching time, and undermine the refinement of the existing system?

Typically it was Johnno who brought everyone back down to earth:

'Okay, everyone knows the system we use, but no team had proved that they have what it takes to break us down. Our records show that.

'You were right to introduce the idea Phil, but I don't see why we should take an unnecessary gamble this close to the big prize.'

Neil looked over at Johnno and smiled: 'First time I have heard you talk any sense,' he said. Backy looked visibly more relaxed – he knew at that moment he had won his battle.

The will to 'keep going up' was still present, even if not all the potential improvements turned out to be viable. One area of clear development in this long training phase occurred in the kicking game, and on both sides of it. The 'no second chance' atmosphere of World Cup matches tends to accent the importance of the kicking game, with teams unwilling to give anything away by making mistakes with the ball in hand.

We concentrated on pressurising opposition kickers and we planned to do it at every opportunity, using second-rows to charge down box kicks, back-rowers to pressure exit kicks – in fact our aim was to pressurise every kick the opposition made. Meanwhile Dave Alred improved both the kicking of all of the backs, and the catching skills of the whole team. His catching clinics would introduce a fundamental concept which DA would then tailor towards receiving a pass, catching a lineout throw or receiving a kick that had been launched high into the sky. Gradually the pressure placed on the players was intensified and the aerial battles between lineout jumpers, and the receivers and chasers of high kicks became quite spectacular. In response, I worked harder on legally blocking the chaser on all high kicks in order to reduce the pressure on the catcher when the ball came down. Every little improvement stimulated a positive response, and another small step forward in the team's overall capability.

Dave's work on the positioning of the hands when receiving the ball also improved the crispness of our passing as both passers and receivers became more conscious of the ideal spot for the receipt, so there was a pay-off in our attacking game too. Andy Robinson introduced the 'shotgun' formation with a forward riding inside Jonny Wilkinson in case the opposing number 7 tried to rush Wilko, as Serge Betsen had done with such success in our 2002 Six Nations game against France in Paris. When he felt the pressure in his face, Jonny would dump the ball off to the forward underneath him so that he could be available at first receiver on the next phase.

Above all, the coaching staff all paid attention to the constant improvement of fundamental skills. I had been persuaded once and for all of the importance of skills coaching after watching the 1982 Kangaroos in training. There are many knowledgeable people from both codes of rugby who believe that the coaching of rugby league in Australia is the most advanced in the world at every age group level, because of its emphasis on skill acquisition.

When I'm asked to address coaching conferences and visit schools and junior clubs, I feel an unspoken expectation that I will at some point divulge 'the big secret' – some previously-unknown coaching method or team drill that will bring my hosts instant success. In fact the solution is, and always has been both more prosaic and difficult to accept. *Simply spend more time on improving the basic skills of all the individuals in the team.* This is 'the secret', what is uncertain is the determination of the playing and coaching group to drive towards the achievement of that ultimate aim. There are just too many glittering distractions along the way…

As Vince Lombardi put it, in the game of American football that is so similar and yet so different to our own: 'Some people try to find things in this game that don't exist, but football is only two things – blocking and tackling.' American football, like rugby in both codes is basically a humble game. If tremendous gains were made during this training period with England, they were only made for the most part in the fundamentals of the game – the simple skills of passing, catching, kicking and tackling. Nothing more.

* * * * *

England's qualifying group contained one side out of the very top tier in the form of South Africa, a very dangerous second tier nation in Samoa, and two of the developing countries in Georgia and Uruguay. The first two games [against Georgia and South Africa], were due to be played on the Subiaco Oval, in a western suburb of Perth; the third [versus Samoa] shifted ground to the Docklands stadium in Melbourne, with England finishing up with a match against Uruguay at Lang Park in Brisbane.

Three of the four games therefore were scheduled to be played on ovals, which bounced the focus all the way back on England's lineout throwing and their goal-kicking. As Steve Thompson had discovered at Wellington, the circular shape of the stadium could cause disorientation at lineout time, while the goal-kickers often found their 'spots' in the crowd behind the posts too far back to function as targets. At Melbourne and Subiaco at least, grandma's coffee was safe from the left-footed attentions of young Jonny! The fact that England had already played two games at Wellington and Melbourne four months previously would provide an insurance policy, as would the visualisation exercises prescribed to the hookers and goal-kickers likely to play in the group games at Subiaco and the Docklands. But nothing was certain, as the game against Samoa would prove.

The two 'minnows' were comfortably dispatched by a combined aggregate of almost 200 points, and South Africa were clearly still suffering from the inferiority complex built up by their four successive defeats against England since the summer tour to the Republic in June 2000. The Springboks had lost their last two games to England by a combined score of 82-12 and they had failed to register a try in either encounter. Phil Larder and Andy Robinson had first noticed abnormal signs of stress in the Springbok party at a local function held a few days before the game:

> Robbo and I had seen what we thought was a chink in their armour when the teams met the Perth city dignitaries in the Town Hall. There was a palpable presence, and a sense of easy self-confidence around our players as they walked into the main hall and were introduced to the mayor and his colleagues, and it affected even some of the more established South African players quite obviously. They did not look at all comfortable in their own skins, and the impression was reinforced by the sight of Springboks crashing into tackle bags emblazoned by England jerseys – with the numbers 10 and 4 receiving most of their attention. They appeared unusually worried about us and at that point I realised we held a winning hand. Most of the battles you fight are won before you ever step on the field.

With Sherylle Calder helping to unpick the Springbok lineout with her knowledge of Afrikaans and our emphasis on kick blocks paying immediate dividends – their outside-half Louis Koen had his clearance kick charged down by Lewis Moody and Will Greenwood hacked the ball on to score – we were able to pull away to a comfortable 25-6 win. Furthermore we held the Springboks try-less for the third consecutive occasion, and Jonny Wilkinson's last two drop goals to seal it provided a satisfying sense of symmetry and a modest revenge for what had happened to us in the 1999 World Cup quarters against the same opponents. We had made 163 tackles with our back-rowers Lawrence Dallaglio, Neil Back and Lewis Moody combining for 55 of them, and we'd hit our 95% success ratio. I felt Will Greenwood had come of age as a Test match defender, and looking to the future we were confident that we had now guaranteed an easier route to the final, one which did not feature New Zealand at the quarter-final stage or the hosts Australia in the semis.

As it turned out, England's most testing challenge in the group stages was mounted by the Samoans. Perhaps there was not the same whiff of gunpowder in the air as there had been against the Springboks, maybe England's six changes in personnel resulted in a slight but significant loss of co-ordination, or the Samoans simply had one of those days on which they can beat any side in the world. However much of the full story was embodied in those three elements, the result was a major scare for England and major fillip for their potential opponents in the knockout stages.

Samoa were never behind in a first half which ended with a narrow 16-13 lead for the Pacific islanders, and they were still leading the game by 22 points to 20 as late as the 62nd minute. It was only in those final 18 minutes that England took control, scoring 15 unanswered points to claim victory 35-22.

Neither the England lineout thrower Mark Regan nor their goal-kicker Jonny Wilkinson were their usual consistent selves at the Docklands oval and England's fractured composure was expressed in a series of penalties for side entry or offside in and around the breakdown. They conceded 14 penalties overall, six of which were kickable and resulted in 15 points for Samoa. In addition the Samoans played outstandingly well, as Martin Johnson pointed out immediately after the match: 'They played fantastically well and they could have beaten us.

We haven't played a team who's played that well in the first 20 minutes for as long as I can remember. We need to take a long hard look at ourselves because that performance was not good enough and it won't win us anything...'

England's temporary loss of composure was most clearly evidenced in an incident that occurred in the twilight moments of the match. Mike Tindall had received a knock near the far touchline and left the field to receive treatment, leaving England temporarily down to 14 men. Dave Reddin, who was responsible for the substitutes' bench and in communication with Clive Woodward up in the stands, was under immediate pressure to get a replacement on. The transcript of the World Cup enquiry shows that the fifth official Brett Bowden asked Reddin not to make the substitution on five separate occasions. Inevitably, substitute Dan Luger ran on to the field just as Mike Tindall trotted back into position, blissfully ignorant of what had already occurred on the other side of the pitch. For half a minute or so, England had 16 players on the field.

> When we studied the recording of the incident afterwards we found that it lasted for exactly 32 seconds, and neither the result of the game nor the play in that short period were affected demonstrably – although Dan Luger did concede a penalty which helped Samoa!
>
> It was the proverbial storm in a teacup. It was an administrative error on our part, which was rightly punished by administrative means. We were fined £10,000 and Otis had his touchline accreditation withdrawn for two games, while the fourth official Steve Walsh, who had needlessly involved himself in a spat with Dave afterwards, squirting water at him and trying to trip him in the tunnel, was also suspended for one match. An RWC statement said: 'Mr Walsh has subsequently been suspended for inappropriate behaviour during an exchange with a member of the England management team.'
>
> As far as we were concerned, there the issue rested. As usual in Australia however, the press tried to inflate it in order to destabilise one of their major opponents in the tournament. The fact that it involved the Poms only added an extra edge. Mike Cleary summed it up well in *The Daily Telegraph* when he said:
> 'What initially appeared to be a cock-up is assuming momentum beyond its significance, fuelled in part by a gloating

media happy to see England in the dock... Having 16 men on the field is not a heinous offence. It even happened during the Australia–Namibia match on Saturday and, if the referee sees fit, is sanctioned by just a penalty kick. England though is accused of an action that strays into the territory of bringing the game into disrepute.'

Toutai Kefu, the Australian number 8 who had been ruled out of the World Cup by injury, felt England should have had their five winning points deducted, which would almost certainly have redirected us through the tougher half of the knockout draw. What a surprise.

It was perhaps typical that Clive, who had probably caused the problem in the first place with his insistence on getting Luger on to the field at all costs, should also provide the 'save'. As usual, he had covered all eventualities by appointing a high-profile QC, Richard Smith, as England's legal advisor.

'QC' was superb on tour, never in the way but always aware of what was happening, highly intelligent and always with a great feel for the mood in the camp. Clive told us that QC had convincingly won the argument before the disciplinary committee and had ensured that the range of the debate was held to its true proportions. That was all we needed to be able to move on and start looking towards the quarter-finals.

Another example of Clive Woodward's awareness of the critical non-essentials was in his positive management of the players' partners and families. Many of the wives and partners had joined the England group towards the end of the group stages, during their stay on the Gold Coast at the time of the final pool game against Uruguay.

There is no doubt in my mind that Clive was one hundred per cent right in allowing families to join us for the latter stages of the competition. I had experienced the loneliness of being separated from Anne and my young family for several weeks on my first [rugby league] tour of the southern hemisphere and I was well aware of the dangers. Happy players who don't have any worries at home to distract them function far better than those who have their focus split two or three different ways. 'Home' results tend to be infinitely better than 'away' results for this very reason, and anything that can be done to replicate the home scenario had to be a step in the right direction – particularly as the players always had the sanctuary of their own hotel rooms to escape to whenever they wanted some peace and quiet!

There were no equivalents to soccer 'WAGs' in the party, no women jockeying for media attention on the backs of their partner's sporting profiles, they all understood their supportive role and Jayne Woodward was the key figure in the prompting, and the reminding of that understanding. Anne had done a great job with the partners of the England RL team during the 1995 World Cup, but Jayne was operating on an entirely different plane. Jayne ensured that the players' families embraced and enjoyed 'the England experience'. Regular meetings were arranged throughout the year, and when for example Dr Adam Carey was appointed to manage our diets, Jayne organised seminars for the partners so they could understand all the potential spin-offs. Jayne is both approachable and astute and she was able to spot issues before they arose. Figures in the spotlight at the forefront of the stage often project much larger shadows in the background, and Jayne played a huge, if hidden, part in our success as a group.

The big danger of England's forthcoming quarter-final against Wales was complacency. The England second XV had gone down to Cardiff and administered a 43-9 thrashing to the Wales 'firsts' during the warm-up schedule in August, and there was a worrying sense within the England camp that they had only to turn up to win. Even some of the coaches, as Andy Robinson later acknowledged, had turned their attention to a potential semi-final clash against France and paid too little attention, preparation-wise, to the stepping stone right in front of their noses.

Before the press conference after the final pool win over Uruguay, both Clive Woodward and Phil Larder were looking up at the big screens in the media village. On those screens, giant versions of Shane Williams, Ceri Sweeney and Tom Shanklin were to be seen, slashing and sidestepping their way past groping All Black defenders as Wales recovered from a 10-28 deficit after half an hour to lead 37-33 just 30 minutes later. The game was an orgy of spectacular attacking rugby, with New Zealand pulling away in the final quarter to win it 53-37. But as Clive Woodward and Phil Larder looked across at each other, both could feel the ice-shelves moving and an avalanche in the air:

Up until the New Zealand game, Wales had struggled to produce much quality rugby. I had analysed all their recent games, and in all honesty their performance against New Zealand was completely out of character. The feeling of some in the camp was that it was a one-off, and that New Zealand under-performed. But I could not get rid of a nagging sense of worry. Wales had played as if the shackles had been removed and attacked New Zealand at every opportunity, throwing the ball about with a smile on their faces and a complete disregard for field position. They reminded me of the St Helens rugby league team, who would run and support the ball in a kind of emotional frenzy. A play-off semi-final with Widnes seeped back into my memory. Despite finishing the regular season with the best defensive record in the competition, Saints had turned up 'in frenzy' and taken us apart. I hoped the same would not happen again if Wales started the game in the same mood in which they had taken on New Zealand.

The IRB had quite rightly scheduled kick-off time for 8pm, which meant that our usual walk-through would take place at noon, with the sun directly overhead and the temperature well in excess of 30°C. The backs tended to do some light work and would finish well before the forwards. I usually enjoyed watching the forwards going about their business but the sun was so strong that I left them to it and returned to the hotel with the backs. When the forwards finally came in for their pre-match meal, they looked totally shattered.

At the beginning of the game the signs of torpor were confirmed. England's defensive line-speed was poor, their forwards looked sluggish moving across from the set piece and the Welsh attack thrived on the space it was given. Wales broke the line from a midfield scrum in the fifth minute and nearly scored out on the England left, with Robert Sidoli dropping the ball in the action of placing it over the goal-line. After a kick return a couple of minutes later England were stretched to the absolute limit to contain the Welsh counter and prevent Shane Williams touching down after a kick-through to the opposite corner. With Wales winning turnovers from the breakdown and mixing the running and kicking games with intelligence, Jonny Wilkinson's penalty to put England ahead in the 18th minute was probably against the run of play. It was then that England felt their footing slip and saw the avalanche pounding down the mountainside.

> With both Will Greenwood and our right wing Dan Luger still close to the breakdown after the previous phase, Mike Tindall looked up and kicked towards the far corner of the Wales 22. It was a rugby version of suicide. The kick was designed to be caught by Ben Kay out on the right – but instead it was Shane Williams who received it in acres of space, and Shane was the most elusive and dynamic runner in the Welsh team. Even if Ben had caught the ball he would have been turned over because the nearest support was on the other side of midfield. The danger of practising unit skills like the cross-kick, but failing to develop the thinking process behind them, reminded me of Wilko's midfield bomb at Wellington. The technical skills [coached by Dave Alred] were there, but the appreciation of when and where to use them was absent. In this respect, we just had not learned.
>
> Although we scrambled back as best we could, Williams skirted around Ben easily and Wales scored after a magnificent five-pass move converted by the man who started it all. As if that was not enough, they doubled their lead to 10-3 just before half-time. There was another turnover penalty and the Welsh captain Colin Charvis smelled blood. He ordered a kick to the corner from which Wales scored their second try with a lineout drive very similar to the one which they'd used against New Zealand. Charvis touched down on both occasions too, and when the referee's whistle went for half-time, I knew that the seven-point margin did not flatter them in the least.

With the sheds unusually quite at half-time, Clive Woodward made the crucial decision to pull off Dan Luger, shift Mike Tindall to the right wing in his place and bring on Mike Catt at inside centre to share the kicking responsibilities with Jonny Wilkinson. As Mike Catt says, 'Clive Woodward sent me on to provide the second kicking option which was an important but simple tactical switch. We then stood either side of the scrums, Jonny left and me right, hoofed it 60 metres downfield to get us on the front foot and the nature of the game soon changed.'

With the pressure firmly back on Wales, it was suddenly Jason Robinson rather than Shane Williams who became the main kick-returning threat in the game. Robinson returned a Welsh exit kick in the 45th minute, beating five defenders before setting up Will Greenwood for a try in the same corner where Rob Sidoli had failed to touch down in the first half. Back level at 10-10, neither the England forwards nor their kickers spared a glance back over their shoulder. With the game being played in Welsh territory, the penalties accrued and Jonny began to hit grandma's coffee-cup unerringly. 10-10 became 25-10 with five successive Wilkinson kicks before Wales scored a consolation try nine minutes from time, to make the final score 28-17 to England.

I was like a bear with a sore head afterwards, and the frustration was only partly allayed by a return to my favourite hotel, the Manly Pacific in Sydney. Our defence had not achieved any of the six World Class Performance Standards. We'd missed 15 tackles giving us only an 88% success rate. It was our worst defensive performance in recent memory and it had allowed the Wales attack to dominate much of the game. We had finished the pool stages with the best defensive record of all, but we had now been overtaken by Australia who had conceded four tries to our five.

I had several individual chats with key players and they were all extremely confident of beating France. They understood the reasons for our poor first-half performance against Wales and were determined not to make the same mistake twice. Both Johnno and Backy emphasised that everyone in the team understood their roles in the defensive pattern and there was no need to panic. 'Trust us, Phil,' said Backy, 'just keep the sessions sharp and short.'

The main priority was therefore to learn from our mistakes in preparation against Wales and turn up for the match full of energy. Training time was restricted to a minimum and rest and recuperation emphasised. Dave Reddin was highly instrumental in ensuring that the players did not spend too much time out in the sun; took on energy via fluids rather than solids when appetites were low; and followed post-training 'warm-down' routines to the letter. Meanwhile the jewel in our administrative crown, Louise Ramsay, had followed the NSW meteorological reports like a hawk and revealed rather surprisingly, that torrential rain was predicted for Sunday.

The game against France would therefore likely come down to forward play, the kicking game and mental toughness in the battle of wills. France were capable of generating an expansive attack off their set pieces, moving the ball wide off lineout through their backs and then coming back all the way to their dangerous ball-playing back-rowers Olivier Magne and Imanol Harinorduquy on the nearside touchline, and their scrum-half Fabien Galthié was expert at bringing his back-row into the game from scrums. They had beaten all their opponents by large margins, beating Fiji (61-18), Japan (51-29), Scotland (51-9) and USA (41-14) in the group stages before thrashing Ireland in the quarter-final 43-21. But the truth was that it was never going to be an expansive game as the quarter-final against Wales had been. The weather would see to that.

After England opened the scoring with a Jonny Wilkinson drop goal off his 'wrong' right foot, France scored a try from one of their own lineouts near the England 22. A gap appeared in England's defensive 3-3-1 formation between the rear lifter in the second pod of 'three' [Lawrence Dallaglio] and the 'one' at the tail [Richard Hill] after a French decoy jump in the middle. With the England pod shuffling down the line, Serge Betsen caught the ball and looked as surprised as anybody as he went straight through the gap between Dallaglio and Hill to score, despite the attentions of Jason Robinson.

France led by 7-3 after 10 minutes, but they did not know then that they would be held scoreless for the remaining 70 minutes of the match. With England's aggressive line-speed and kick-blocks forcing a stream of errors out of the French, Jonny Wilkinson and Mike Catt at 10 and 12 slowly began to turn the screw with the kicking game. Hitherto unsuspected fissures in French discipline began to appear, with Christophe Dominici yellow-carded for a trip on Jason Robinson in the 24th minute and Betsen sin-binned for a late charge on Jonny Wilkinson in the 53rd. Wilkinson kicked a penalty after a mistake by the French full-back Nicolas Brusque, then dropped another goal off his right foot before adding his second penalty after a lineout steal right on half-time. It was 12-7 and England had no intention of relinquishing their grip on the match. By the end of the second period, Wilkinson had kicked five penalties and three drop goals to account for all of England's 24 points, while his opposite number Freddie Michalak had only succeeded with one out of his five attempts at goal. The game had emphasised the ultimate importance of experience and mental toughness in claustrophobic tournaments like the World Cup, a setting in which there was no way to hide psychological fragility. Seven of the England forwards who had endured the quarter-final loss at the hands of South Africa in 1999 were either still starting four years later or coming off the bench regularly [Jason Leonard] – only hooker Phil Greening was missing. Apart from Martin Johnson, the pack contained four other players with experience of captaining England – Neil Back, Lawrence Dallaglio, Phil Vickery and Jason Leonard. In the backs, that leadership experience extended to Matt Dawson, Kyran Bracken and Jonny Wilkinson.

Over the last four World Cups the average age of the winning squad has always been between 27 and 28 years of age, with the total number of caps as follows: Australia 1999 [622 caps], England 2003 [638], South Africa 2007 [668] and finally New Zealand in 2011 [709]. Allowing for the steady increase in the number of international fixtures, the figures are nearly identical. In 2003, there were nine players in the England squad with a minimum of 50 caps, and one of those [Jason Leonard] had passed 100 caps. In 2011, New Zealand fielded exactly the same number of players as England with over 50 caps [nine], and their two most experienced players [Richie McCaw and Mils Muliaina] totalled a nearly identical cap-count to England's top two in the same bracket [Jason Leonard and Martin Johnson] – 194 caps compared to 197. Leadership and decision-making experience under pressure was paramount.

> The France game emphasised the importance of selection more than anything else. Ever since the 1999 World Cup, I had been bemused by the barrage of criticism of our selections in the media. The criticism always took on the same hue – that we did not select, or persevere with some of the more naturally skilful and elusive players in the Premiership, like James Simpson-Daniel of Gloucester, and therefore we were too 'conservative'. Although I understood the need for creative game-breaking types very well, by far the overriding principle in selection is to restrict it to those players who can handle the intense pressure that is generated in the big games. That is the alpha and the omega of the situation, even if the press boys don't always understand it so well.
>
> France had not pursued this policy and they had suffered like many other teams before them, including ourselves. We knew we would make a lot of mistakes in the prevailing weather

conditions in the Sydney stadium, but our players simply picked themselves up off the floor and got on with it, psychologically-speaking. They made the invaluable 'second effort', and they did it quicker and more decisively than their French counterparts. By comparison, some of the key French players were completely thrown off their game by the pressure we exerted, and didn't come back with positive responses of their own. That was the difference. While it is always the gladiators in the arena who win the big games, the coaches play a hugely significant role in selecting those with the required levels of mental toughness, and then developing their all-round game around those core psychological strengths.

France went into the game as the form team of the competition but were unable to adapt their tactics to the conditions and they paid the price. Wet weather football is all about playing the game as close to the opponent's 22 as possible, keeping possession when it has been won, being disciplined and taking every opportunity to score. The Scotland grand slam game in 2000 had taught us that lesson.

We won the territorial battle. Jonny Wilkinson handled the ball on 49 occasions while the two French outside-halves only handled the ball 22 times between them. As a result we only had to make 79 tackles. We conceded six penalties to France's 11, and France played for one quarter of the match with 14 men on the park.

We had picked up the tag of 'Dad's Army' in the media, but we did not care. What does 'too old' mean for a sportsman? Robbo once told me that he decided to retire because he was no longer first to reach the breakdown. I retired at 37 years old because I had lost my enthusiasm for the game, while Roachy finished because he was picking up too many injuries. None of this applied to the older members of the England squad. The physical conditioning programme, particularly the work they had completed through the three training periods, resulted in every player flying to Perth in the best condition of his life. Our oldest player Jason Leonard had recorded test results before departure, that were not bettered by any England player up to and including the 2011 World Cup, when the same tests were still being carried out. The 2003 World Cup squad was the most enthusiastic group that I had coached in both codes of rugby. They gave it everything they had and were a privilege to be with because of that. As Andy Robinson pointed out with a chuckle after the semi-final, 'Those old men certainly know how to win games.'

Another aspect of experience is knowing how and when to switch off completely in pressure-cooker situations. With his family assembling steadily around him as the knockout stages progressed, Phil Larder took the opportunity to relax with a dinner on the Sydney Quays on the day of the first semi-final between New Zealand and Australia.

My youngest son David and his girlfriend Jamie had booked a holiday in Australia to coincide with the tournament. They had joined up with us prior to the quarter-final in Brisbane, and I'd reserved a table on the Sydney Quays to celebrate their arrival. As the four of us enjoyed that seminal journey across the estuary from Manly to Sydney on the slow ferry, I made it known that I did not even want to know the score in the first semi-final. A rugby-free evening meant just that – no rugby.

But immediately upon disembarking we were swallowed up in a massive crowd and the river of people flowed only one way – towards a massive outside TV screen. Dids took one look at the action and could hardly contain his excitement.

With a sense of resignation in the face of the inevitable I said grimly, 'Go on then Dids, tell me the score.'

'No dad, you said you wanted to relax and get away from it all. Let's move on and find the restaurant,' he replied.

It was impossible, there were television screens everywhere, and after one especially loud cheer which seemed to bounce around the walls of the city skyscrapers, I could not contain myself any longer. We pushed open the doors to the nearest pub and enjoyed a few drinks watching Australia book their place in the final.

All along I'd considered New Zealand to be the main threat to our aspirations, so the result of the first semi made me smile. Even though I had wasted an awful lot of time that week analysing New Zealand as our likely opponents in the final, the smile stubbornly refused to leave my face. We had beaten New Zealand home and away in the previous 12 months but they had both been desperately close games which could have gone either way. I knew far more about Australia, having played them four times since

2000 with a 100% winning record. Who would I rather be facing in the final? In all honesty, it had to be Australia.

* * * * *

The theme of conserving energy, and hence focus, continued in the build-up to the final. We only trained twice during the week, playing some touch rugby and running our defensive routine against the reserves at half-pace. Frankly it drove me mad. I was seething. I may have been the only person in the entire coaching group to feel that way, but the thought of preparing for a World Cup Final against Australia without the benefit of any full-speed defensive sessions contradicted everything I believed as a coach. Fortunately Johnno and Backy had the sense to banish me to the stands as I waved one last admonishing finger back at them: 'If you are f***ing sloppy at the weekend', I said, 'it's not going to be on my head.'

'Don't worry Phil,' they replied, grinning. 'It will be okay. Trust us.' And of course, trust them I did.

There were any number of distractions which can agitate you no end in a peak sporting week like the build-up to a World Cup Final. The media are everywhere you go, you are swamped by messages from people you hardly know, and requests for tickets. On top of that, *The Sydney Morning Herald* had encouraged Wallaby supporters to make a racket outside our hotel at night and make nuisance phone calls to the players. They even published a list of their room numbers so that key individuals could be targeted by attractive 'ladies of the night'! Some of the more eager members of the back-room staff selflessly offered to swap rooms with Jonny...

All the razzmatazz and the stream of demands can get you down and drain your batteries, to the point where you lose all your energy to the outside world and have nothing left inside when the big day arrives. Fortunately the media demands were well-regulated by our media office and by Richard Prescott in particular. The family 'cushion' fitted even more snugly when my eldest son Matt arrived in Sydney on the Thursday before the game. We all drove down to Palm Beach for lunch only to find an episode of *Home and Away* being filmed right in front of us! Matt couldn't find a hotel or guest house anywhere in Sydney and ended up sleeping in Dids and Jamie's room during the day while 'feeding' and partying by night. He stayed resolutely on UK time right up until the final, and while I think he had more fun than anybody, he very nearly missed the train to the stadium for the final after oversleeping on Dids's floor!

It all came to a head when I walked into the war-room only to find Johnno playing *Battleships* on a laptop instead of performing Sherylle's vision exercises... With my son living upside-down and Johnno's huge frame hunched over a computer game, I got the message. I knew I had to relax, let go and enjoy the journey.

As the two squads trooped on to the field on Sunday 22 November at around 7.55pm, the reception our players received reminded me of the first Lions Test at the Gabba in 2001. Thousands of English supporters must have travelled to Australia in that final week, because wherever you looked, white shirts and St George flags outnumbered the yellow and gold hats and waterproofs which had been freely issued to Australian fans by the ARU before the match. When Aussie fans began to taunt Dids and Matt that they were going to keep 'Bill' [their name for the Webb Ellis trophy], Matt turned around and told them it had been changed to 'Ours'. Even though the never-say-die attitude of the Australian sportsman can never be discounted, and we were a little wary of the presence of André Watson as referee – every time he had refereed us there had been some controversy, and every game had gone down to the wire – we had an unshakeable feeling that this was our time. Where we had entered the 1999 World Cup in hope, we now knew we were capable of taking the big prize back to England.

The conditions were not dissimilar to those in the semi-final but Australia adapted to the slippery pitch and heavy drizzle far better than France had done on the previous weekend. They deservedly took the lead after dominating the first six minutes of the match. Australia survived a rocky scrum about 30 metres from our goal-line and Stephen Larkham [who had been missing from our 25-14 victory on the summer tour] pumped an enormous crossfield bomb out towards our right corner. Suddenly 5ft 9in of Jason Robinson found himself defending against all 6ft 4in and 102kgs of Lote Tuqiri one-on-one after our right wing Josh

Lewsey had jammed in too far. The idea was for Josh to drift out and legally block Tuqiri's run, but I think his 'Wasps instincts' interfered and the result was that Jason was left out on an island. The kick was perfectly judged and came down in the in-goal area, which forced Jason to compete in the air. It was an unequal contest, Lote won it and suddenly it was 5-0 to Australia.

Andy Robinson: The question I've always been itching to ask Eddie Jones [the Australian coach] is: 'You scored on your first attacking play on a cross-kick with Lote Tuqiri outjumping Jason Robinson for the ball in-goal – why on earth didn't you try it again?'

The game then became a tough struggle dominated by the two best defences in the world in difficult conditions. Because they knew each other inside out, both lineouts came under constant pressure with neither side winning more than two-thirds of their own ball, and this made it hard for either side to maintain possession for long periods. Jonny kicked us into the lead after two rapid-fire penalties – first for a breakdown infringement by Australia and then for an obstruction on Ben Cohen as Ben was running exactly the same line from scrum as he had done to score in Melbourne. That made it 6-5. Our first clear scoring opportunity occurred in the 25th minute of the match. Australia ran the ball rather laboriously from a scrum in their own half and Wilko put in the second of two big tackles on Matt Giteau, who had come on to replace Steve Larkham. While Jonny stayed down with a 'stinger' to his shoulder, Johnno was fast up in the line to force the error, the ball went loose and Richard Hill hacked it through towards the Wallaby line. He managed to recover the ball too. With Tuqiri sucked into the breakdown there was space for Matt Dawson to put big Ben Kay in at the corner, unmarked and only five metres out.

Ben Kay: I'm always asked, 'Why did you drop that pass in the final? England could have won in normal time if you had caught it and scored.' Looking back on it now, the feeling of confidence that we would win the game was stronger than my sense of embarrassment. At no time did I think we weren't going to achieve our goal and that feeling remained beyond the moment when I dropped Matt Dawson's pass over the try-line. But 'Daws' did delay the pass and it was probably a bit forward anyway!

Ben dropped the ball but we kept the pressure on and Jonny kicked another penalty after a massive scrum shunt near the Australian line [9-5]. Up in the commentary booth, ex-Sale and England scrum-half Steve Smith said, 'Let 'em boo all they want' as the kick bisected the posts. The hits were becoming brutal. Matt Giteau took a shot from Josh Lewsey, who had broken one of Mat Rogers's ribs in a cataclysmic tackle at Melbourne. Up in the box, John Taylor commented that 'it ruined Rogers' surfing career. The rib reset but it pokes out a little bit more so now Rogers can't lie flat on his board.' It was that kind of game.

Then we scored our only try from a lineout in the 38th minute. The ball went loose at the back but Ben Kay was quickly down to secure it. Will Greenwood then made a strong hit up off Wilko, making five metres and delivering a quick ball to Matt Dawson at the base. For once the Australian defence was too slow around the corner and Lawrence Dallaglio was able to run at their last defender [Wendell Sailor] before unloading a beautiful inside pass to Jonny Wilkinson. Ben Cohen had a clear run to the posts on his inside, but Wilko weighted another perfect pass for Jason Robinson to scuttle over in the corner. Jason gave it the fist-pump and screamed 'Come on!' as the England fans rose in ecstasy as one.

Jason Robinson: I can still remember everything about that try as if it was in slow motion. Lawrence taking the ball wide, feeding the ball inside to Jonny Wilkinson; then Jonny looking the other way for a moment before putting the ball out on a plate in front of me; the exhilaration of knowing Mat Rogers wouldn't catch me to the corner. That feeling will never leave me. When I'm old I'll always know I scored in a World Cup Final – not many players get the opportunity to do that but the main thing is we won the game.

It was 14-5 at the half and the fate of the game was firmly in our hands. As the second half rolled on however, we made more and more mistakes. First we threw long at a lineout on our own 22, Australia pinched it and Lol went offside trying to rescue the situation at the next breakdown. Then Josh Lewsey got in front of Matt Dawson and was penalised for obstruction after Johnno had stolen his second ball of the night against the Australian five-man lineout. Their goal-kicker Elton Flatley kicked the first of those two penalty attempts and we started to ship some questionable penalties in the scrum. After the third penalty against us in the 58th minute, Steve Smith just said, 'England certainly seem to have supremacy in the scrum… Why they would want to cheat I don't know.' When Phil Vickery was penalised again at a breakdown in the 61st minute, Flatley duly goaled from 45 metres and Australia were suddenly right back in the game at 14-11. By this time the majority of André Watson's refereeing attention was focused on Phil Vickery, and when Phil was pinged at another scrum in the 64th minute, it encouraged Australia sufficiently to engineer their only line-break of the match when Stirling Mortlock went past Will Greenwood from a lineout – even though Mortlock was cut down by Backy immediately after the break.

Lewis Moody: Before the game André had come into the dressing-room and said to our team leaders, 'There won't be any penalties at scrum-time, I'll bet my mortgage on it!' After the last scrum pen, Steve Thompson got up wearily and muttered, 'You must live in a f***ing awful house André…'

In the last seven or eight minutes the tension in the coaches' box was almost unbearable. I have always prided myself on being able to distance myself from the swings of emotion during the game but I must admit that the pressure really got to me and I was watching proceedings through the cracks in my fingers. The penalty count had risen to 11-6 against us, our attack lacked momentum because we were making basic handling errors and all the 50-50 refereeing calls appeared to be going in Australia's favour. As John Taylor pointed out in the commentary box, 'You just cannot believe on the run of play in the second half, that England have lost it 9-0 and that Jonny Wilkinson has not had a single shot at goal.' There was an air of inevitability when our front row was penalised for the fifth and final time in the regular 80 minutes and Flatley sent the game into extra time with the scores tied at 14-14. The coaches all rushed down to the pitch but I was pleased to see that the team leaders had already taken control. Wilko had moved away from the huddle and was calmly practising his goal-kicking, Backy was urging the defence on and reminding them that we were fitter than Australia, but it was Johnno who as always, took the game by the scruff of the neck in a crisis.

Ben Kay: Somehow Johnno gathered the players around him and handled all the pressure. He said, 'If someone had said to us before the tournament started that we would get to the final and be level with Australia after 80 minutes, we would have bitten their hand off.'

Clive made two significant substitutions during the first half of extra time, bringing on Jason Leonard for the harshly-treated Phil Vickery at tight-head and Mike Catt at inside centre for Mike Tindall, which meant that Will Greenwood now had to defend in the unfamiliar role of outside centre. As he had throughout the knockout stages, Mike Catt made a tremendous impact off the bench, making a number of damaging runs which dented the Wallaby defence. Meanwhile Jason had been absolutely itching to get on the field.

Jason Leonard: I was standing near the comms guys and I was shouting at Clive, 'Let me get on the field! Get me on… before we lose the f***ing game!' When the score got to 17-14, he finally mumbled something and sent me on. I looked over and shouted: 'About 20 f***ing minutes too late!' But I knew what had to be done in the scrums. We were dominant but we were giving away penalty after penalty and I think André Watson had taken umbrage because of the chat he was getting from the likes of Johnno and Lol. I came on and told Trevor Woodman to let the Aussies win their own ball, and I told André he wouldn't have any problems with me. From then on, I was good as gold and to be fair, so was he. I just stayed square and straight and there were no more penalties.

Will Greenwood was superb switching to outside centre on defence, first shepherding Lote Tuqiri towards the touchline in our own 22 and then bringing down Mat Rogers as he attempted to take Will on the outside. Rogers was penalised for getting up and going again after being tackled, which temporarily relieved the pressure on us. Although Elton Flatley kicked another goal to bring Australia back level once more, the scene was now set for the final act of the drama.

Will Greenwood: I have never played with my socks down before. How knackered were we? There was a three-minute period when we were just defending, defending and defending for our lives. The referee was giving decisions against us, we were turning the ball over but we never missed a tackle. It seemed as if there were 20 England players strung out across the field. Our defence was so strong!

With only two minutes left before the game went into sudden death Wilko kicked the restart long and Lewis Moody pressurised Mat Rogers, forcing him to slice his kick and giving England a lineout only 30 metres out. We immediately went into 'drop goal routine' mode, a drill we had practised and perfected at the end of each captain's run since losing to Wales at Wembley in 1999. The players realised we were a little too far out for comfort and we needed to make some ground before giving Jonny Wilkinson the drop goal opportunity.

Every player involved had to fulfil his role perfectly in order to set up Wilko for the shot. First, an accurate throw to the back of the lineout with a slippery ball by Thommo, caught at the back by 'Moodos'. Second, a strong run into the heart of the Australian defence by Mike Catt. Third, a clever break up the middle by Matt Dawson with the Wallabies fixating on the threat of Jonny's boot and coming out of the blocks too far and too fast. Fourth, Johnno taking the ball up one more time to allow Matt to get back into position for the pass to Jonny. Fifth, Daws dummying the pass to catch the Australians offside and forcing them to retire as the drop goal attempt is made. Sixth and finally, Jonny putting the ball over off his wrong foot – as Johnno said afterwards, 'Who else would you rather have taking that shot?' Lewis Moody caught the restart, Catty kicked it out and as my son Matt had predicted, 'Bill' became 'Ours'.

Everything after that is a haze as the mind struggles to compute the delirium of the emotions. Hands are shaken and there are congratulations from Eddie Jones and John Muggleton and there is a mutual respect as 'Muggo' says, 'You have done wonders with England's defence. Well done, enjoy the feeling.'

Back in the changing room, Lawrence Dallaglio and Prince William stand in the middle of the floor like a latter-day Sir Lancelot and King Arthur. Jonny Wilkinson is still in his cocoon of concentration with a faint smile on his lips, maybe he's still running through the game in his head? Will Greenwood is roaring at the top of his lungs, at anyone who will listen: 'Flatley kicked all his goals… They'll never be able to say that Australia lost it. We won it!' Meanwhile Lewis Moody slams the door shut with a whooping 'No f***ing women in here', oblivious to the fact it is the Secretary of State for Sport, Tessa Jowell who has come to congratulate the England players and coaches.

Later there will be a trip to an exclusive restaurant on the rocks organised and paid for by Clive and Jayne. As the team coach winds its way slowly into the centre of Sydney and its nightclubs in the early hours of the morning, fans – English and Australian alike – will be banging on the sides of the England coach as if it is a drum; there will be a very special reunion with the family – Anne, Dids and the white ghost himself, who has lived only by night since his arrival in Sydney, Matt. Only Phil's daughter Anna is missing, but she will be there when the entire squad meets the Queen back in London, and when Phil receives his MBE.

The first phone call he receives is from Jack Gibson and Ron Massey, the two coaches who were there at the outset of his coaching journey, before he had ever contemplated a move into rugby union. It is a reminder that, beyond the celebrations and awards, the real satisfaction for Phil Larder is far, far quieter. Clive Woodward's words, 'How do you want to be remembered?' are still echoing in his mind, as the 16-8 loss to Australia in the 1995 Rugby League World Cup Final finally slips away into the background of his professional memories. Phil realises with a jolt, that it is no longer the defining moment of his coaching life. To win in Sydney, in a World Cup Final against Australia in the sister code, means everything now.

Above all else, there is the same overwhelming sense of relief – shared by all the players and the other coaches – that Joe Brown felt when he reached the summit of Kangchenjunga back in 1955, the relief that 'we didn't have to keep going up'. The ascent was complete, even if the next three years were to show that the summit neither would, nor could not remain conquered.

Chapter eleven
Now it's our turn

IT IS Thursday 27 April 2006, and Phil Larder is making the familiar drive up the winding road that leads to the Pennyhill Park Hotel. As his Mercedes crackles along the gravelly surface, the thick, pungent smell of pine needles snakes in through his open window. There is the comforting sight of the gigantic old cedar tree, pre-dating the hotel and every other part of its grounds by at least 500 years. There is however nothing of comfort in the meeting to come. The England head coach Andy Robinson has scheduled a succession of face-to-face meetings with Dave Alred, Joe Lydon and Phil Larder. At the end of those meetings, none will still have a job with the RFU as part of the elite performance squad set-up. Phil already knows that his head is on the block, due to a press leak a few weeks before. He is the second man in to see Robbo, at 8am:

> All three of us were given our marching orders, although Joe Lydon was given the opportunity to move sideways into the National Academy, one which he rejected. I was well aware that our replacements had already been approached. Robbo apologised to me with tears in his eyes and told me that he had fought hard to keep me in position but that it had been a decision made by Francis Baron and the management board. I didn't accept that. We'd already lost 31-6 to France in the middle of March during the Six Nations and I'd gone out to bat with Andy and Joe at the press conference afterwards. There were some harsh questions asked and it was an uncomfortable experience, but I felt I could

not let Robbo face the barrage on his own. That night I told all the coaching staff that I thought the players needed a new stimulus and offered to resign. Robbo had said, 'No, that's not what I want.'

As a head coach I had always insisted that I had total responsibility for hiring and firing my staff, and had indeed turned down the opportunity to coach the Great Britain rugby league team in 1994, when the then CEO Maurice Lindsay offered it to me, for that very reason. So rightly or wrongly, I felt that it should have been Andy Robinson making the decision as to whether my services were still required, but the decision-making process seemed to be occurring all around him and above him. I wanted it to be him making the decision, for better or worse.

In hindsight, perhaps I was too harsh in criticising Andy. Jack Gibson had given me the soundest advice of my coaching life when he had told me that there were only two kinds of coaches – 'Those that are sacked and those who are waiting to be sacked. Don't pick up the coaching reins if you can't handle that reality.' I had followed this advice implicitly and only took charge as a coach when my three children were in the final years at school. Robbo in contrast had become a coach when all of his four children were still well-entrenched at private school. He was between a rock and a hard place and understandably chose the security of his family over that of his staff. It's hard to blame any man for protecting his family. At the time I didn't fully understand the nuances of the background politics, and so Andy's survival when everyone else around him was dropping made little sense to me.

An awful lot of political reality had been compressed into one five-minute meeting. Around the same time that Phil and Dave Alred were sacked and Joe Lydon resigned, Phil's old mates Dave Reddin and Phil Keith-Roach were redeployed to the elite performance department, which meant that they could only assist Andy Robinson on a part-time basis. The number of full-time coaches was now reduced to three – one each for attack, defence and the forwards – so the American football- style specialist backroom staff that Woodward had built had been comprehensively dismantled. Meanwhile performance director Chris Spice resigned his position and Robinson was informed that he would have 'revised responsibilities' with a rugby director likely to enter at a level above him, in order to set out overall strategy for the coming season and assist with team selection and some aspects of administration. It appeared to be an opportunity ready-made for the return of Sir Clive Woodward.

Woodward himself had resigned his position at the beginning of September 2004, less than one calendar year after achieving the ultimate success in Australia. The background to his departure is a complex story with many different chapters. The most obvious subplot was the disappearance of England's core of senior players. England's outstanding captain Martin Johnson retired immediately after the World Cup, and England's winning ratio during the Woodward years dwindled by a colossal 30% when he was not leading the team. Johnno was the heart and soul of the side and the perfect earthy complement on the field to Clive Woodward's ideas and lateral thinking off it. As the chief executive of the Rugby Players' Association, Damian Hopley says, 'The Johnno leadership figure has never really been replaced. Some outstanding captains followed him but he was such an all-encompassing force and presence on and off the field. It's bloody hard to fill those shoes.' The alliance of heart and brain [between captain and head coach] was not as balanced when Lawrence Dallaglio and Matt Dawson were leading the side in the Woodward years and opponents were not as wary of those combinations against them.

Apart from Martin Johnson, the other two central bolts in the World Cup machine had been Neil Back and Jonny Wilkinson. Neil Back was Phil's defensive captain and the key figure in England's organisation without the ball. However Neil had been omitted from the first squad selection of the Six Nations in 2004 – with Richard Hill and Joe Worsley starting ahead of him at flanker and Chris Jones on the bench – and it had given him a lot of time to contemplate his future at the age of 35. When Clive Woodward called to say that he had been reinstated for the second round match against Scotland on 21 February, it was already too late.

Given Clive's insistence that every player picked during the Six Nations had to be available for the summer tour of Australasia, Neil Back declined the offer and was never seen in an England shirt again. England's evergreen prop Jason Leonard, who had successfully spanned the amateur and professional eras and earned over 100 caps for his country, benched for the first two matches of the Six Nations before being told by Clive Woodward before the third game against Ireland that he would be replaced by the simply green Matt Stevens. As Phil says,

> Sport is a tough uncompromising business which is driven by results. As time moves on and the player becomes older decisions have to be made which are not at all pleasant. Selection is all about the here and now and must be made on present form and not past glories.

Jonny Wilkinson meanwhile was hit by a succession of injuries which were to limit him to roughly 15 and a half hours of game-time in 18 months, until an attempted comeback on the British & Irish Lions tour of New Zealand in 2005. Wilkinson was England's main source of points, and in the knockout stages of the World Cup he had been responsible for 62 of England's 72 points [86%] and ended the tournament as the highest points scorer overall.

Although Lawrence Dallaglio soldiered on as the new captain up to and including the summer tour of Australia and New Zealand, he too retired [albeit temporarily] from international rugby at the end of August 2004. Kyran Bracken and Dorian West had retired after the World Cup, Trevor Woodman was forced to quit the game with a persistent back injury in 2004, at the age of 29 and while still in his propping prime. Richard Hill and Will Greenwood were both out with long-term injuries in the autumn of 2004, the list went on and on…

Were England's losses to retirement worse than those suffered by other World Cup winners in the professional era? Probably not in terms of numbers, but the individuals concerned proved more critical to the overall welfare of the team. In 1999, Australia lost their tight-head prop Andrew Blades and a world-class centre in Tim Horan to retirement, but they had a ready-made replacement for Horan in the shape of Jason Little.

Therefore they were able to win the tournament following the World Cup [the 2000 Tri-Nations] and beat a very strong Lions outfit in a three-Test series one year later. In 2007 South Africa lost their first-choice loose-head prop 'Os' du Randt to retirement and suffered a temporary dip in the tournament immediately after the World Cup, finishing bottom of the 2008 Tri-Nations. However by 2009 they had beaten the Lions in another three-Test series and won the Tri-Nations later that summer with a 100% winning record. In 2011 Brad Thorn retired from the All Blacks after winning the World Cup, but New Zealand was able to maintain its success with another perfect record in the 2012 Rugby Championship.

England were however unable to recover from the loss of Johnson and Wilkinson in particular, finishing third and fourth respectively in the 2004 and 2005 Six Nations with a 50% winning record across both tournaments. The core of leadership and playing ability, and mental toughness represented by Martin Johnson, Jonny Wilkinson and Neil Back could not be adequately replaced by the players who followed them, and the scheduling of the World Cup during the northern hemisphere autumn only magnified their absence:

> The World Cup players were running on empty. The scheduling of the World Cup assists the southern hemisphere teams because the end of the competition coincides naturally with their close season [typically an eight-week break in New Zealand for example]. That affords them a long, natural recovery period in which to recharge their batteries and embark progressively on essential pre-season strength and conditioning programmes. This break simply did not exist in England with the double-barrelled demands from both club and country. England had been the fittest team in the World Cup after following a rigorous strength and conditioning programme, which gave the players huge self-confidence and had enabled them to play the added 20 minutes of extra time in the World Cup Final without missing a solitary tackle. It was completely different eight months later. I remember having one-to-one discussions with players like Ben Cohen, who had completely lost their appetite for the game, and could not get it back because they had been so over-played. When I looked at Ben a blankness stared back at me, and his form over the next 12 months dropped like a stone because there was no energy left to rediscover interest in the game which [all things being equal] he loved so much. Ben just wanted, and needed to go home.
>
> England has been the only northern hemisphere team to win the World Cup, and neither the RFU nor the England management group predicted the difficulties that would occur. Upon arriving back in England the players immediately rejoined their clubs who were already engaged in important Premiership league fixtures. Furthermore, they resumed international training as early as February for the start of the 2004 Six Nations, and were looking at another demanding tour of the southern hemisphere in the summer before they could have a legitimate break for R & R.

The political background between the 2003 and 2007 World Cups was undoubtedly a decisive factor in undermining the success that had been achieved. The next Elite Playing Squad agreement between the RFU and the PRL Ltd, the body representing the clubs, was due to be signed on 5 September 2003. In practice the document still remained unsigned, and in the process of negotiation and counter-negotiation more than eight months later. The clubs, who had given so generously of the players' time during World Cup year, now wanted something back. As one director of rugby in the Premiership would tell England's head-coach-in-waiting Andy Robinson, 'Now it's our turn...' The club owners' expectation was directly contradictory to that of Clive Woodward, who viewed the generosity in the latter half of 2003 as merely a platform for further concessions.

In line with the original Cotton/Brittle plan back in 1998, Clive Woodward wanted the introduction of central contracts for England international players, which would give 'Team England' primacy of control instead of the directors of rugby. There was actually far less chance of this happening in 2003 than there was in 1998, with the club owners' investments now firmly embedded another six years down the line and associated ideas, such as the revival of divisional competition, having fallen by the wayside in the meantime. As Premier Rugby Ltd re-emphasised in 2005, 'PRL and the clubs have confirmed unanimously their opposition to any form of central contracting and reiterated that any RFU ownership in a club is prohibited under the Long Form Agreement.' In business terms, Clive Woodward was effectively attempting to control and direct employees who were paid by, and therefore belonged to another company, or group of companies.

The second major issue in the proposed EPS agreement was the number of training days allotted to 'Team England' in the course of a full season. Where Clive wanted unlimited access to England squad members, the clubs offered no training days at all. When Woodward scaled down his request to 24 days, the clubs offered 16.

Additionally, there was a substantial and significant amount of grey in important areas such as:

- The 'cap' for the number of club matches a player could play in a season – the clubs suggested 32, but that didn't include appearances off the bench.

- The 'R & R' block – Woodward wanted one continuous 11-week rest and recuperation block but the clubs wanted it to include fragmentary 'off' days and weeks throughout the season.

- Control of England training days – the clubs offered a majority of un-useful days early in the week, during which the players would still be recovering from their exertions over the weekend.

In the event, the new EPS agreement was not signed until the end of the 2004 summer tour to New Zealand and Australia, almost one full year after it was supposed to have been all neatly wrapped up and delivered. Even after Woodward had agreed to the clubs' 16 day training day release proposal, on condition that he could cherry-pick the days, the agreement was further modified by the chief executive of the RFU Francis Baron, who reduced the number of release days to 14 or 15 as part of a cost-cutting exercise. Even after the agreement had been signed, arguments persisted and in October 2005 it appeared inevitable that legal process would be required to resolve them. PRL's lawyers issued the RFU with a writ to reclaim a total of £120,000 that had been allegedly withheld from Guinness Premiership clubs Sale, Leicester and Wasps in compensation for the British & Irish Lions tour, and the RFU responded by insisting that the three clubs had broken the 11-week rest and recuperation rule by fielding their English Lions ahead of schedule. Regardless of agreements signed or unsigned – and the RFU and the clubs were still limping along on interim agreements at the time – the real issue of primacy of player control was still very much alive and kicking. As Francis Baron noted, at that stage there were only two years remaining before the 2007 World Cup, and that was generally accepted as the minimum amount of time needed to develop a winning international team: 'In planning terms we are at the 11th hour. It takes two years to develop a team, and we have only two years left.'

Andy Robinson recalls that,

In 2005 the RFU and Premier Rugby Ltd were embroiled in threats of legal action against each other, and it got to the stage where the players were working to [club] rule. Seventeen England players were in action only one week before our opening game against Wales at the beginning of February. Our wing Mark Cueto played no less than 39 matches in the 2004/05 season, and one year later it was even worse. We had defeated both Wales and Italy handily in the two opening rounds of the 2006 Six Nations. Wales had completed the grand slam the year before, but we beat them 47-13 at Twickenham. But in the middle of the two-week break between the second and third rounds of the tournament the wheels began to fall off. Mike Tindall for example was required to play for his club Gloucester on the Sunday, giving him only six days' recovery and preparation time ahead of the away fixture against Scotland. There were a number of other players in that position. They weren't rested and they were not properly prepared, so our build-up to the match was just not right. It destroyed our momentum in the tournament as a whole, and as a result we lost to Scotland in a try-less game.

After the winning of the World Cup, the RFU's vision of a scaled-back investment in the national game infuriated Woodward, to the point where he had been excluded from negotiations with the clubs on the EPS agreement. This pushed him further towards a path he had already been treading before the 2003 World Cup, a path which involved the marginalising of the RFU in the development of Team England, even to the extent of removing it completely from the negotiating table in the quest for new funding.

After being knighted in the 2004 New Year's honours list and with his profile as a World Cup winning coach elevating him to the status of a sporting celebrity, Woodward was able to appeal to an entirely different range of potential sponsors without channelling that appeal through the RFU. His connection with Tessa Jowell, the Minister for Culture, Media and Sport, led to an introduction to Camelot and the National Lottery's corporate sponsorship department. The project under discussion was a proposed £10 million development at Pennyhill Park which was to feature a 'Pressure Dome', a centre of excellence in which all the players in all the England teams could be assessed while playing under pressure.

In her biography of Clive Woodward, Alison Kervin recounts the startling impressions made by Clive Woodward's presentation on the three representatives from the National Lottery sponsorship department. One of them, Tim Stemp recalled:

'We walked in and there were three chairs in the middle of the room. Around us sat the coaches and the owner of Pennyhill Park. We were surrounded. It was a very odd set-up.

'It was all very surreal because the project had nothing to do with the RFU at all – it was an independent project that they wanted to do for Team England... We had to say "No" because it is difficult to back something that did not come from a governing body… There was just one individual in charge. If he left, would it all stop?' *[Kervin, p.276]*

The corporate sponsors were quite literally 'ring-fenced', and the negotiation had been removed from the auspices of the Rugby Football Union where it properly belonged. There could be no more elegant metaphor for Clive Woodward's tendency to see 'Team England' as a separate entity with its own rules and needs, or for the potential issues that Tim Stemp foresaw so clearly with his position as a transformational leader. What would happen if Clive Woodward suddenly departed the scene? Could anyone realistically replace him in the unique role he had designed so successfully for himself? All hope for change had become invested in Clive Woodward's persona, for better or worse. The bare minimum requirement for a transformational leader like Woodward was that he stayed connected to the institutions he wanted to change, but by the middle of 2004 the links with both his own administration and the club owners had been fractured beyond repair.

The ring-fencing of the Team England environment had also resulted in a failure of connection between the England coaches and the clubs. What they were learning and the innovations they were making at the elite level were not getting passed along to the club game, which had been Don Rutherford's main criterion in employing them in the first place.

It also ensured that they did not find a home in English club rugby when the coaching set-up under Woodward began to break up. Dave Alred moved his deep knowledge of biomechanics and performance psychology into golf, and the main testimonies to the work he does now come from Luke Donald and Padraig Harrington on his website. Dave Reddin first followed Woodward to the British Olympic Association as head of performance services for the 2012 Olympic Games in London before shifting to a similar role at soccer's FA in 2014. Sherylle Calder returned to her homeland and was ironically part of the South African squad who beat England twice at the 2007 World Cup, while Phil Keith-Roach took his comprehensive knowledge of the scrum to places as far afield as London Welsh and Scottish, Stade Francais and Russia after the 2007 World Cup. Andy Robinson moved to Scotland, to coach first Edinburgh and then the Scottish national side after resigning his position as head coach with England in 2006, while Phil Larder himself brought forward his plans for retirement while working part-time at Worcester Warriors.

In all these cases the coaching legacy of 2003 was largely lost to the grass-roots game in England when it should have been informing it. Moreover, the huge influx of new enthusiasts for the game sparked by the World Cup triumph was wasted because the preparatory work had not been done in the four-year cycle between the 1999 and 2003 World Cups. After peaking at 255,000 in 2003, the number of active participants in rugby in England fell to 190,000 two years later. The same mistake will not be made in 2015. As the incumbent England head coach Stuart Lancaster says:

> I'd never really thought about the absence of legacy before I moved from Leeds to Twickenham, but it became very obvious to me when I joined the RFU in September 2008. Martin Johnson had started roughly at the same time as I was appointed head of elite player development, and I very much saw it as my role to connect all my areas of responsibility – the 14 club academies, all the England age-group sides and the England Saxons [the equivalent of England 'A'] – to the senior England side. It was my job to provide the conduit through which talent could flow to the highest level – or if it didn't, I was at least trying to ensure that it had the best chance of doing so.

Lancaster's role could be described as the effort to 'connect upwards' from root level and it was totally organic. It was the same role he'd had up at Leeds, connecting the academy to the senior side, and the only change was one of scale, from club level to national level. Although Leeds had not been very interested at the time, that role – with one foot in each house as it were – was critical, and he knew it inside out.

> Although there was a club/country divide at senior level, the relationship at academy level was much closer, partly because the union part-funded the 14 academies. The primary interest of all the academy managers was the same – to develop world-class performers for England. There was a unity of purpose at that level, even if it fragmented further up the food chain.
>
> When I became England manager after the World Cup in 2011, it was only natural for me to make the development of relationships with the clubs, and in particular with the director of rugby at each club, my top priority. Many of those directors were not English, and I knew from both the Professional Game Board

report and my own observations that they were highly critical of the RFU. So the initial effort was simply a lot of legwork: making the effort to visit each club and its director of operations, establish a relationship and connect my philosophies to theirs. I made some concessions – allowing players to participate in games from which they might previously have been excluded – as a badge of good faith, did what I said I was going to do and kept the lines of communication open.

The July 2007 EPS agreement was a huge improvement on its predecessor in 2004, and it was the first fully detailed and comprehensive document of its kind. Compared to 2003 for example, when England were heading off to Australasia on a two-Test tour in June, we now have a much longer build-up period with the players in training in 2015 – one which was negotiated between the clubs and the RFU in the more positive environment that has existed since 2007. England international players no longer play any club rugby during the Six Nations' window, there is now a facility for me [as England head coach] to request that a player be rested for a week in the Christmas holiday period and there are week-long training camps in August, before the autumn internationals and the Six Nations tournament.

Moreover, there is now full co-operation between the clubs and England on individual player development plans, encompassing diet, conditioning and training. That plan is now a shared one, and it is player-centred. The data from every England training session gets shared with the clubs and they share their data with us. The players are capped firmly at 32 games per season and that is a black-and-white situation based on the number of minutes they spend on the field. There is no grey area any more.

Stuart Lancaster's role is, and will continue to be about connection and relationship – connecting the bottom of the game to the top and ensuring organic growth between the club and international levels. This sense of relationship is grown from a point firmly within the union, there is no future in positioning 'Team England' out on its own island, unrelated to what is happening with the clubs and junior levels of the game in the country. This is not someone's else's job, it is an integral part of Lancaster's role, even if that role is probably unique in global rugby.

Like Alan Jones in the mid-1980s in Australia, Clive Woodward tended to tackle the administrative issues from the outside-in, rather than from a point within the host union. This rendered his approach more revolutionary than evolutionary and eventually isolated him from the environment in which he was operating. When Clive Woodward announced his resignation at the beginning of September 2004, it therefore became clear that there was nobody within the existing coaching group who could perform the same function in the political arena, and that put the entire succession plan at risk. Both Andy Robinson and Phil Larder were teachers and coaching educators who were far more at home on the training field than in negotiating around a boardroom table.

At the end of August 2004, I was shocked to receive a telephone call from Clive informing me that he was about to resign. He'd had several meetings with the RFU and felt that it was going to be impossible to move England forward within the new restrictions. In the six months after the World Cup more than half the run-on team had been replaced because of retirement and injuries. As coaches we were starting with a new group of players but were not being given the time to prepare them. There was going to be less training time outside Test weeks, which meant that we would be severely handicapped in comparison with Australia, New Zealand and South Africa, who had always provided the benchmark for our own performances. Perhaps having so much preparation time with the players during the summer and early autumn before the World Cup had spoiled us all and created an unrealistic sense of expectation, but at least the advantages of that time together were there for all to see.

Clive thanked me for the work that I had done, and said he felt either Robbo or myself should step up as the next head coach. I replied that I wasn't interested in the top job. I felt Clive was too big an act to follow but pledged my total support to Andy if he was appointed. Anne and I were both hugely disappointed at Clive's decision. We had been on an unbelievable journey during his time in charge and had a massive amount of respect for both him and his wife Jayne.

Although I was delighted that Andy Robinson had been appointed as Clive Woodward's replacement on 15 October 2004, in all honesty I felt it was a huge ask for him to step into Clive's shoes. He had done a magnificent job working for Clive as a coach and I'd enjoyed working alongside him, but I knew that heading up the process required entirely different attributes and I was not sure that he had them. That was the very reason I had refused to allow my own name to go forward as a candidate for the head coaching role after Clive left. I was determined to give him my total support and promised to help him in every possible way, but that determination could not entirely dispel a sense of foreboding about the future.

With the benefit of hindsight, Phil Larder believes that he also made some mistakes in judgement when planning for life with a new group of players at the beginning of 2004:

The players had now achieved all their goals. They had been ranked the number one team in the world, they had won a grand slam and now they had won the World Cup. Defensively we had been the top side in the world for four successive seasons. What was left for them to do?

I began to look for another challenge for them but in retrospect perhaps I was naïve to underestimate the impact of the loss of key players to retirement, injury and loss of form. In reality, the challenge that lay ahead of us was one of consolidation rather than immediate improvement; to build a new team and maintain the standards we had set rather than to make another big leap forward.

Instead, I looked to raise the bar even further and turned back to Australian rugby league to provide the inspiration. On the return journey from an International Board Conference in Auckland in January 2004, I made a detour and dropped off in Sydney. Sydney City Roosters had won the Grand Final and by all accounts they had the most aggressive defence in the ARL. A former England international back-row forward, Phil Clarke, had played for the Roosters and he opened the door to the club for me to observe training.

I immediately realised that I had come to the right place. I arrived at training early on Monday morning and met big Adrian Morley, the former Leeds Rhino and Great Britain international who had signed for the Roosters in 2000. Adrian was now considered to be the best forward in Australia. He introduced me to Brad Fittler who had captained Australia to their 16-8 World Cup Final win over England in 1995. Both Adrian and Brad were adamant that I was wasting my time. The Roosters' head coach Ricky Stuart was renowned for keeping his thoughts to himself and his tactics up his sleeve. Ricky was as tight as a drum, or so the theory went.

After observing training I had lunch with Ricky and his assistant John Cartwright, and our reminiscences about shared experiences in league gradually changed colour to technical comment about the game. Our defensive coaching was similar, based on an up-and-out system with fast line-speed and decisive communication. When I finally threw out the bait and explained that we had experimented with an up-and-in defence prior to the World Cup, I saw a glint of recognition in Ricky's eyes and his whole demeanour sharpened. I realised that I had touched on a relevant issue. After a moment or two where he was clearly weighing up the wisdom of unveiling his plans, Ricky stated unequivocally that he was seriously considering combining the two systems for the season ahead.

We agreed to keep in touch and stay abreast of developments. Over the four days I stayed with the Roosters, it was the defensive sessions that really grabbed my attention. There was a demand that every tackle had to be both perfectly executed in a technical sense, and an expression of physical dominance. The defender had to knock the ball-carrier backwards and finish with his body on top of him. As far as I was concerned, this added fuel to the fire that had already been burning before the World Cup. The up-and-in pattern, with its emphasis on decisive frontal tackles, had to be included in my defensive programme for 2004, along with other ideas I'd garnered from watching Ricky Stuart's sessions – like dividing the pitch into three defensive zones, with completely different patterns and objectives in each zone.

The 2004 Six Nations was a disappointment, with England losing two games in the tournament [at home by 13-19 to Ireland and away to France in Paris by 24-21] for the first time since 1993, in the Geoff Cooke era. Although England only conceded six tries in their four games, it was still one more than France, and a small but significant sign that they were beginning to fall behind the French and their Dave Ellis-coached defence.

Although he was never a great friend of mine, I recognised that Dave Ellis had done a great job with the France 'D', and more importantly I had begun to feel a sense of unease with our own defensive preparation. This was confirmed when we toured New Zealand and Australia in June. Both New Zealand and Australia had been able to recover and embark on important and essential pre-season strength and conditioning programmes so they were fully prepared for the challenge. The England players in contrast had not had the benefit of either a break or a proper off-season. The result was a disaster. We conceded 14 tries in three games, in the worst set of defensive performances with which I had been associated.

I felt that I had underperformed as a coach and missed several points that I should have corrected between matches. In particular, the 'up-and-in' defence that we tried to incorporate in certain circumstances was poorly executed for a number of reasons:

- I had little training time to introduce it adequately. Despite Clive's statement that 'defence is the number one priority', the coaching time that I was allocated during the week was reduced drastically. The improvement of individual technique also takes considerable time. Our tackle misses in the three games were 20, 21 and 21 respectively – in comparison to a mere six in the 100 minutes of the World Cup Final.
- 'The Wasps problem'. The 'up-and-in' system operated by Wasps was vastly different to England's and made it difficult for their players to adapt. Lol, Josh Lewsey and Joe Worsley were all familiar with the differences but Tom Voyce, Simon Shaw, Fraser Waters, Stuart Abbott and Tim Payne all required far more time to adjust. On too many occasions we were sidetracked into discussions about the validity of the two systems which were ultimately irrelevant.
- The loss of Robinson, Greenwood, Wilkinson, Vickery, Kay, Johnson and Back saw their replacement by players who often did not fully understand their roles in the existing defensive system, let alone the hybrid I was attempting to introduce!

I believe I should have kept faith with the system that had served us so well in the past, and consolidated my teaching process rather than branching out in a new direction. I should also have opposed the selection of Mike Catt at centre far more vigorously. Mike had done an outstanding job in the World Cup but then he was defending outside Jonny Wilkinson. To have Charlie Hodgson and Mike defending side-by-side in the line against such a dangerous attacking team as New Zealand was asking for trouble.

After Clive Woodward's resignation the downhill momentum continued to accelerate. Although England still had the Indian sign over South Africa, defeating them 32-16 in the end-of-year Test series in 2004, they slipped further back into the *peloton* in the 2005 Six Nations tournament, winning only two of their five games – the first time since 1987 that England had finished with a negative win-loss ratio.

After our return from the British & Irish Lions tour of New Zealand in June/July 2005, the customary England coaches and management meeting took place at Runnymede on the southern bank of the Thames. Runnymede actually means 'meeting place in the meadow' and was of course the birthplace of *Magna Carta*, the first great declaration of the rights of the individual in England.

Ironically, it turned out that Andy Robinson was planning his own version of that declaration, and introducing a form of democracy within the playing squad. Much to my astonishment, he announced that our approach was going to change radically. Andy said that the environment was to become player-driven and that the players were going to have far more influence on all aspects of the coaching organisation with England. I was not sure if he had discussed this with any of the other coaches but it took me completely by surprise!

I was aware that governing bodies in different parts of the world had adopted policies driven by extreme educationalists, who had radically changed the way these sports were coached. Several coaches working both in the UK and Australia had mentioned these changes to me, and the consensus was that it was a passing trend concocted by people who had never been at the sharp end of professional team sports.

Part of the new package was that the players would now take on responsibility for analysis of the opposition and decide on the content of the training sessions. It's fair to say that I was vigorously opposed to the idea and we had some heated exchanges during the meeting. I didn't feel we had the players to implement such a policy. Most of our leadership core, and the players who were most self-reliant and best embodied our work ethic – Martin Johnson, Neil Back, Richard Hill, Jonny Wilkinson, Lawrence Dallaglio and Jason Leonard – had recently been lost to retirement or long-term injury, so it seemed to me to be the very worst time to introduce such a policy. The players we had to work with weren't as advanced in either leadership skills or their ability to self-manage as those players. I felt that asking a new playing group to analyse their upcoming opponents' last three matches was an unrealistic expectation on top of all their other responsibilities.

It however became obvious that Andy had already discussed the empowerment issue with some of the senior players and that his mind was already made up, whatever I said. I felt that Andy was taking a wrong turn that would have serious repercussions for the England team in the long term, and I rang my wife Anne that evening to tell her that I was considering resigning. Anne told me to calm down and take a deep breath; she persuaded me [rightly] to honour my promises to both Clive and Robbo and continue to support him, whatever the outcome.

The progress to a more *participative* approach to leadership might have worked well if the players Phil mentions had not been absent in 2004/05 and able to head up the change. Most winning teams who boast the 600+ caps apparently needed to win the World Cup also feature a strong core culture of self-reliance, and a number of strong, independent characters within the team – people who are willing and able to make decisions under pressure. The England playing and coaching group of 2003 had that. They had strong on-field leaders like Martin Johnson, Neil Back and Will Greenwood who were empowered to make tactical changes on the field, while the coaches functioned autonomously off it in the coaching structure established by Clive Woodward.

New Zealand rebuilt themselves on the basis of this method in the years between 2004 and 2011, but they called it 'dual-management' rather than participative leadership. As Graham Henry says, 'I was pretty authoritarian. But it moved on after 2004, to a group of people trying to do something together, rather than two separate groups, one of coaches and another of players. Now it's much more consensus; there's a consensus home environment, there's a consensus educational environment.'

The idea was to spread the burden of responsibility around. Firstly to create the same sense of shared leadership among the coaches that Clive Woodward had encouraged – Wayne Smith says that 'Steve [Hansen] and I always felt like head coaches within Graham's team. We always felt we had the accountabilities, the responsibilities, of head coaches'; and secondly to further empower a core group of senior players who already knew what it took, for example, to keep a training day running at maximum efficiency.

Henry had a core leadership group of Richie McCaw, Mils Muliaina, Conrad Smith, Dan Carter, Brad Thorn, Keven Mealamu and Andrew Hore who arrived at the 2011 World Cup with more caps than any other team in the history of the competition. They were therefore fully primed to expand both the range of their responsibilities and the enjoyment they derived from them.

The chief requirements of 'player-empowerment' – analysing the opposition or their own performances, giving presentations to the group or establishing training priorities for the week ahead – comes naturally to a veteran group at a mature stage of their rugby development. The fit with England circa 2004/05 was not so good.

One of the immediate casualties of the new policy was the training time devoted to individual one-on-one tackling technique, which had always been the bedrock of Phil's teaching:

> I could not have disagreed more strongly with the reduction in the amount of time allocated to coaching the fundamental core skills of the game which was driven by the players. My experience researching elite teams in England, America and Australia, my ten years experience as coaching director in rugby league, and 22 years of coaching Great Britain and England in both codes at the highest level had convinced me of that. Even my recent trip to the Sydney City Roosters had re-emphasised its critical importance. Rugby is a far simpler game than some coaches give it credit for, it is practical and not theoretical, and teams that are successful are the ones that perform the simple fundamental basic skills of the game under pressure most effectively.

One-on-one tackling drills had now become an optional extra at the end of training sessions proper, and players who wanted to do them could come to me afterwards. Although three or four would always pitch up, they were seldom the ones I needed to work with. Ironically, we lost the 2005 autumn international to New Zealand partly because of two missed one-on-one tackles by Martin Corry, who, along with Matt Dawson, had been one of the main drivers behind the discarding of sessions on individual technique.

In fairness the delegation policy to new leaders within the team did not work too badly, with Lewis Moody and Mike Tindall offering to step up and fill the huge void left by retirements after 2003. Both Lewis and Tinds developed greater insight into our strategic aims and were unafraid to voice their opinions. On the other hand, the players' analysis of the opposition tended to be mediocre, it would rely more on generalisation than detail and often have big holes or omissions in it. Therefore our knowledge of our opponents was often spotty and incomplete.

Even with the continued teething problems with the up-and-in pattern, our defence performed reasonably well in 2005, co-leading my table with France for the fewest number of tries conceded and lowest average per game. Ironically it was to be France who sounded the death-knell on my England coaching career. After two wins in the first two rounds against Wales and Italy, we lost to Scotland in another Edinburgh rainstorm and then we were swept away by France 31-6 in Paris. Matt Dawson, Mike Tindall, Steve Thompson, Lee Mears and Tom Voyce were all laid low by a gastroenteritis bug on the eve of the game and Andy Gomarsall had to be flown in as emergency cover for Daws. Although this was a strong mitigating factor, it is also the kind of event that tends to occur when all is not right in the state of Denmark. The writing was already on the wall.

I accompanied Andy to the press conference, I offered to resign after the game, and before I knew it I was making the drive up to Pennyhill Park for the final time as an England coach. Only seven short months after our five-minute meeting, Andy resigned his own position as England head coach. The circle was complete.

* * * * *

Neil Back is drawing patiently on a piece of blank paper. There is one big circle, then smaller circles dropping down on either side of the page, linked by straight lines but making their own progress down to the bottom of the page independently. The two sets look like separate strings of pearls, and the only place they meet is in the big circle at the top.

'This is my diagram of the 2005 Lions tour to New Zealand,' explains Neil.

'Two separate coaching teams and playing squads moving around the country independently of each other…

'On the Lions tours of 1997 [to South Africa] and 2001 [to Australia], the Saturday Test team worked with the midweek side on the Sunday, the day after the main game, with the situation reversed in the middle of the week. In 2005 there was no connection between the two teams because they were in different parts of New Zealand. In my opinion it was a big mistake because the Wednesday boys could never mount a challenge to the Saturday players in training or feel that they were even competing for a place. It went against the essence of the Lions ethos.'

The 2001 and 2005 British & Irish Lions tours were the first two fully-professional tours in Lions history. Both were in essence experimental, and neither hit the winning mark in terms of preparation – although the 2001 squad came considerably closer in terms of both results and quality of performance. Neil Back's comments are just one example of a gamble in preparation that misfired spectacularly during this period of groping in the dark.

> The Lions is a wonderful concept and I am sure that it will continue to prosper as it embraces the rapidly-developing professionalism in the sport, but many aspects of the 2001 tour to Australia and the 2005 tour to New Zealand were not only disappointing, they were definitely inferior to the preparation that was being implemented by some of the home nations at the time.
>
> There has necessarily been a reduction in the length of Lions tours in the professional era [generally to 10 or 11 matches] with fewer games between the start of the tour and the first Test, and no midweek games after the Test series begins. This has increased the emphasis in the media on winning the Test series itself.
>
> In my opinion, in order to make the brand viable, the Lions must
>
> 1. play an enterprising 15-man game, and
> 2. win 50% of the Test series in which they engage.

If they do not satisfy those aims, I don't feel the Lions can continue to capture the imagination of their supporters in the long term.

It is a difficult proposition. Where the southern hemisphere sides enjoy the streamlined ease of preparation that comes with central union-hosted contracts, the British & Irish Lions are selected from four separate international teams, each with their own coaching methods and tactical approaches. Blending them together into a cohesive unit capable of beating Australia, New Zealand and South Africa in the very short time available is a huge challenge.

The tours also take place at the end of a long and demanding season when the players are likely to be tired and carrying injuries, which in turn makes it even more likely that they will be invalided home at some point during the tour, or suffer a major injury breakdown after it.

In reality there is next to zero meaningful preparation time for a Lions tour, and the situation is definitely not improving in this respect. There were only nine days separating the English Premiership Final in 2005 and the Lions' first 'tour' match against Argentina; there were 14 days between the 2009 Premiership Final and the Lions' first match against a Royal XV in Rustenburg in 2009, and in 2013 the situation had deteriorated even further. The Leicester Tigers beat the Northampton Saints 37-17 at Twickenham on 25 May, only six days before the Lions' first scheduled tour match against the Barbarians in Hong Kong.

A top player in the UK is effectively required to peak, mentally and physically, on at least three potential occasions in the northern hemisphere season – during the autumn internationals against the southern hemisphere nations, during the Six Nations in the spring and potentially in the middle/end of May for his club or province in domestic competition. To add another, even bigger 'fourth peak' in June for a Lions tour, makes little sense coming so soon after the climax of the club season.

In 2013 the International Rugby Players' Association or IRPA, very sensibly suggested that the current June Test window be moved to July. This would not only enable the Super Rugby competition to be completed before a British & Irish Lions tour began, it would also give potential Lions players a gilt-edged opportunity to both recover from a long domestic season and provide a longer prep window for the tour itself.

'The idea would see the British & Irish Lions from the 2017 series in New Zealand onwards touring in a clear window after Super Rugby,' said the IRPA, 'with an improved ability to deliver full-strength midweek games.' Ever since 2001, Lions tours have been devalued by under-strength opposition in the crucial first six matches of the tour, particularly with all the potential Test players from the host union withdrawn from those games. Certainly in Australia in 2013, those withdrawals were augmented by the absence of other key players who were deemed essential to success in the Super Rugby tournament which would resume after the Lions tour was over.

The Lions' own selection values were severely downgraded as a result. On the four tours since 2001, the Lions have won the crucial first six games of the tour [or seven on the 2005 tour] by an average score of 42-14. That average includes three narrow defeats and one draw, although there were only two other games in which the winning margin finished within seven points.

> The vast majority of players on a Lions tour are experienced internationals at the top of their profession and one of the most difficult tasks of the coaching staff is selection. Selection was made difficult to the point of impossibility by the very variable quality of the opposition on the two tours I went on as a coach. In both 2001 and 2005 we only faced one serious top-quality opponent before the first Test – Australia 'A' in 2001 and the Maori in 2005 – and we lost both games. All the Australian or New Zealand players who were in contention for the Test series were removed from all the other games except those two. We beat every other team in 2001 and 2005 either quite easily or very easily, which meant we had very little material to compare the performances of players vying for the same position in the Test team. They had quite simply not been put under any pressure and no questions had been asked of them. In my opinion, there should be no under-strength teams in the build-up to the Tests and that should be a condition of the touring agreement. The Test 23 in the host international matchday squad should be involved against the Lions up to a fortnight before the first Test is played, and the remaining members of the squad should play in all matches against the Lions unless promoted into the 23.

In 2005 the selection problem was compounded by the fact that we effectively had two separate teams touring New Zealand and no less than 46 different players to accommodate in selection. Although the most obvious criterion of selection is play in live matches, it is a massive help to those selecting the team to get to know players in training, to see how well they perform the basic fundamentals and core skills, and how they react to pressure first hand. It is important to understand their characters, how they relate to team-mates, and the man-management skills required to get the best out of them before and during the game. It is also essential to build in an element of trust between coach and player, one which works both ways.

Because of the split organisation in 2005, each coach could only relate to half of the playing squad, so the element of comparison was entirely lacking. Having two teams with two separate sets of coaches simply did not work. Paul O'Connell said that he never felt he had the time to get to know other players well because they were always on a different track around New Zealand, and he wasn't sure of the functions of half the people on the management team!

As a result there was no equality of opportunity for the players, no common standard of judgement available to the selectors and only a superficial level of trust between coaches and players. It was an impossible situation.

Despite support from all three of the southern hemisphere nations, genuine positive interest from both England and France in the north and support from leading players on the global stage from both sides of the world like Richie McCaw and Jonathan Sexton, the IRPA idea did not survive the block vote of the Six Nations committee. Wales was apparently instrumental in defeating the proposal and keeping the status quo. It was a tragic outcome for both the British & Irish Lions and top international players from the four nations, who are expected to find one more mountainous 'peak' in their season when all the administrative circumstances of the game are collaborating against it.

The sorry tale of mass long-term injuries and collapses in form after a Lions tour only reiterates the chronic lack of balance in the situation. After the Lions tour in 2013, all nine of the England players who participated in the tour as first choices had either succumbed to long-term injury or severe loss of form, with only Owen Farrell among them contributing anything of significance to the following Six Nations tournament. The Wales side who provided no less than ten of the starters for the Lions third Test victory over Australia could manage no better than a third-place finish behind Ireland and England in that same Six Nations tournament seven months later. The same tale could have been told after the three previous tours in 2001 [in which 16 injuries occurred in the course of the tour, aside from the carnage thereafter], 2005 and 2009. If you tell players that selection for the Lions is the highest accolade to which a player from the four nations can aspire, then you have to behave as if that statement means something in terms of the organisation of, and administrative approach to the tour itself.

Phil Larder is adamant that the selection processes in both 2001 and 2005 were fatally compromised:

> On both tours I believe we got the crucial selection period before the first Test wrong. All the players should have an equal opportunity to make their case for inclusion in the Test squad, and selection for the early games should be carefully planned to do just that. Perhaps in these early games, the good of the individual should take precedence over the good of the collective. Once the first Test team has been selected however, the entire squad should have one goal only, and that is to win the Test series. Weekly preparation should all be geared to that aim, even if the performance of the midweek team becomes a secondary priority. This should be spelled out in black and white.
>
> In 2001, there was at least one player in the first six matches who had played in three different positions and complained, quite rightly in my opinion, not to have been given a realistic chance of selection. One of the two Welsh scrum-halves to be part of the 2005 squad that toured New Zealand, Gareth Cooper, played in the first 'home' match against Argentina at the Millennium stadium on 23 May and didn't start again until 21 June against Southland, only four days before the first Test against New Zealand. He therefore had no opportunity to put down a marker for selection in the Test team or even the matchday 22.
>
> In 2001 Andy Robinson and I had problems with some of the English players on the tour who thought that they should have been in the Test team, and their immature revelations in the media before the first Test was an unwelcome distraction.

Graham Henry experienced similar issues with the Welsh squad both at the end of the tour and after it, but at least the Welsh players had the common sense not to jeopardise our chances of beating Australia while we were there.

In my opinion the attitude to selection before both tours was also skewed by the loyalty of the coaches to players who had served them well. In a sense it's natural to pick players you are already familiar with, because you've learned to trust them in your own national environment. Nonetheless, in 2001 I felt we took too many Welsh players on tour when England was far and away the dominant force in the Six Nations. In 2005 the opposite was the case. We didn't take enough Welshmen after they had won their first grand slam in 27 years, and in retrospect we took too many English players, some of whom were coming out of international retirement [like Lawrence Dallaglio and Neil Back] and others who were coming off serious long-term injuries [like Jonny Wilkinson and Richard Hill].

Making a success of an international team in the professional era more often than not is a four-year journey involving a long-term plan and countless training weeks outside Test match preparation. The Lions coach does not have the luxury of time to plan and develop his campaign. His skill is to select a group of players, develop immediate chemistry between them, and produce a winning formula in a very short time frame. I am not suggesting that he cuts corners but he must be able to develop a simple but effective game-plan that tests the opposition immediately. For this reason, the coach best suited to head up the Lions may not be the most obvious choice.

Phil's comments raise the question of whether the Lions coach should be the current coach of any of the four nations, or have any obvious affiliation to them at national level. After all, he must be free to undertake all the planning necessary in the year before the tour takes place without distractions and have the time to study all the latest tactical trends and developments in the game in the southern hemisphere.

Another of the major issues that tends to crop up on Lions tours in the professional era is that of 'security of information'. If the issue of the loss of intellectual property to other home nations is a long-term problem after the tour is over, in the short term there is the difficulty of protecting team secrets from the hosts.

A security team to protect the squad from the industrial-level spying that occurs on Lions tours is essential if the Lions are serious about winning the Test series.

One of Clive Woodward's strengths was that he covered all eventualities and left nothing to chance. When he heard that the 2001 Lions had been the targets of regular spying and filming missions by the Australians, he decided that it would not happen to either England in 2003 or the 2005 Lions.

In 2001, our security was virtually non-existent. Scott Johnson [later to become a coach with Wales and now director of rugby with the SRU] was an analyst with the Wallabies at that time, and he could be seen kneeling down near every lineout in every Lions tour match up to the first Test, noting down all the lineout calls with pencil and pad. Before the decisive third Test, one of our most important training sessions occurred at Keirle Park in Manly. We disembarked from the coach only to find ourselves in a public park with ordinary Aussie citizens out for a walk with their dogs! There were no enclosures, and there was nowhere we could practise without being in full view of any passer-by who happened to take an interest in proceedings. I believe it was during this session that our lineout practice was filmed – and of course the result of the whole series eventually turned on a five- metre lineout where Justin Harrison stole a 'banker' throw when we were primed for a winning drive in the final seconds.

In 2003, after taking advice from Nathan Martin, an ex-Marine who joined the RFU as head of performance services in 2000, Clive had appointed four ex-Special Forces personnel to be responsible for our security during the World Cup. They had given the whole playing and coaching group a questionnaire which exposed the insecurity of our hotel environments:

Where do you hold team meetings?	War Room
Do you have another team room?	Social Room
How many people stay in the hotel overnight?	400+
How many restaurants in the hotel?	Three
How many people pass through the hotel every day?	1,000+
How many staff does the hotel employ?	100+
Who cleans your rooms?	Cleaners
Do they have access to your room?	Yes

Do you discuss tactics useful to the opposition?	Yes
Could this be the difference between winning and losing?	Yes
Do any of you make notes in team meetings?	Yes
Do any of you leave vital information in your bedrooms?	Yes
Do you see a problem?	WE DO NOW!

The Special Forces guys then pinned all the sensitive bits of paper they'd picked up that very morning from the war-room, the social room and some of the players' and coaches' bedrooms to a wall in front of us. Our collective jaws dropped open when we realised that they covered every aspect of the way we planned to play at the weekend. That by itself could have made the difference between winning and losing.

After that meeting, whether it was for England or the Lions, every Clive Woodward team paid great attention to how they disposed of papers and documents, training areas were secured behind walls with pitch patrols, and critical plays were never included in final team runs, which tended to occur at the matchday venues where security could more easily be compromised.

However by 2005, Clive Woodward had maybe become a little too anxious that New Zealand had inside information. Right at the beginning of the tour, the training ground had been sealed off behind an eight-foot tall red fence and even a small group of schoolchildren were ushered out. Woodward was convinced that the All Blacks had tapped into the Lions' lineout signals, so they were changed throughout the week before the first Test. Ian McGeechan pointed out that the confusion was so widespread that players were coming up to the coaches at half-time asking what the calls were! With that confusion the Lions lost the match, and realistically all chance they had of winning the series. In fact the All Blacks had known Andy Robinson's lineout calls ever since the middle of 2003. Steve Hansen [at that time the head coach of Wales] knew about them then and the constant stream of Welsh analysis since had verified that very little had changed by 2005.

While the issue of security, and the protection of important data was very much a relevant one, it did carry with it an attendant danger. Lions tours in the amateur era were founded on a reciprocal generosity between hosts and tourists, and that generosity of spirit tends to evaporate when suspicion becomes the dominant theme of the touring experience. Unfortunately the presence of Alastair Campbell as the press officer in 2005 epitomised that guarded attitude towards external factors and tended to undermine the sense of enjoyment on which the tour should have been based. The scripted answers at media sessions presented by Campbell to the players and coaches, the media overkill after the Brian O'Driscoll 'spear-tackle' in the first Test and the pre-planned 'walk' with Clive Woodward and Gavin Henson later in the tour, all implied a closed attitude of control rather than one of generosity or engagement.

The first changes made by Sir Ian McGeechan on the following tour of South Africa in 2009 were to reduce the touring party from 46 players back down to 37 with a single management team, shared rather than single rooms for the players and an open rather than a scripted or closed attitude to the media. 'We went back to being open with each other and the media,' said McGeechan, and it is indeed hard to look past Sir Ian, or someone very like him, as the ideal Lions head coach of the future. McGeechan was and is responsive to Lions tradition – indeed he had contributed a large portion of it himself as both a player and coach – he paid attention to both emotional and technical needs equally, and he was current with trends in the modern professional game. Above all else he was not affiliated directly to any of the home nations and free to do the job. But heading up a Lions tour requires a unique set of attributes from its head coach, make no mistake.

For Phil Larder, the ultimate sporting fulfilment occurred not with the Lions but with England in 2003, and perhaps that too is a lesson of the professional era. After all, what is the effort of a couple of months compared to the effort involved in a four-year World Cup cycle? What is the effort of four years compared to seven years spent developing the England rugby union team into an outfit worthy of lifting the World Cup trophy, or seven years spent reconstructing British Rugby League with solid brick, to the point where its house no longer collapsed at the mere sight of an Australian wolf?

Phil's mentor Jack Gibson once said, 'The day that God invented rugby league, he didn't do anything else but sit around and feel good.' God must have felt the same way when he invented rugby union too, and Phil Larder is one of the few who have experienced that pleasure, in both codes and at the highest level. It has been a unique journey, and a unique rugby life. 'Played strong, done good', as Jack would have undoubtedly said.

Bibliography

Size Doesn't Matter: My Rugby Life, Neil Back (Milo 2002)

Transformational Leadership, Bernard M. Bass (Psychology Press 2005)

White Gold : England's Journey to World Cup Glory, Peter Burns (Arena 2013)

Landing on my Feet: My Story, Mike Catt (Hodder & Stoughton 2008)

The Winning Way, Bob Dwyer (Rugby Press Auckland 1992)

Path to Victory: Wallaby Power in the 1980's, Mark Ella (ABC 1987)

Jack Gibson: The Last Word, Jack Gibson (ABC 2003)

Up and Over: A Trek through Rugby League Land, Dave Hadfield (Mainstream 2005)

Landry: the Legend and the Legacy, Bob John (Word Publishing U.S 2001)

Legacy, James Kerr (Constable 2013)

Clive Woodward: the Biography, Alison Kervin (Orion 2005)

Run to Daylight!, Vince Lombardi and W.C.Heinz (Simon & Schuster 2014)

Daring to Dream: the Story of Keighley Cougars, Brian Lund (Reflections of a Bygone Age 1998)

Building the Happiness-Centred Business, Paddi Lund (Solutions Press 1995)

Heroes All: The Official Book of the Lions in South Africa 1997, Ian McGeechan, Mick Cleary and Willie-John McBride (Hodder & Stoughton 1997)

Kanchnejunga: the Story of an Unprecedented Mountaineering Experience, John Tucker (Elek 1955)

Problem Athletes and How to Handle Them, Thomas Tutko & David Ogilvie (Pelham 1966)

Global Challenge: Leadership Lessons from 'The World's Toughest Yacht Race', Humphrey Walters (The Book Guild 1997)

Supercoach: the Life and Times of Jack Gibson, Andrew Webster (Allen & Unwin Academic 2013)

Winning!, Clive Woodward (Hodder 2005)